Feminist Economics Today

Feminist Economics Today

Beyond Economic Man

Edited by

Marianne A. Ferber and Julie A. Nelson

The University of Chicago Press
Chicago & London

The University of Chicago Press, Chicago 60637
The University of Chicago Press, Ltd., London
© 2003 by The University of Chicago
All rights reserved. Published 2003
Printed in the United States of America

12 11 10 09 08 07 06 05 04 03   1 2 3 4 5

ISBN: 0-226-24206-4 (cloth)
ISBN: 0-226-24207-2 (paper)

Library of Congress Cataloging-in-Publication Data

Feminist economics today : beyond economic man / edited by Marianne A. Ferber and
    Julie A. Nelson.
        p. cm.
    This is a follow-up volume to the 1993 publication, titled Beyond Economic Man, on
    which it builds.
    Includes bibliographical references and index.
    ISBN 0-226-24206-4 (cloth : alk. paper) — ISBN 0-226-24207-2 (pbk : alk. paper)
        1. Feminist economics.   2. Economic man.   3. Economics.   I. Ferber, Marianne A.,
    1923–   II. Nelson, Julie A., 1956–
    HQ1381 .F465 2003
    330'.082—dc21
                                                                            2003006766

⊗The paper used in this publication meets the minimum requirements of the American
National Standard for Information Sciences—Permanence of Paper for Printed Library
Materials, ANSI Z39.48-1992.

Contents

Ten years ago, we coedited the book *Beyond Economic Man: Feminist Theory and Economics.* In it, we collected essays that began to explore possible connections between feminist scholarship and the discipline of economics. Drawing attention to the fact that the topics, assumptions, and methods of contemporary mainstream economics reflect distinctly masculine concerns, the volume raised questions about the presumed objectivity of this one-sided practice. We argued that biases which give market relations pride of place over family and social relations, emphasize heroic individualism while ignoring interdependence, and define rationality so narrowly that even verbal analysis is excluded leave the discipline impoverished.

During the intervening decade, feminist economics has grown into a field of its own, with its own journal, diverse international organization, lively conferences, and fresh voices. At the request of our editors at the University of Chicago Press, we have compiled this follow-up volume to update readers on these developments in feminist economics. It does not in any way replace the original volume, but rather builds on it. Our aim is to include some of the most vibrant streams of research that have flourished in these ten years and point to significant new questions that are being raised.

We also attempt to document how much influence feminist thought has had on actual economic practice, in the United States and elsewhere. While *Beyond Economic Man* has been referred to as the "manifesto" of feminist economics, any feminist revolution is far from complete. The mainstream has remained rather resistant to relatively conventional goals of feminists, such as advancing women in the profession and attending to the importance of gender as a factor in labor markets. The more subtle—and also more radical—theoretical critiques advanced in *Beyond Economic Man* have received even less attention among mainstream economists. These critiques have, however, had more of a hearing among practitioners of public policy, the other social sciences, women's studies, and the humanities.

Will "improvements in economic practice," the goal emphasized in the preface to *Beyond Economic Man*, ever be achieved within the mainstream of the discipline? Or might it prove more effective to bypass this intransigent group and construct a more balanced analysis of real-world economic problems on a different disciplinary base? Perhaps another ten years will tell. In the meantime, the essays in this volume testify to the continuing vitality of the engagement of serious analysis of gender with the study of the basis of the provisioning needed to maintain and improve life.

This book could not have been written without the help and support, both personal and professional, of many friends and colleagues. We thank Nancy Folbre, Jane Humphries, Robert Solow, Myra Strober, and our editors at the University of Chicago Press, Geoffrey Huck and John Tryneski, for their suggestions on topics for this volume. We appreciate the help of Elisabetta Addis, Robin Bartlett, Prue Hyman, Edith Kuiper, Friederike Maier, Jean Shackelford, and Diana Strassmann in providing details of institutional history. We thank Linda Lucas for putting our questionnaire for members of the International Association for Feminist Economics in the newsletter, and we are grateful to the following people for their thoughtful responses to that survey: Ronald G. Bodkin, Debbie Budlender, E. A. (Nora) Cebotarev, Marjorie Griffin Cohen, Matthias Gysler, Suzanne Helburn, Katja Hokkinen, Prue Hyman, Alison Jaggar, Yoshiko Kuba, Margaret Levenstein, Daniele Meulders, Perry Patterson, Ellie Perkins, Paddy Quick, Ingrid Robeyns, Judy Robinson, Sumitra Shah, Irene van Staveren, Diane-Gabrielle Tremblay, Marjolein van der Veen, Brigitte Young, and Eiman Zein-Elabdin. We also thank the fifty-four department heads and faculty members who responded (anonymously) to our survey of economics departments. We appreciate the comments received from those who attended the session on this volume at the 2001 Conference on Feminist Economics, June 22–24, Oslo, Norway, and the comments received from Randy Albelda and an anonymous reader of this manuscript. We thank Anne Ford at the University of Chicago Press for assisting with the logistics of publication. Julie Nelson acknowledges the financial support of the Charlotte Perkins Gilman Fellowship for Research on Caring Labor, the Foundation for Child Development, and the Center for the Study of Values in Public Life at Harvard Divinity School. All decisions, and all errors, of course, remain entirely our own.

Beyond Economic Man, Ten Years Later

. . . Marianne A. Ferber and Julie A. Nelson

In the introduction to *Beyond Economic Man* (*BEM*), we sought to expose and explain the links between the social construction of gender and the social construction of the contemporary discipline of economics. We explained that gender, which should not be confused with biological sex, refers to the way societies attribute "masculinity" or "femininity" not only to various people, but also to various activities and even concepts. Likewise, the discipline of economics is a creation of groups of people, reflecting the way they have come to think about economic life. Hence the discipline is malleable over time and inevitably influenced by the interests and biases of its creators. We pointed out how, in the social construction of contemporary mainstream economics, culturally "masculine" topics, such as men and market behavior, and culturally "masculine" characteristics, such as autonomy, abstraction, and logic, have come to define the field. Meanwhile, topics such as women and family behavior as well as characteristics of connection, concreteness, and emotion are all considered "feminine." In a sexist culture they are denigrated, sometimes even by women themselves, and largely excluded from mainstream thinking. In *BEM*, we challenged the view that the "masculine" topics are inherently more worthy and the adequacy of using only "masculine" assumptions to analyze *anyone's* behavior. We challenged the definitions of economics based on rational choice theorizing and markets and suggested instead a definition centered around the provisioning of human life. Feminist economics differs from standard economics not only

1

because it gives serious attention to women and challenges the common con-
fusion of gender with sex, but also because it challenges this definition of the
discipline in masculine-only terms.

Ten years later we find that this point still needs constant reiteration.[1] A
perennial struggle for feminist economists thus has been to find the energy
to both survive and provide a basic theoretical education (a sort of Sex and
Gender 101) in a generally hostile discipline, while at the same time expanding
the frontiers of their field and developing positive and progressive examples
of the important contributions a less gender-limited view of economics can
offer. The purpose of this volume is to document both the battles and the areas
of growth. This introduction points to many signs of feminist progress and
evaluates the effect of feminist theory on economics over the last ten years.

From Isolated Voices to Active Organization

At the time we began to work on *BEM,* an individual academic who put "feminist" and "economics" in the same sentence tended to feel as though she or
he were the only person in the world who did not find this silly. Certainly, the
major accomplishment since that time is the joining together of feminist voices.

We begin our introduction, as before in *BEM,* with an update on women's
status in the economics profession. We do this *not* because all female economists
are feminist economists, or because none of the men are. The discipline includes both nonfeminist women and feminist men. The continued dearth of
women in economics is, however, one indicator of the persistence of cultural
sexism, which manifests itself in the composition and behavior of the economics profession as well as in the core assumptions and methods of the
discipline.

Economics: Still Dominated by Men

We are most familiar with the situation in the United States, where progress
in recent years has been rather uneven. The share of degrees in economics
awarded to women rose from 8 percent of B.A.s in 1949–50 to 34 percent in
1985–86, but was only 32 percent in 1997–98. Meanwhile, during the same

---

1. For example, one of us recently pointed out at a seminar that elegant but empty abstractions,
accompanied by sloppy empirical work, can be seen as reflecting the association of using concrete data
with less "toughness" and hence lesser worth. A (male) listener interrupted to say very defensively, "I
don't think just men lie. Women lie too, you know."

years, the proportion of M.A.s increased from 12 percent to 26 percent and 33 percent, while the proportion of Ph.D.s rose from 5 percent to 20 percent and 28 percent (U.S. Department of Education 2000). However, the proportion of female faculty in economics departments at all Ph.D.-granting institutions increased only from 12 percent in 1993 to 15 percent in 2000. Further, the share of women among tenured full professors actually declined marginally from 8 percent in 1996 to 7 percent in 2000 (Bartlett 2001), while the proportion of women was as high as 48 percent in 1997 among the growing proportion of faculty who are not on tenure track (26 percent in 1997). In addition, it is worth noting that among the 333 departments with five or more faculty members listed in the most recent (1997) directory of the American Economic Association (AEA), 52 had no faculty listed who had recognizably female names.

Reports in the 2002 *Newsletter of the Committee on the Status of Women in the Economics Profession* show that there were essentially no further changes by 2001. Kahn (2002) emphasizes that there have been "major setbacks in the status of women in the economics profession" since the early 1990s, most notably in attaining tenured positions at colleges and universities. Ginther (2002) emphasizes the extent to which "promotion differences are much larger than those found in the sciences and humanities" (6–7).

Information concerning economics faculty in several other countries (see table 1) from various years between 1997 and 1999 shows that the situation in the United States is by no means unique. On the contrary, it appears to be rather typical. Although the ranks in different countries are not entirely comparable,[2] it is nonetheless possible to draw some general conclusions. The proportions of women in Australia, Austria, and the United Kingdom are clearly lower than in the United States. Among the others, however, the proportion of female professors is relatively high in Germany; the proportion of female associates is

---

2. A private communication from Friederike Maier, for instance, made clear that there are substantial differences even between the relatively similar systems in Austria and Germany, let alone between them and the others. For instance, while in both these countries a "habilitation," unheard of in the English-speaking countries, is required in order to reach the highest professorial rank, Austria has three such ranks, while Germany has four. Also, Booth, Burton, and Mumford (2000) list somewhat different categories for the United Kingdom, although the data they report are broadly consistent with those shown in table 1: 4 percent of professors, 11 percent of senior lecturers or readers, 17 percent of permanent lecturers, 28 percent of fixed-term lecturers. They also report that 33 percent of Ph.D./research students are women. We were also able to obtain some information about Sweden from Nyberg 2001 which suggests that women have made even less progress in the economics profession there. During the ten years from 1989–90 to 1999–2000, women earned 17 percent of doctoral degrees and made up 2.6 percent of professors, 10.3 percent of associate professors, and 11.3 percent of senior lecturers at Swedish universities, Stockholm Business School, and Jönköping Business School.

relatively high in Germany and Italy; and the proportion of female assistants is relatively high in Italy.

It is also interesting to note that the ratio of the proportion of assistant professors who are female to the proportion of professors who are female ranges from 3.1 in Germany to 4.1 in Australia, 4.3 in the United States, and 4.6 in the United Kingdom; it is as high as 5.8 in Austria and 6.7 in Italy. The high ratio in some countries could be the result of a rapid increase in young women entering the field during recent years or of women being promoted more slowly than men in these countries. The two interpretations are, of course, not mutually exclusive. On the one hand, there is ample evidence that the number of women in academia has risen more rapidly than that of men. On the other hand, research in the United States suggests that there continues to be discrimination in promotions against women in economics, as well as in academia in general (Ginther and Hayes 1999; Hornig 2002; McDowell, Singell, and Ziliak 1999; Ward 1999; see also "Study on the Status of Women Faculty" 1999).[3]

We also noted in BEM that women had not been doing well within the AEA, the premier professional organization for economists in the United States, in terms of honors received and offices held. No woman had received the highly regarded John Bates Clark medal. This is still true today. Similarly, only one distinguished fellowship has been bestowed on a woman—Anna Schwartz in 1993—since Margaret Reid received that honor in 1979, and to date, only two women have been selected to present the prestigious Ely lecture—Joan Robinson in 1971 and Alice Rivlin in 1974. On the other hand, while in earlier times women's representation among AEA officers was thin—there was only one woman on the Executive Committee through all the years before 1972— there have been women on the Executive Committee in all but two years since then, and there have also been female vice presidents in eleven of those years. We also noted in BEM that the only female president of the AEA (since its founding in 1886) had been Alice Rivlin in 1985; she has now been joined in this distinction by Anne Krueger, elected in 1996.

There is moderately encouraging news concerning female authors in the regular issues of the American Economic Review (AER), the most highly rated economics journal in the United States, and the other well-established journal of the AEA, the Journal of Economic Literature (JEL), which is devoted to review papers and book reviews. An examination of a sample of issues of AER (consisting of the June issues for every fifth year between 1970 and 1995 and every

---

3. These studies are particularly interesting because qualifications—such as publications, grants, etc.—are generally taken into account.

Table 1. Women as a Percentage of Economics Faculties in Six Countries

Professor[a] (%)		Associate[b] (%)		Assistant[c] (%)	
Australia	2.9	Australia	4.5	Australia	11.8
Austria	3.7	Austria	4.7	United Kingdom	18.9
United Kingdom	4.1	United Kingdom	11.2	Austria	21.3
Italy	5.1	United States	15.1	Germany	25.2
United States	6.5	Germany	19.2	United States	27.8
Germany	8.1	Italy	22.0	Italy	34.4

Source: Margreiter, Kocher, and Sutter 2001.

[a]Professor (Australia, Austria, Germany, United Kingdom); full professor, tenured (United States); ordinari (Italy).

[b]Reader and senior lecturer (United Kingdom); associati (Italy); reader and associate professor (Australia); Dozent and wissenschaftlicher Mitarbeiter (Austria, Germany); associate professor, tenured (United States).

[c]Lecturer (United Kingdom); senior lecturer (Australia); Assistent (Austria, Germany); ricercatori (Italy); assistant professor, untenured (United States).

issue between September 1998 and December 2000) shows that through 1985 there were no papers published that had a clearly identifiable female author or coauthor. Since then, there have generally been two per issue, and in June 2000 there were four. Progress has been slower in the *JEL*. A similar sample of issues over the same period shows that through 1995 the proportion of books reviewed that had at least one identifiably female author fluctuated around 10 percent; it was not until 2000 that it rose to 15 percent.[4] But in 2001 it was as high as 36 percent.

CSWEP: A Challenge from Within

The first organization in the United States to critically examine the position of women in economics was the Committee on the Status of Women in the Economics Profession (CSWEP). The Committee was founded in 1972 as the result of the efforts of a group of women who began to meet in the late 1960s. Before long, they formed the Women's Caucus and requested that the executive committee of the AEA take action to remedy the gender imbalance in the profession. The AEA responded by instituting CSWEP. Its charge was to "monitor the progress of women in the profession and to engage in activities

4. There is no way of determining how many potentially eligible books with female authors or coauthors were not reviewed. We did, however, find a good many such books, reviewed favorably in *Feminist Economics* as well as other economics journals, that were not reviewed in *JEL*.

that would help to further this progress."[5] Among the first steps the AEA took in response to CSWEP's requests was to open up its annual meetings by no longer relying as heavily on invited papers and giving CSWEP the opportunity to organize several sessions at the annual meetings. These actions help to explain the increase in the proportion of papers presented by women (as sole authors or coauthors) at these meetings as well as among the papers published in the annual *Papers and Proceedings* issue of the *AER*. The proportion of papers by female sole authors or coauthors rose from about one-tenth in 1970 to about one-quarter in 2000.[6] The representation among paper givers is now similar to that of women in the profession.

The AEA also resolved to appoint female economists as members of the editorial boards of its journals and to actively encourage the appointment of women as program chairs and participants at future meetings. To the extent these resolutions were implemented, they may have contributed to the results noted above.[7]

Thus, CSWEP has had some success in achieving the primary goal of "affirmative action" feminists of improving women's status in the economics profession in the United States. In addition, CSWEP's recent efforts to provide mentoring for female graduate students may help to improve the situation further by increasing the number of women earning Ph.D.s in the field and assisting them in getting a better start.

There have, however, always been feminists in the field who were not satisfied with this goal, but who also wanted to change the very nature of the field. Further, many were also considerably more interested in collaborating with like-minded colleagues from throughout the world. These activists have also been aware that CSWEP is a creature of the AEA establishment, which appoints its officers, albeit in consultation with CSWEP members. Not surprisingly, the AEA officers have tended to choose individuals who do not deviate too far from established orthodoxy. While most officers of CSWEP have nonetheless been welcoming to more nonconformist feminists, such openness has never been guaranteed. Hence, as time went on, it became increasingly clear in the United

5. This information is excerpted from Bartlett 2001. The record of much of what CSWEP has done can be found in its annual reports in the May issues of the *American Economic Review*.

6. The sample examined was for every fifth year during this period. The one exception to the steady increase is that the highest figure was 35.3 percent in 1994, when Amartya Sen organized the meetings, while the lowest since 1970 was 10.7 percent in 1996, when Anne Krueger was the organizer.

7. These resolutions by the AEA were not universally supported. For example, Milton Friedman told Carolyn Shaw Bell in 1973 that, while he was sympathetic to the objective of equal treatment of all people, he regretted that the AEA took these steps because they would lead to discrimination in favor of women (Friedman 1998). In 1998 he suggested that this had, in fact, been the case.

States, as elsewhere, that there was room for another, more independent and more heterodox organization.

Feminist Economics: A More Radical Challenge

While the publication of *BEM* in 1993 was one visible sign of the rise of critical feminist voices in the early 1990s, it was only one piece of a much larger flowering of organizing and publishing activity around feminist economic concerns.

The International Association for Feminist Economics

In 1990 a few dissidents in the United States got together and discussed their ideas for starting an organization of their own. Taking advantage of the large attendance at a panel organized by Diana Strassmann entitled "Can Feminism Find a Home in Economics?" Jean Shackelford and April Aerni invited members of the audience to sign up to start a new network with an explicitly feminist slant. Two years later, this network was transformed into the International Association for Feminist Economics (IAFFE). It is independent of the AEA,[8] and open not only to female and male economists but to academics from other fields, as well as activists who are not academics (Aerni and Nelson 1995).[9] Jean Shackelford was the first president (and has been executive secretary ever since), followed by Marianne A. Ferber, Myra Strober, Barbara R. Bergmann (all from the United States), Rhonda Sharp (from Australia), Jane Humphries (from the United Kingdom), Nancy Folbre (from the United States), and Lourdes Benería (from Spain and the United States). The next president will be Bina Agarwal (from India). Today, IAFFE has more than five hundred members from over thirty countries, as well as links to a number of affiliated organizations throughout the world.

While IAFFE shares many goals with CSWEP, its objectives include the more radical aim of challenging the masculinist biases in the now well-entrenched neoclassical economics. Feminist economists have questioned such fundamental neoclassical assumptions in economics as the "separative self," the ubiquity of self-interest, the primacy of competition over cooperation, and the primacy of efficiency concerns over concerns for equity. They have tended to

8. IAFFE has, however, greatly benefited from the generosity of CSWEP in initially letting IAFFE use their rooms for the first business meeting and inviting them to join all their receptions at national and regional meetings.

9. This intent is reflected in the decision to use the phrase "for feminist economics" rather than "of feminist economists."

define economics in terms of real-world issues of concern to women, men, and children, rather than as merely the examination of choice under conditions of scarcity. Many want to counter the worldwide takeover by neoclassical economics not only of economics departments, but also of governments and international organizations, such as the World Bank and the IMF.

From the beginning, IAFFE also took the "I" in its name seriously and, for the most part, has been successful in this respect. By the year 2000, in addition to the presidents from the United States, Australia, and the United Kingdom, it has had vice presidents and members of the board of directors from countries on all continents. While the initial 1992 organizational meeting was in New Orleans, Louisiana, United States, and was attended by only "a few Europeans and Canadians" (Aerni and Nelson 1995) and the first conference (organized by Barbara Bergmann) was in Washington, D.C., conferences have since been held in the Netherlands, France, Mexico, Canada, Turkey, and Norway, some attended by members from over thirty countries.[10]

Important tools for communicating, across this wide geographical dispersion have included the regular IAFFE newsletter, the IAFFE-sponsored e-mail listservs, and the IAFFE Web page (www.facstaff.bucknell.edu/jshackel/iaffe/).

Organizations across the Globe

Simultaneously with the organization of IAFFE, but independently, Dutch women were planning a conference on feminist perspectives on economic theory. The result was the Out of the Margins conference in Amsterdam in 1993, organized by Edith Kuiper and others. Many who attended, from around the world, remember this with delight as their first meeting with substantial numbers of international colleagues concerned with the same issues. Since then, international activities and regional organizations have grown in various parts of the world, some associated with IAFFE and some independent of it.

The 1993 conference provided a great opportunity for feminist economists from many countries to meet and make plans for continued cooperation. For example, a network formed at the conference gradually evolved into the Australian and New Zealand Association for Feminist Economics (ANZAFFE), a chapter of IAFFE. This organization continues, sporadically organizing feminist sessions at professional conferences and sending out occasional newsletters. Prue Hyman also started a small feminist economics group in Wellington, New Zealand; most of its members are not academics, but rather government employees or independent researchers.

---

10. IAFFE has made considerable efforts to raise funds to provide subsidies for members who would not otherwise have been able to attend these conferences.

Not long after the Amsterdam conference, a small group of Dutch econo-mists met in The Hague and founded a Dutch Network on Feminist Economics, FENN. It holds an annual dinner, organizes three seminars, and sends out three newsletters. By 2000 the membership had risen from forty to eighty. The board still consists of young economists at the beginning of their careers, mostly promising Ph.D. students and young civil servants. Even so, FENN is gaining growing attention among both private and governmental organizations, and its views are sought by them.

At the second Amsterdam conference in 1998, IAFFE Europe was orga-nized. It had its first meeting in Brussels in November of that year, attended by twenty-five participants from ten countries. As a result of that meeting an e-mail list was developed, a report was sent to interested participants, and plans were made to organize sessions at European conferences. The group has continued to meet, and its members organized panels at the meetings of the European Asso-ciation for Evolutionary and Political Economy (EAEPE) in 1999 and 2000.

In the United States, IAFFE members organize regular sessions at the an-nual meetings of the AEA and frequently at meetings of regional associations as well. Reports of additional activities have come from many places through-out the world. In November 1999 a conference on Women and Economics (Wirtschaftswissenschaften): Gender Specific Aspects of the Science was held in Berlin, and a workshop on feminist economics took place in Vienna in March 2001. In March 2000 the Economics, Feminism, and Science network (EFAS) was established in Germany. It plans to have meetings and a newsletter and to participate in developing a data bank that will provide information useful for doing research on women. The organization Marché du Travail et Genre (La-bor Market and Gender) of the Centre National de la Recherche Scientifique in France engages in interdisciplinary work on gender (Daniele Meulders, per-sonal e-mail communication, March 16, 2001). The Robert Schuman Centre European University Institute sponsored conferences in the fall of 2002 related to feminist economics in France, Italy, Portugal, Spain, and the United States. A group at Tokyo Gakugei University, Japan, is currently compiling a book series on economics and gender (Kuba Yoshiko, personal e-mail communication, July 20, 2001). The introduction to *BEM* has been translated into German (Regen-hard, Maier, and Carl 1994), and the full text was published in Korean (by Hankuuk University in 1997).

Publications of Our Own

Not long after it was founded, IAFFE began discussing the possibility of publishing a journal, and in the spring of 1995 the first issue of *Feminist Eco-nomics* made its appearance. In an editorial in that issue Diana Strassmann

(1995, 1), the founding editor, announced that the purpose of the journal would be to celebrate open debate as the best way to develop scholarship of the highest quality. By opening the gates that had for so long protected economic theories from fundamental critique and by subjecting all ideas addressed in this forum to critical scrutiny, *Feminist Economics* has from the beginning encouraged the emergence of a more intellectually resilient economics.

The growing readership of the journal, its availability in more than three hundred libraries throughout the world, and its selection as best new journal in 1997 (by the Council of Editors of Learned Journals) all attest to its success. Articles published in the journal include some that employ a neoclassical-style economic analysis of topics of concern to feminists, many that offer a critique of neoclassical economics, and a considerable number that have applied innovative approaches to economics.

Following close on the heels of *BEM* came another landmark book, *Out of the Margin: Feminist Perspectives on Economics* (Kuiper and Sap 1995), which brought together many of the best papers from the 1993 Amsterdam conference of the same name. Soon individual works and anthologies multiplied. For example, *The Elgar Companion to Feminist Economics*, edited by Janice Peterson and Meg Lewis (2000) drew together contributions on ninety-nine topics from eighty-eight authors in eight countries.

It is not possible to list all the important recent feminist economics publications, but, happily, technology has made this largely unnecessary. Review articles have appeared in many venues, the IAFFE e-mail lists allow for quick communication, and—at least among the electronically linked—electronic search engines can quickly compile bibliographies to specification.

At the same time, the very history and structure of the various summaries and databases provide further evidence concerning the progress of feminism in economics. Certainly, the request from a mainstream economist to write a section on feminist economics for the new *International Encyclopedia of the Social and Behavioral Sciences* (Meulders 2001) is a sign of some recognition. Popular success is evidenced by the appearance of "Feminist Economics" as a subject category at on-line bookstores such as Amazon.com. Yet, in the standard *Journal of Economic Literature* classification codes used in the discipline, no such category exists at the time of this writing. Work in feminist economics is frequently awkwardly placed in such often inappropriate categories as "Economics of Gender" or the overly general "Economic Methodology." This is also generally the case in the leading *EconLit* electronic database, though in this case, a very few publications are placed under the additional (probably newer) subject heading of "Feminism." *BEM* cannot, however, be found under any of those subject headings. *EconLit* (mis-)classifies it under "Time Allocation, Work Behavior, and Employment," "Labor Markets," and, perhaps most ironically, "Manpower Training and Development."

The Effect of Feminist Economics on the Mainstream

This leads us to the question of to what extent critical feminist voices have been heard within the economics mainstream, and whether feminist voices have improved economic practice. To provide some evidence on whether feminist interests have been noted, expounded, and cited, we look to journals, books, reports, citations, textbooks, and the views of leaders in the discipline. Our investigation of this issue concentrates on English-language and particularly U.S. evidence not only because of our own limitations as scholars but also because economics in the United States tends to play a dominant role in setting standards for the discipline internationally.

Case Study: *The Journal of Economic Perspectives*

The winter 2000 issue of the *Journal of Economic Perspectives* included a special "millennium" section intended to "look back at key developments in the economy and economic thinking" as well as to look forward to the "future of the subject of economics" (Krueger, De Long, and Taylor 2000, 4, 5). As this is an official publication of the AEA, with a blue-ribbon advisory board, this is a suitable touchstone for noting the effect of feminist thinking.

Remarkably, the neglect of feminism was complete, the neglect of disparities by sex nearly so, and the coverage of anything to do with women extremely limited. No mention was made of feminist theorizing, even in articles where it would have been particularly relevant. Richard H. Thaler (2000) asserted that rational and unemotional *Homo economicus* will evolve into *Homo sapiens,* a quasi-rational, emotional human being, yet he failed to discuss the obvious gender connotations. Feminist insights on pedagogy were likewise overlooked: William Becker (2000) failed to note that different teaching methods and ways of testing students have very different results for male and female students. The dramatic changes in women's labor-force participation and economic status over the last century were apparently not seen as worthy of an article and merely received two sentences in an article on policies toward workers. A discussion of socialism versus capitalism omitted any mention of the differential impact on women and men of the transition from communism to capitalism, including the dismantling of the social safety net. Women briefly appeared in the discussion of fertility in an essay on the standard of living, but gender disparities were not mentioned in the sections on literacy and political democracy. Among the eighteen articles, only the one on U.S. welfare policy paid sustained attention to women. Of the twenty-one authors, only one was female.[11] Further, there was virtually no analysis of disparities by race, class, or sexual preference, and heterodox schools of economics also received scant attention.

Interestingly, apart from the millennium issue, the *JEP* has given more space to feminist concerns and feminist writings than have many other journals. Over the years, *JEP* published, for instance, "Discovering Diversity in Introductory Economics" (Bartlett 1996), "Feminism and Economics" (Nelson 1995), and "Bargaining and Distribution in Marriage" (Lundberg and Pollak 1996). Further, it has published a number of sections on what are considered to be women's issues, such as "Wage Inequality" (1997, vol. 11, no. 2, 21–98), "Discrimination in Product, Credit, and Labor Markets" (1998, vol. 12, no. 2, 23–74), and "Women in the Labor Market" (2000, vol. 14, no. 4, 75–164). Of course, papers on topics of concern to women are by no means always written from a feminist point of view, but some of those published in *JEP* were authored by leading feminists, such as Robin Bartlett (1996), Barbara Bergmann (1989), and Nancy Folbre (Folbre and Nelson 2000).

Case Study: A Review of Economic Paradigms

We have found that, outside of the top mainstream journals, feminist concerns are increasingly mentioned when writers are describing "alternative" approaches to economics—though not always with great accuracy. For example, in a chapter entitled "Some Other Paradigms" in the 1999 volume *Economics: The Culture of a Controversial Science,* Melvin W. Reder (professor emeritus in the Graduate School of Business at the University of Chicago) devotes two pages to feminism. After briefly discussing rational actor bargaining models of the household, he goes on: "There is already a considerable feminist . . . literature designed to elucidate the structure and behavioral characteristics of households in the context of (claimed) gender domination. However, the analyses are decidedly and intentionally interdisciplinary, and not aimed at creating an economic paradigm" (139–40). The reference he gives for this presumably nonparadigmatic work is, oddly, *BEM.*

---

11. This was Beth Allen, whose contribution on microeconomics did not mention gender, but rather encouraged economic theorists to increase their attention to mathematics and abstraction, and expand cooperation with engineers.

Case Study: A World Bank Policy Research Report

One sign of progress is the recent report by the World Bank. Its very title, *Engendering Development* (2001), suggests that this work has been influenced by feminist thinking (and two decades of lobbying), as does the fact that, along with many traditional mainstream economists, no less than twenty-seven publications of authors who are members of IAFFE are cited. In addition, while the general tenor of the book is quite neoclassical, the first two sentences of the preface indicate that the authors are fully aware of the role that disparities between women and men play in holding back economic and social progress: "Gender inequalities undermine the effectiveness of development policies in fundamental ways. Yet this is an issue that often lies only at the periphery of policy dialogue and decision making, both in national and international arenas" (xiii). Furthermore, the report focuses on human rights, not merely economic efficiency, and takes a considerably more activist approach toward bringing about the desired changes than is common among neoclassical economists as indicated by its conclusion that the "evidence presented in this report makes a compelling case for the state to intervene to promote gender equality" (271).

Citations: A Measure of Recognition by the Profession

For some time now, it has been common to use patterns of citations—that is, the appearance of references to a work in later publications—to gauge the recognition scholarly work has achieved. In thinking about ways to use this approach to estimate the impact of feminist economics, we considered and rejected several ideas. One was trying to identify and count citations to papers on gender topics (as done in Rodgers 1996), but we discarded the idea because, as already noted, many papers on gender topics are not written from a feminist point of view. In addition, feminists are concerned with subjects that are not "gender topics," such as problems of race and ethnicity, the environment, and a good many others. We also decided that it would be unrealistic to try to categorically determine which papers were written from a feminist point of view, whatever the topic. Because of diverse views on topics, methodology, and policy issues, such decisions would, inevitably, be too controversial. In the end, we decided to examine citations of three influential, explicitly feminist books and of articles in *Feminist Economics*.

Three Feminist Books

The books we considered were Barbara Bergmann's *The Economic Emergence of Women* (*EEW*), published in 1986, *Beyond Economic Man* (*BEM*), published in 1993, and Nancy Folbre's *Who Pays for the Kids? Gender and the Structures of Constraint* (WPK), published in 1994. To make the data comparable, we examined the citations for each book over the first eight years after its publication. Using the *Social Sciences Citation Index* and the *Arts and Humanities Citation Index*, we found a total of 109 citations of *EEW*, 108 of *BEM*, and 136 of *WPK*. These numbers do not suggest that there is a substantially greater interest in feminist economic issues than in feminist theory. Also, in most respects, the patterns of the citations for the three books were rather similar. A large proportion of the citations for each of these books (more than half of those for *EEW* and *WPK* and more than one-third of those for *BEM*) were found in noneconomics publications, many of them either interdisciplinary or in sociology, feminist studies, and, to some extent, law. On the other hand, fewer than 10 percent of the citations were in the most highly rated general economics journals. Interestingly, each of the books was cited in a fair number of journals whose readers would not necessarily be expected to be interested in the subjects of these books, such as *Fortune,* the *Academy of Management Review,* the *Deutsche Zeitschrift fur Philosophie, Geoforum,* the *Millennium Journal of International Affairs, Ocean and Coast Management, Housing Studies,* and *Environment and Organization.*

To put this record in perspective, we also looked at the citations of two gender-related books written by prominent nonfeminist economists, Victor Fuchs's *Women's Quest for Economic Equality* and Edward P. Lazear and Robert T. Michael's *Allocation of Income within the Household,* both published in 1988. During its initial eight years, the Fuchs book received seventy citations, seven of them in top economics journals and many in labor economics, law, and sociology journals. The Lazear and Michael book was cited fifty-one times—also seven times in top economics journals, and often in labor economics, law, and sociology journals. On the basis of this evidence, one may well conclude that the books written by the feminists were very successful in attracting attention from the scholarly community and only somewhat less in being cited in the top economics journals.

Feminist Economics

Again using the *Social Sciences Citation Index* and the *Arts and Humanities Citation Index*, we examined the pattern of citations of articles in *Feminist Economics* from 1997 (when the journal began to be listed in these citation indexes) until 2000 (the last complete year available when this research was done). For purposes of comparison, we also collected citations of articles from the *AER*, one of the most widely read mainstream economics journals; as well as the *Journal of Human Resources* (JHR), a mainstream but more specialized journal;

and two journals whose critical stance toward mainstream economics may be said to resemble FE, the *Review of Social Economy (RSE)* and the *Journal of Post Keynesian Economics (JPKE)*.

Table 2 shows a comparison of the number of citations of articles in these journals. Even the most casual inspection of the data in this table shows that the articles published in *AER* are cited far more often than any of the others and that this is true during each of the three years. This is hardly surprising since this is the official journal of the AEA, received by most members of the association as part of the package they receive when they pay their dues. Information for this journal is included here as a benchmark of the highest number of citations that could most likely be expected for papers in any journal. The number of citations of papers published in *JHR,* one of the most highly regarded mainstream labor economics journals, is a good deal lower, but nonetheless well above that of papers published in the three "dissident" journals.

This serves to confirm the widely held view that the various heterodox schools, which have managed to form associations, to hold regular meetings, and to publish journals, have nonetheless failed so far to take the discipline by storm. Among dissident voices, however, feminist ones seem to be registering relatively well in the general social science literature.

Feminist Theory in the Classroom

In addition to the effects of feminist economics on research, we were interested in understanding what effect it has had on the teaching of economics.

Introductory Texts: The Impregnable Bastion

A review of the leading introductory texts shows that there has been little change in this area. We reviewed six of the current best-selling introductory economics texts: Case and Fair 1999a, 1999b; Mankiw 2000; McConnell and Brue 1999; Samuelson and Nordhaus 1995; and Stiglitz 1997. We believe that their content is a good indication of what is the generally accepted dogma in the field and what subject matter is considered most important. Earlier reviews (e.g., Feiner and Morgan 1987; Feiner 1993; Ferber 1998) had noted a neglect of women and feminist concerns.

Women continue to be only slightly visible in introductory economics texts, while feminist theory is entirely excluded. The proportion of women mentioned among economists, other professionals, and celebrities ranges from less than 5 percent (Case and Fair 1999a, 1999b; Stiglitz 1997) to 27 percent (McConnell and Brue 1999). The role of women in the economy is given minimal attention, even when their role is particularly relevant. Typically, these

Table 2. Citations of Articles in Journals

Journal and Year	Number of Articles	Number of Citations	Citations per Article
Feminist Economics			
1997	21	38	1.81
1998	27	32	1.19
1999	26	7	0.23
Total	74	77	1.04
American Economic Review			
1997	54	508	9.41
1998	66	348	5.27
1999	63	120	1.90
Total	183	976	5.33
Journal of Human Resources			
1997	30	112	3.73
1998	30	74	2.47
1999	31	23	0.74
Total	91	209	2.30
Review of Social Economy			
1997	24	21	0.88
1998	11	3	0.27
1999	19	4	0.21
Total	54	28	0.52
Journal of Post Keynesian Economics			
1997	37	32	0.86
1998	40	19	0.48
1999	35	29	0.57
Total	112	80	0.71

Source: Compiled from the *Social Sciences Citation Index* and the *Arts and Humanities Citation Index.*

books mention nonmarket work in only a few sentences when discussing GDP. They may mention women's increasing labor force participation and some reasons for its rise and the fact that poverty disproportionately affects women. They typically mention the possibility of labor market discrimination against women, but usually leave the impression that market competition should cause discrimination to disappear. Feminist theory of the sort discussed in *BEM* appears nowhere in the introductory textbooks.

Other Feminist Sources

Some instructors have, however, made use of resources other than introductory textbooks to give students access to feminist economic thought.

Having thought of BEM as a book primarily for our economist colleagues, we were rather surprised to hear how frequently it has been used for teaching both undergraduate and graduate courses. Our formal and informal survey of IAFFE members and their course syllabi has found that attention to feminist theory (and, to a degree, the use of parts of BEM) is making some inroads in economics departments, usually in courses with titles like "Gender and Economics," "Methodology of Economics," or "Political Economy." Nevertheless, such courses are far from standard and feminist theory is not always included.

Our evidence suggests that feminist theory is more often taught in programs other than regular economics departments. We have reports of serious attention to feminist economics in some graduate programs such as public policy (at the University of Minnesota, United States), family studies (University of Caldas, Colombia), rural development (Colegio de Postgraduados en Ciencias Agropecuarias, Montecillo, Mexico), and in women's studies courses in feminist methodology (University of Colorado at Boulder, United States). Alternatively, at times feminist economics comes to the attention of students through visiting speakers and papers or books they happen to come across and at times pass from hand to hand. BEM, for example, has the distinction of having been the target of a (rare) theft from the library of the institute of women's studies at the Åbo Akademi university in Finland (Katja Hokkinen, personal e-mail communication, March 24, 2001). Thus, the exposure of students to feminist economics, ten years after publication of BEM, seems to depend as much or more on grassroots activities as on formal instruction.

Feminist Pedagogy

As little impact as feminist economics has had on *what* is taught in introductory economics courses, it appears that it has had even less impact on *how* economics is taught. In recent years, however, as concern has grown about the small proportion of women (and minorities) among students who take any economics beyond the required introductory courses and their even smaller proportion among those who major in economics, some feminist economists (e.g., Aerni and McGoldrick 1999; Bartlett and Ferber 1998) have turned their attention to improvements in pedagogy that might help to remedy this situation. As Bartlett (1999, 601) explains, "Feminist pedagogy questions the neutrality of positivism and objectivity; realizes the importance and legitimacy of personal experience for learning; explores the intersections of race, gender and class and their impact on the subject matter; establishes non-hierarchical interactions between the instructor and the students and between and among students; and empowers students to be active and contributing members of the political process." She goes on to contrast this with conservative pedagogy, so common among economists, which emphasizes hierarchically structured, unidirectional teaching, and also notes that multiple choice and short answer questions are the norm in such classrooms. This practice continues as widespread as ever in spite of evidence that women tend to get lower grades on such examinations, but not on essay examinations (Ferber, Birnbaum, and Green 1983). Bartlett concludes by recommending that the content should be expanded, the interactions redefined, and the students be given the opportunity to provide evidence of what they learned in a variety of less constrained ways. As long as most beginning undergraduate courses are as large as is currently the case, however, the chances of such reforms being adopted are not great.

A Survey of Department Heads

After an extensive survey of a random sample of members of the AEA conducted in 1992, Albelda (1997) reported that up to that time feminism had little impact on economics. At the same time, she found that three out of ten respondents thought that feminism had made more than a little impact on economics. She concluded that there is reason to be optimistic about the future, mainly because of the growing body of literature, especially in the area of labor economics, and because of the journal *Feminist Economics* (4). We next discuss whether and to what extent her optimism was justified.

In order to obtain relevant information, in 2001 we sent e-mail questionnaires to the heads of economics departments in 34 colleges (all those with at least five members listed in the AEA directory), to all 45 top-ranked departments, and to 44 other departments in universities (every fifth university with at least five members listed in the AEA directory that is not among the 45 top-ranked), for a total of 123 questionnaires. After sending a second copy of the questionnaire to nonrespondents as a reminder, we received 44 responses: 10 from colleges, 14 from top-ranked departments, and 20 from departments in universities that are not top-ranked. In addition we received 10 responses to a very brief follow-up questionnaire we sent to the remaining nonrespondents. We are told by experts on survey data that this is a respectable response rate, especially since the respondents are likely to be very busy people. It should be noted that three of the respondents asked another faculty member to respond to the questions about the department, as we had suggested they might want to do.

Even so, the question of possible nonresponse bias raises its ugly head. A priori, it is not clear what that bias is likely to be. More sympathetic individuals may have been more likely to respond; but we cannot discount the possibility that hostile individuals took the opportunity to vent their views. A few negative comments (cited below) suggest that at least a few people did that. The only other evidence we can provide on this thorny issue is derived from the answers of individuals who did return the brief follow-up questionnaire although they had not responded to either of the first two requests. Because they would have been nonrespondents if we had not sent the additional request, it is reasonable to assume that they are more like nonrespondents than those who responded earlier. They were no different in terms of general familiarity with feminist economics or in reporting interest among faculty members in their department than those who responded to one of the first two complete questionnaires we had sent to them. Nor were the few comments we received from them notably more friendly or hostile.

One goal of the survey was to learn to what extent department heads themselves are familiar with feminist literature and organizations in economics and what they think of feminist economics. In the text accompanying the survey, we defined "feminist economics" as "including both work concerning women's and men's roles in the economy that has a liberatory bent, and critical work concerning possible biases in the focus and methodology of the discipline." Another goal was to determine the extent to which faculty were interested in work on women and feminist work and how many departments had courses on "women, gender, or feminism." In addition, we were also interested in seeing how many of the departments in any way put neoclassical thought in context, either by teaching the history and methodology of the discipline or by including in their curriculum courses that focus on heterodox schools.

The first section of the questionnaire asked respondents to report how familiar they were with five publications and two organizations. The publications included *BEM*, the journal *Feminist Economics*, and three textbooks widely used in courses about women and the economy. As the title implies, *Race, Gender, and Work: A Multicultural Economic History of Women in the United States* by Amott and Matthaei (1996) has considerable emphasis on race as well as gender; it also provides considerable historical background and takes a Marxist perspective. *The Economics of Women, Men, and Work* by Blau, Ferber, and Winkler (1st ed. 1986; 4th ed. 2002) has long been the standard text for such courses (Conrad 1992). While it is written from a feminist perspective and frequently offers critiques of existing approaches, it generally presents conventional analyses (Blau, Ferber, and Winkler 2002, 2). Jacobsen's *The Economics of Gender* (1998) is a more recent entry covering much of the same ground, but it is rather less critical of neoclassical theory than Blau, Ferber, and Winkler. Familiarity with one or the other of these books would indicate at least a rudimentary awareness of work that is concerned with women's issues, if not feminist economic analysis.

Table 3. Department Heads' Familiarity with Feminist Economics Publications and Organizations ($N = 44$)

Publications and Organizations	Familiarity				
	1	2	3	4	5
Beyond Economic Man[a]	26	8	5	2	3
Feminist Economics	19	12	8	2	3
Race, Gender, and Work[b]	37	5	0	1	1
Economics of Women, Men, and Work[c]	19	7	7	3	8
Economics of Gender[d]	36	3	1	1	3
IAFFE	27	11	3	2	1
CSWEP	2	5	19	11	7

Note: For publications, 1 = no familiarity at all; 5 = very familiar, have used it in a class or recommended it to students. For organizations, 1 = no familiarity at all; 5 = very familiar.

[a]Ferber and Nelson 1993.

[b]Amott and Matthaei 1996.

[c]Blau, Ferber, and Winkler 2002.

[d]Jacobsen 1998.

The answers to the first set of questions, using a scale of 1 (no familiarity) to 5 (very familiar), can be seen in table 3.[12] Among the publications, only the Blau, Ferber, and Winkler textbook and the journal *Feminist Economics* were familiar (to any degree) to a majority of respondents (i.e., received scores higher than 1). The number of respondents "very familiar" with (i.e., giving a score of 5 to) any publication was small. Similarly, few of the respondents had any substantial familiarity with IAFFE. On the other hand, almost all of them were at least somewhat familiar with CSWEP. This is not unexpected since, as noted previously, CSWEP has been a visible presence at the annual meetings of the AEA as well as the regional economic associations for many years now, and a CSWEP report is published annually in the *AER*.

In another section, we asked a series of questions about the department as a whole: whether any courses are taught on women, gender, or feminism; whether there are any faculty members who are interested in feminist economics; whether any students (undergraduate or graduate) have expressed an interest in feminist economics; and whether the department offers courses

---

12. We also separately examined the information obtained from the fourteen respondents who were heads of top-ranked departments and from the seven respondents who were women. While these numbers are clearly too small to establish whether any possible differences by departmental rank or sex of respondent were statistically significant, a careful inspection of the data revealed no strikingly different distributions.

in the history of economic thought, philosophy and/or methodology of economics, or heterodox economics (e.g., Marxist, institutionalist). Only 24 (out of 54) department heads reported that any faculty members were interested in feminist economics and far fewer, 13 and 8, respectively, reported any interest on the part of graduate or undergraduate students. Of course, it may be that they are not always well-informed about such interests, particularly if faculty or students think that expressing such an interest would not further their standing in the department. In any case, these figures neither point to the complete absence of interest in feminist economics nor suggest a groundswell of enthusiasm.

We also learned that courses on women, gender, or feminism are taught in 19 of these 54 departments, but only in 11 of them as often as once a year. The corresponding figures are 23 and 12 for history of economic thought, 7 and 3 for philosophy and/or methodology of economics, and 7 and 5 for any heterodox economics. This shows that, on the one hand, it is not unusual for such courses to be taught at least occasionally, but that, on the other hand, there are many departments where they are not taught at all. The difference between gender-related economics and the others is, however, that the number of gender-related courses has been increasing in recent years, while the opposite is clearly true for history of thought and a number of the heterodox schools.

We further included four open-ended questions, directed to the department head: "Are you familiar with other feminist work in economics? (please describe)," "Are you familiar with feminist work in other disciplines? (please describe)," "We would especially appreciate if you would very briefly describe your view of the merits of a feminist approach to economics," and "Do you have any other comments for us?" Among the 44 respondents who answered the question about other feminist work in economics, 21 reported some familiarity; and among the 38 who answered the question about feminist work in fields other than economics, 18 did so. Of the 24 who answered the third question and the 5 who chose to make other comments, 7 merely explained that they did not have enough information to have a view, and 4 more prefaced brief comments with a declaration that they really did not know much about feminist economics. Among those who expressed a view, there were about equal numbers that may be classified as negative, positive, and ambivalent. Several responders replied that they valued the more conventional types of analysis of women's economic position in the labor market or women's role in developing countries. Often, however, this was combined with an implication that feminist analysis beyond such bounds is not valuable. Here are examples of such comments:

I see little merit outside labor economics.

Useful only for developing economies.

Favor "liberatory" work but not some of the "critical" work.

I understand and find merit in "work concerning women's and men's roles in the economy that has a liberatory bent." I don't understand or value some of the critical work concerning possible biases in the focus and methodology of the discipline.

I would welcome models and data analyses that explain gender, racial, and other differences in performances or rewards. But that is standard economics. I do not understand why one would call it feminist economics.

Others expressed more openness to critical feminist analysis, though some of them also professed ignorance or disagreement:

To say that I am "suspicious of" or "skeptical about" feminist economics is by no means to say it isn't valuable to the profession. As a neoclassical economist I think feminist economics is important as a way of keeping neoclassical economics honest.

I am not well enough informed to have a well-developed view specifically on feminist economics. I do think that economics should be more open to alternative perspectives than it is. Under-representation of women is part of that problem.

To the extent that feminists have directed the profession's attention to questions that have sometimes been neglected, it has been a good thing. However . . . I have yet to see anything in feminist epistemology or feminist economic methodology that has affected the way in which I approach problems in macroeconomics and monetary economics.

Only a few comments seemed to be entirely dismissive, such as:

It's silly.

I hold the conventional view that gender differences, per se, do not have much, if any, relevance to the practice of economics.

Some respondents appeared to have their own definitions of "feminist economics":

I have a prejudice (and that's all it is really) that "feminist" translates as "anti-capitalism," "anti-market," and "anti-neoclassical."

Many merits, but no great achievements so far. I do not agree with your definition of feminist economics. What is meant by a "liberatory bent"? Why should all work that is critical of economics be "feminist"?

Other comments were wholly positive, and some were even enthusiastic:

Expands research agenda to important issues that men seem not to have thought of, attracts more women to the profession.

Teaching this material has been rewarding.

The merit of what I see as the feminist approach to economics is that it attempts to address areas that are either ignored by mainstream economics, or defined into irrelevance.

Don't have time to do this justice—but I like its epistemological stance, definition of economics, attention to institutions, critique of national income accounts, attack on homo economicus, its attention to the household, and economics of caring labor, etc.

To these observations we would only add that we believe the number of respondents who took the trouble to let us have their views, the proportion who saw at least some merit to feminist economics, and last but not least the thoughtful nature of many of the comments suggest that Albelda's optimism about the future of feminist economics may, at least to some extent, have been justified. It would be interesting to have someone do another such survey ten years from now to enable us to determine the truth of this conclusion with greater certainty.

The State of Feminist Economists

The information we have provided so far—about women's slow progress in economics, about feminists in the profession, and about the effects (or lack thereof) of feminist economics on the mainstream—provides only parts of the picture. Young scholars with feminist tendencies may legitimately give considerable thought to the question of whether they can expect to survive, let alone thrive, in economics—whether mainstream, heterodox, or applied in other programs. Because feminist economics recognizes the social construction of the discipline and places considerable emphasis on the personal, social, and institutional forces involved in disciplinary change, we believe that recounting some personal histories of feminist economists may lead to a greater appreciation of the diversity of feminist thinking as well as the effect of being any kind of feminist economist may have on careers. Therefore, we thought it would be of interest to our readers to learn about the careers of the contributors to BEM during the intervening decade.

The BEM Authors, Ten Years Later

Five of the authors represented in BEM have also contributed to the current volume. Rebecca M. Blank, who offered a commentary in BEM, was in 1993 a professor of economics at Northwestern University and until 2000 a member of the President's Council of Economic Advisers. She is now Dean of the School of Public Policy at the University of Michigan and continues to publish research on labor markets in many books and top-ranked journals. Paula England left her position as professor of sociology at the University of Arizona to accept full professorships first at the University of Pennsylvania, then at Northwestern University. She has also served as editor of the prestigious *American Sociological Review* and continues to publish extensively on labor-market issues, the family, and caring labor. Marianne A. Ferber retired from teaching in 1993; since then, she has spent two years at the Public Policy Institute at Radcliffe and continues as professor emerita of economics and women's studies at the University of Illinois, Urbana-Champaign. She remains active in research and editing projects, on issues including nonstandard labor, women in academia, economic education, and women in the Czech Republic. Nancy Folbre remains a professor of economics at the University of Massachusetts, Amherst, in a department that now includes a number of feminist economists. For her incisive work, she received a distinguished MacArthur Fellowship (popularly known as the "genius grant"). She continues to publish on issues of distribution, feminism, and caring labor. Julie A. Nelson was promoted to associate professor with tenure at the University of California, Davis, in 1993. She was, however, denied tenure in her subsequent position at Brandeis University. Although she had published in journals like *Econometrica* and the *Journal of Political Economy*, the Brandeis administration claimed that her research was inadequate and her feminist work was "narrow" (Nelson 2001).[13] She has, nonetheless,

13. Meanwhile, a male departmental colleague whose top-ranked publication was in *World Development* was tenured and five new faculty members, all male, were hired. Nelson filed a sex discrimination complaint with the Equal Employment Opportunity Commission and the Massachusetts

continued to publish in feminist economics and has been a Fellow at Harvard Divinity School. She is now at the Global Development and Environment Institute at Tufts University working on an alternative microeconomics textbook that gives serious treatment to topics of human well-being, household labor, and the environment.

Some of the contributors to *BEM* do not rejoin us, in order to make space for new voices. Ann L. Jennings, who in 1993 was an assistant professor of economics at the University of Wisconsin at Green Bay, moved on to become an assistant professor of economics and management at DePauw University. She has continued to write on institutionalism. Helen Longino, who wrote a commentary, has moved from Rice University to become professor of women's studies and of philosophy at the University of Minnesota. She continues to write on feminism and science. Donald N. McCloskey, then professor of economics at the University of Iowa, surprised many in 1996 by becoming Deirdre McCloskey (McCloskey 1999). She is now Distinguished Professor of Economics, History, and English at the University of Illinois at Chicago and Tinbergen Professor of Economics, Philosophy, Art, and Cultural Studies at Erasmus Universiteit Rotterdam. She continues to write extensively about the state of economics. Robert M. Solow, who offered a commentary, has retired and is now professor emeritus of economics at the Massachusetts Institute of Technology. He continues to publish widely on topics including economic growth and policy. Diana Strassmann, at the time *BEM* was published an assistant professor in the Center for Cultural Studies at Rice University, is now a senior research fellow at the same institution. Much of the success of *Feminist Economics* can be attributed to her dedication as editor. The field of feminist economics is poorer for the untimely death in November 2000 of Rhonda M. Williams, professor of Afro-American studies at the University of Maryland, College Park, who contributed a fourth commentary to *BEM*. Her impressive work on gender, race, and class will be long remembered.

Some Reflections by IAFFE Members

In order to learn more about the progress of feminist economics, we not only conducted the survey of department heads discussed above, we also invited members of IAFFE (through its newsletter) and subscribers to FEMECON-L (an IAFFE-sponsored listserv) to share with us stories about the effect of feminist economics on their own lives and how they see its impact on

---

Commission on Discrimination. After lengthy preliminary investigation, the commission reached a finding of "probable cause" (Nelson 2001).

economics. We also asked for information about their courses and organizations to which they belong. We are indebted to the twenty-three respondents from eleven countries for much of the information discussed above.

These responses confirmed what we had already learned from conferences, e-mail discussions, and submissions to *Feminist Economics*: people interested in feminist economics are involved in a wide variety of activities, of which academic development of feminist theory (the focus of *BEM* and the current volume) is only one. Some approach feminist work motivated primarily by a concern for policy issues, whether they are mainly interested in labor, development, or the environment. Many work, either as consultants or employees, for local and national governments, political parties, or nongovernmental organizations. Still, as we had hoped would be the case, a number noted that the groundwork of the methodological and epistemological critique set out in such early writings as *BEM* has been useful in their work, both intellectually and in terms of helping them to bring about institutional change. A number of academics mentioned that having such a book as *BEM* published by a major university press gave them increased respectability, more opportunity to follow their interests, and increased leverage in efforts like getting new courses approved.

Still, a substantial proportion of respondents also mentioned that being a feminist economist can be a rather lonely existence, that they face an "uphill fight" in their academic departments, and that at times students as well as colleagues are hostile toward feminist work. A substantial proportion also noted that being active in IAFFE helps them persevere, whether they work on improving the practice of economics from inside or from outside the mainstream discipline.

New Contributions to Feminist Economics

In this volume, we include one revised and updated essay from the original *BEM* and seven new essays that review developments over the last ten years and point to exciting new directions. Although all the authors in this volume are feminists, we are not trying to present a unified view. Our intent rather is to have a variety of viewpoints represented. The first six chapters largely build on the sort of feminist theory presented in *BEM*, updating and extending it to issues of caring work, the theory of the firm, race, globalization, and education. In addition, we include an essay on policy making written from a largely neoclassical point of view and an essay on postcolonial thought and feminist economics, in order to give fuller exposure to the diversity and richness of this field.

Paula England has revised and updated her essay "The Separative Self" for the current volume. This essay, much cited in the intervening ten years, provides a cogent critique of the concept of "economic man." England explores how neoclassical assumptions of self-interest, exogenous tastes, and the impossibility of interpersonal utility comparisons reflect androcentric bias. Adding to her original essay, she examines the extent to which recent discussions in feminist theory and in economics (particularly concerning social norms, the formation of preferences, and household bargaining) do, or do not, modify her analysis.

Paula England and Nancy Folbre begin a dialogue between feminist economics and "new institutionalist economics." They argue that new institutionalist theorizing about social and labor contracts can provide insights into difficulties currently experienced by caregivers and care recipients. They argue, as well, that the use of the language of contracts provides a way for feminists to influence mainstream discourse. After reviewing feminist conceptualizations of care, they explore distinctive characteristics of markets for caring labor, including missing markets, monitoring problems, and endogenous preferences.

Julie A. Nelson's contribution extends the critique of the "separative/soluble self" to the conception of firms as isolated agents driven only by the forces of impersonal market competition. She argues that standard models of business organizations, like the model of *Homo economicus*, reflect an androcentric blindness to the complexity of relational existence. Nelson uses feminist theory and empirical evidence from law, the social sciences, and business to outline a view of firms—as well as the markets in which they are embedded—as webs of individuals-in-relation of social and ethical consequence.

Lisa Saunders and William Darity Jr. note that traditional economic theories about racism are inadequate for the task of explaining racial inequality, because they attribute unequal treatment by race to premarket events, exogenous preferences, or information asymmetries. In their chapter they examine how feminist theory and innovative theories about institutions and economic incentives for racial discrimination could help explain race and gender norms and their persistence. They further suggest that while feminist and antiracist scholarship have much in common, feminism will not succeed in being relevant to all women unless it contains a racial component and antiracist theory will not be relevant to all members of minorities unless it includes consideration of feminist issues.

Lourdes Benería examines the extent to which globalization has made what Karl Polanyi called "market society" more dominant and more pervasive. She examines the gender dimensions of this transformation, both in terms of its effects on women all over the world and in terms of how market thinking is intertwined with gendered norms of human behavior. She argues that a more people-centered notion of development, far from being "soft," "idealistic," and "female," presents a truly democratic challenge to the advance of uncontrolled global markets.

Myra H. Strober compares educators' notions of well-being with the narrower views commonly propounded by neoclassical economists. She examines how the colonizing application of certain neoclassical constructs (including scarcity, self-interest, competition, market value, efficiency, and choice) to education undermines educators' goals. She goes on to note, however, the recent progress that has been made in the development of feminist pedagogy within economics and suggests that its emphasis on inclusiveness, interdisciplinary work, provisioning, and the use of cooperative and service learning provide a superior alternative.

Rebecca M. Blank and Cordelia W. Reimers are both empirical economists and policy analysts. In their essay they reflect on how feminism affects "our choice of models, our choice of topics, how we present our work, and our behavior in our other professional roles." In brief, they accept neoclassical models as useful, but are skeptical of them in their pure form, in which it is assumed that markets "are frictionless and everything works for the best." Instead, they take account of the many imperfections in markets, such as transaction costs, discrimination, and externalities. Like many other feminists, they are also open to nontraditional models and perspectives from other disciplines.

S. Charusheela and Eiman Zein-Elabdin argue that feminist economic thinking can be improved by engaging with postcolonial theory. They point out that both women and people in countries historically colonized by Europeans are marginalized within conventional discourse. Noting that the modernist notion of "development" reflects a normative ideal of a postindustrial capitalist economy, they argue that this too often undergirds even the analysis of feminist economists. They provide an overview of the postcolonial critique, discuss its relations with feminism, and review recent developments in postcolonial feminist economics.

Conclusion

Grounds exist both for being impressed by the headway feminist economics has made and for being discouraged because to date it has had little impact on the mainstream of the profession. On the one hand, there are observers such as Michael Steinberger (1998, 57) who wrote, "From quiet rumblings on the fringes of several economics conferences in the 1980s, feminist economics has evolved into a full-blown insurrection, complete with its own organization (the International Association for Feminist Economics), its own journal (*Feminist Economics*), and its own manifesto (*Beyond Economic Man: Feminist Theory and Economics*)." The new contributions in this volume, as well, indicate the continued vitality of feminist economic theory. On the other hand, there is a widespread perception that feminist economics has barely caused a ripple within the increasingly conservative core of the profession.

One may well ponder whether feminist economics has a better chance of creating change by head-on confrontations within the mainstream or in more indirect ways, such as proving its superior usefulness for social, political, and economic analysis in the other social sciences and public policy. Some feminist economists asked more than a decade ago, "Can Feminism Find a Home in Economics?" The answer is still unclear. There is considerable evidence, however, that lack of progress to date is more due to deeply entrenched biases in the discipline than to a lack of insight, organization, vitality, and mutual support on the part of feminist economists.

References

Aerni, April L., and KimMarie McGoldrick, eds. 1999. *Towards feminist pedagogy in economics.* Ann Arbor: University of Michigan Press.

Aerni, April L., and Julie Nelson. 1995. A brief history of IAFFE. *IAFFE Newsletter* 5:1.

Albelda, Randy. 1997. *Economics and feminism: Disturbances in the field.* New York: Twayne.

Amott, Teresa, and Julie Matthaei. 1996. *Race, gender, and work: A multicultural economic history of women in the United States.* 2d ed. Boston: South End Press.

Bartlett, Robin L. 1996. Discovering diversity in introductory economics. *Journal of Economic Perspectives* 10 (2): 141–53.

———. 1999. Pedagogy. In *The Elgar companion to feminist economics*, edited by Janice Peterson and Margaret Lewis, 600–608. Cheltenham, U.K., and Northampton, Mass.: Edward Elgar.

———. 2001. CSWEP: Twenty-five years at a time. Paper presented at the IAFFE conference in Oslo, June 22–24.

Bartlett, Robin L., and Marianne A. Ferber. 1998. Humanizing content and pedagogy in economics classrooms. In *Teaching undergraduate economics: A handbook for instructors*, edited by Phillip Saunders and William Walstad, 109–25. New York: Irwin McGraw-Hill.

Becker, William. 2000. Teaching economics in the twenty-first century. *Journal of Economic Perspectives* 14:109–20.

Bergmann, Barbara R. 1986. *The economic emergence of women.* New York: Basic Books.

———. 1989. Does the market for women's labor need fixing? *Journal of Economic Perspectives* 3 (1): 43–60.

Blau, Francine D., Marianne A. Ferber, and Anne E. Winkler. 2002. *The economics of women, men, and work.* 4th ed. Englewood Cliffs, N.J.: Prentice-Hall.

Booth, Alison L., Jonathan Burton, and Karen Mumford. 2000. The position of women in U.K. academic economics. *Economic Journal* 110:312–33.

Case, Karl E., and Ray C. Fair. 1999a. *Principles of macroeconomics.* Upper Saddle River, N.J.: Prentice-Hall.

————. 1999b. *Principles of microeconomics.* Upper Saddle River, N.J.: Prentice-Hall.

Conrad, Cecilia A. 1992. Evaluating undergraduate courses on women in the economy. *American Economic Review* 82:565–69.

Feiner, Susan F. 1993. Introductory economics textbooks and the treatment of issues related to women and minorities, 1984–1991. *Journal of Economic Education* 24:145–62.

Feiner, Susan F., and Barbara A. Morgan. 1987. Women and minorities in introductory economics textbooks, 1974–1984. *Journal of Economic Education* 18:376–92.

Ferber, Marianne A. 1998. Gender and the study of economics: A feminist critique. In *Introducing race and gender into economics,* edited by Robin L. Bartlett, 147–55. London: Routledge.

Ferber, Marianne A., Bonnie G. Birnbaum, and Carole A. Green. 1983. Gender differences in economic knowledge: A reevaluation of the evidence. *Journal of Economic Education* 14 (2): 24–37.

Ferber, Marianne A., and Julie A. Nelson, eds. 1993. *Beyond economic man: Feminist theory and economics.* Chicago: University of Chicago Press.

Folbre, Nancy. 1994. *Who pays for the kids? Gender and the structures of constraint.* London: Routledge.

Folbre, Nancy, and Julie A. Nelson. 2000. For love or money—or both? *Journal of Economic Perspectives* 14 (4): 123–40.

Friedman, Milton. 1998. A comment on CSWEP. *Journal of Economic Perspectives* 4:197–99.

Fuchs, Victor. 1988. *Women's quest for economic equality.* Cambridge, Mass.: Harvard University Press.

Ginther, Donna K. 2002. Women in the economics pipeline: How do we compare to other disciplines? *Newsletter of the Committee on the Status of Women in the Economics Profession* (winter): 6–7.

Ginther, Donna K., and Kathy J. Hayes. 1999. Gender differences in salary and promotion in the humanities. *American Economic Review* 89:397–402.

Hornig, Lilli, ed. 2002. *Women at research universities.* New York: Plenum/Kluwer.

Jacobsen, Joyce P. 1998. *The economics of gender.* 2d ed. Malden, Mass.: Blackwell.

Kahn, Shulamit. 2002. The status of women in economics during the nineties: One step forward, two steps back. *Newsletter of the Committee on the Status of Women in the Economics Profession* (winter): 5.

Krueger, Alan B., J. Bradford De Long, and Timothy Taylor. 2000. Reflections on economics at the turn of the millennium. *Journal of Economic Perspectives* 14:3–5.

Kuiper, Edith, and Jolande Sap, eds. 1995. *Out of the margin: Feminist perspectives on economics.* London: Routledge.

Lazear, Edward P., and Robert T. Michael. 1988. *Allocation of income within the household.* Chicago: University of Chicago Press.

Lundberg, Shelly J., and Robert A. Pollak. 1996. Bargaining and distribution in marriage. *Journal of Economic Perspectives* 10 (4): 139–58.

Mankiw, N. Gregory. 2000. *Principles of macroeconomics; Principles of microeconomics.* New York: North Publishers.

Margreiter, Magdalena, Martin Kocher, and Matthias Sutter. 2001. Women in top journals of economics. Working paper, Institute of Public Economics (Finanzwissenschaft), University of Innsbruck.

McCloskey, Deirdre N. 1999. *Crossing: A memoir.* Chicago: University of Chicago Press.

McConnell, Campbell R., and Stan Brue. 1999. *Economics.* New York: McGraw Hill.

McDowell, John M., Larry D. Singell Jr., and James P. Ziliak. 1999. Cracks in the glass ceiling: Gender and promotion in the economics profession. *American Economic Review* 89:392–96.

Meulders, Daniele. 2001. Feminist economics. In *International encyclopedia of the social and behavioral sciences,* edited by Neil J. Smelser and Paul B. Baltes, 8:5451–57. Oxford: Elsevier Science.

Nelson, Julie A. 1995. Feminism and economics. *Journal of Economic Perspectives* 9:131–48.
————. 2001. Fact sheet: Julie A. Nelson v. Brandeis University. Accessed July 23, 2001, at users.erols.com/julie.nelson/fact.html.
Nyberg, Anita. 2001. Feministiska ekonomer och feministisk ekonomi: Exemplet nationalekonomi (Feminsit economists and feminist economy: The example of economics). *Kvinnovetenskaplig Tidskrift* 3–4:5–24.
Peterson, Janice, and Meg Lewis, eds. 2000. *The Elgar companion to feminist economics.* Aldershot, U.K.: Edward Elgar Publishing.
Reder, Melvin W. 1999. *Economics: The culture of a controversial science.* Chicago: University of Chicago Press.
Regenhard, Ulla, Friederike Maier, and Andrea-Hilla Carl, eds. 1994. *Ökonomische Theorien und Geschlechter-verhältnis.* Berlin: Ed. Sigma.
Rodgers, Yana van der Meulen. 1996. The prevalence of gender topics in U.S. economics journals. *Feminist Economics* 2:129–35.
Samuelson, Paul A., and William D. Nordhaus. 1995. *Economics.* New York: McGraw Hill.
Steinberger, Michael. 1998. The second sex and the dismal science: The rise of feminist economics. *Lingua Franca* 8:57–66.
Stiglitz, Joseph E. 1997. *Economics.* New York: Norton.
Strassmann, Diana. 1995. Editorial: Creating a forum for feminist economic inquiry? *Feminist Economics* 1:1–5.
Study on the status of women faculty in science at MIT. 1999. *MIT Faculty Newsletter* 11:4.
Thaler, Richard H. 2000. From Homo economicus to Homo sapiens. *Journal of Economic Perspectives* 14:133–42.
U.S. Department of Education, National Center for Education Statistics. 2000. *Digest of education statistics, 2000.* Accessed June 2001 at nces.ed.gov/pubs2001/digest/tables/PDF/table257.pdf.
Ward, Melanie E. 1999. Salary and the gender salary gap in the academic profession. IZA Discussion Paper 64. University of Bergen, Department of Economics Institute for the Study of Labor (IZA).
World Bank. 2001. *Engendering development.* Washington, D.C.: World Bank.

Separative and Soluble Selves: Dichotomous Thinking in Economics

. . . Paula England

Hidden assumptions related to gender have affected the deep theoretical structure of neoclassical economics. Economists have had one notion of the self for market behavior—individuals are atomized and self-interested, with preferences that no one can change. But there is a very different image of the self for the family, albeit as often tacit as explicit. The family is seen to form our preferences when we are young, and family members are seen to share money and care for each other, with little regard to narrow self-interest. The two spheres are dichotomized, with analysis of the market taking an extreme "separative" view of the self and analysis of the family an extreme "soluble" view.

In this chapter, I review feminist theorizing that criticizes the separative/soluble dichotomy that permeates thinking about the self in Western thought. I then apply these insights to a criticism of neoclassical economics.[1]

This chapter is a revision of my contribution ("The Separative Self: Androcentric Bias in Neoclassical Assumptions") to *Beyond Economic Man* (Ferber and Nelson 1993) and was prepared at the request of the editors. The earlier essay focused largely on the feminist critique of the separative self; this essay reiterates that and also more fully develops the feminist critique of the other side of the dichotomy—the soluble conception of self. Thus, I hope this essay makes clearer that the important point is to develop theories that eschew unnecessarily dichotomous thinking. This chapter also discusses newer work in economics not considered in the earlier version on bargaining in marriage, endogenous tastes, and care.

1. For valuable criticisms of neoclassical assumptions that do not draw upon feminist theory, see Pollak 1970, 1976, 1978, 1988; Sen 1970, 1982, 1987; Elster 1979; Akerlof 1982, 1984; Granovetter 1985, 1988; Hogarth and Reder 1987;

I call one notion of the self "separative" because it presumes that humans are autonomous, impermeable to social influences, and lack sufficient emotional connection to each other to feel any empathy. I argue that three of the most basic assumptions in neoclassical economic theory imply a separative notion of the self. The three assumptions are that interpersonal utility comparisons are impossible, that tastes are exogenous to economic models and unchanging, and that actors are selfish (have independent utilities). While each assumption is occasionally challenged, most mainstream economists accept them without much consideration. I argue that they are grounded in a general tendency in Western thought to posit and valorize the separative self. Because it ignores the inexorable interdependency of human life and the importance for human well-being of connection, feminists have criticized this model of the self as inaccurate and as not worthy as a moral ideal.

In contrast, however, when economists talk about the family, they seem to have an image of selves so soluble that they have no independent will or interest. It is all for one and one for all. This is explicit in Becker's 1991 work *A Treatise on the Family,* usually credited as starting the "new home economics."[2] He posits selfishness in markets but altruism in the family, with family members acting as if they are maximizing a single family utility function. Conflicts of interest between family members and self-interested maneuvering for advantage are ignored, or at least downplayed. Drawing on the feminist critique of the "soluble" pole of the separative/soluble dichotomy, I apply this to economic work on the family, arguing that economists exaggerate the connective empathy and altruism within families.

I then consider recent developments in economics that provide a partial corrective to this dichotomous notion of the self. I discuss bargaining models of the family, which acknowledge conflicts of interest and self-interested maneuvering within the family. I also consider efforts by mainstream economists to relax the assumption that preferences are exogenous and unchanging. I argue that both are useful correctives to overly dichotomized thinking, in that the theory of endogenous tastes assumes a less impermeable self, while bargaining theories bring in some degree of separation between family members. I also

Frank 1988, 2000, chaps. 7–8; Hahnel and Albert 1990; Mansbridge 1990; Hausman and McPherson 1993; Pollak and Watkins 1993; Ben-Ner and Putterman 1998; and Sober and Wilson 1998. There are now too many feminist critiques and reconstructions to mention all; but in addition to the essays in this volume, some that I find especially valuable are Folbre and Hartmann 1988; Sen 1990; Nelson 1992, 1995, 1997, 1999; Ferber and Nelson 1993; Folbre 1994; and Nussbaum 1995.

2. There is a case to be made that Margaret Reid (1934) should receive credit for starting the "new home economics," but the credit is usually given to Becker. (See the special issue of *Feminist Economics* in fall 1996 on Reid, especially Yi 1996.)

argue, however, that if we really want to eschew dichotomies, the unmet challenge is a model of behavior across family and market spheres that captures both the individuated and connective aspects of life.

Finally, I consider how recent work on care by feminist economists has tried to meet this challenge. Work on caregiving (parenting, paid child care, teaching, nursing, counseling, and so forth) represents an attempt, still in progress, to eschew the separative/soluble dichotomy and theorize work done in both families and markets as involving both altruistic and narrowly self-interested motives.

Feminist Critiques of the Separative/Soluble Dichotomy in Conceptions of the Self

Before applying a feminist critique to economic theory, it is first necessary to clarify what I mean by feminist theory. One result of the entry of women, often feminists, into the academy in the last twenty years has been the allegation that theories in every discipline have been affected by gender bias. Over time, feminist thought has become increasingly diverse and today contains much healthy controversy. However, common to virtually all feminist views is the belief that women are subordinated to men to a degree that is morally wrong and unnecessary. Beyond this, views differ as to the sources of women's disadvantage and the proper remedy.

Two major, though not mutually exclusive, emphases within feminist thinking can be discerned: One body of thought emphasizes the exclusion of women from traditionally male activities and institutions. For example, laws, cultural beliefs, and other discriminatory practices have excluded most women from political office, religious leadership, military positions, and traditionally male crafts and professions within paid employment. These exclusions are significant for women since activities traditionally regarded as male include those associated with the largest rewards of honor, power, and money. The mechanisms of exclusion are sometimes so effective that most women do not choose to enter "male" domains, although a minority has always attempted to do so. Here feminists see the corrective to be allowing women to participate in these spheres on an equal basis with men. This goal is especially emphasized by liberal feminists[3] but is shared by almost all feminists. These "masculine" domains have been seen as allowing and even requiring autonomy and self-interested striving; the sense in which the men in these roles have actually been dependent

---

3. Jaggar 1983 contains an excellent, though critical, discussion of liberal feminism.

on and connected to women and other men has been repressed. But because the domains have been at least rhetorically associated with the separative self, the part of feminism that insists on women's equal right to enter these roles can be seen to encourage the development of a more separated, autonomous self in women.

A second body of feminist thought emphasizes the devaluation of and low material rewards accorded to activities and traits that traditionally have been deemed appropriate for women. The sexism here is in failing to see how traditionally female activities or dispositions contribute to the economy, society, or polity. Examples include failing to see how much child rearing, household work, and volunteer work contribute to "the wealth of nations." Another example is failing to see the extent to which work in predominantly female occupations contributes to firms' profits, the issue raised by the movement for "comparable worth" in wage setting (England 1992; Steinberg 2001). Feminists who emphasize this sort of sexism see the remedy to include changing values that deprecate traditionally female activities as well as allocating higher rewards to such activities. This position is sometimes called "cultural feminism" (Warren 2001),[4] and some socialist feminists argue for this revalorization as well. Because many of women's traditional caretaking activities are embedded in familial relationships and are motivated, at least in part, by altruism or obligation, one can see this strain of feminism as valorizing connection as an ideal.

Sometimes these two feminist positions are thought to be in conflict: the first is seen as advocating that women enter traditionally male activities, while the second is seen to advocate women's continued attention to traditionally female activities. Of course, it is entirely possible to believe that we should acknowledge the value of traditionally female activities and reward them accordingly without believing that women should continue to do a disproportionate share of these activities. Indeed, a culture that valorized traditionally female activities would be expected to encourage men as well as women to acquire these skills and values. Therefore, the two feminist positions can be seen as compatible, since together they would agree that activities traditionally associated with either men or women should be open to both men and women, while simultaneously encouraging more equal valuation of and rewards for both kinds of activities. But there is a tension between them in that the first valorizes separation more and the second valorizes connection more.

---

4. While cultural feminists criticize Western thought for failing to see connection and interdependence between people, a related school of ecofeminism points out the analogous failure to see our interdependence with the natural environment and the fact that our instrumentalism toward our environment now threatens the planet and human life (Nelson 1997; Warren 2001).

Could we valorize both connection and autonomy? Could we imagine male and female selves that were both connective and yet somewhat individuated? Implicitly or explicitly, the weight of Western thought answers both questions with a "no." The terms *separative* and *soluble* were coined by theologian Catherine Keller (1986), who discussed their link to pervasive gender dichotomies in Western thought. In the simplest (sexist) formulations, men are seen as naturally separative, individuated, autonomous, and dominating, while women are seen as naturally soluble, yielding, connected, and dominated.

In such dichotomous thinking, the only choices are to be either thoroughly masculine and separative, or thoroughly feminine and soluble. Separation and connection are seen as representing opposite poles that war with each other. To the extent that one is separate, one is not soluble, and vice versa. To the extent that one is feminine, one is less masculine (as in the preandrogyny conception of gender), and vice versa.

In this view, to valorize one pole implies less value for the other. Historically, only men were considered fully human, since women seem to give up most of what is seen as valuably human in order to bear the burden of connection. No wonder then that liberal feminists thought the only corrective was to seek separation and autonomy for women, and no wonder that men saw only fearful loss in pursuing connection. This way of looking at things was undoubtedly influenced by the hierarchical organization of actual gender relations, such that men had authority over women and devised systems of thought that valorized their own activities.

This dichotomous thinking about the self does not allow recognition of the ways in which some degree of individuation may enhance intimacy, or that empathy may actually be enhanced by being in touch with the desires underlying one's own self-interested striving. The feminist position that I draw upon here argues for delinking separation/connection from gender in prescriptions, and for seeing that individuation and connection are not necessarily at war with each other. The nondichotomous position might be called "individuals-in-relation" (see Nelson, chap. 3 in this volume) or "relational autonomy" (Mackenzie and Stoljar 2000).

But because separation had been so glorified in western thought, at least for men, and had been held out as the only fully human model of the self, the feminist critique had to start with an attack on the valorization of the separative self and of its descriptive accuracy for men or women, and particularly for women. This feminist critique of the separative self model was first applied in a number of disciplines other than economics. Seyla Benhabib (1987) traces the ideal of separative autonomy through liberalism in political philosophy. This tradition (whether the version of Hobbes, Locke, Rousseau, Kant, or Rawls) discusses moving from a "state of nature" to the metaphorical "contract" to set up the state. While the contract is seen to increase civility and justice, men are seen as separative and autonomous both before and after the contract. Authors failed to recognize that men are *not* entirely autonomous—that no man would have survived to adulthood but for the nurturing of a woman. Women's nurturing work was taken for granted and excluded from political theory; women and family bonds were seen as "part of nature" within a metaphysic that denigrated nature. Women's activities did not count as "moral"; only exercising "autonomy" in the public sphere did. Thus the separative self was valued, while nurturant connection was ignored or deprecated.

Psychologists have pointed out a similar emphasis on separation in developmental psychology (Chodorow 1978; Gilligan 1982). Carol Gilligan points out that Freud, Jung, Erikson, Piaget, and Kohlberg, despite their differences, all viewed individuation as synonymous with maturation and viewed connection to others as developmentally regressive. They did not acknowledge learning the capacity for intimacy and nurturance as part of maturation.

The separative self is glorified in the philosophy of science as well. Evelyn Fox Keller (1983, 1985) argues that objectivity has been defined in terms of the separation of the subject (the scientist) from the object of study. Emotional connections with one's subject matter are seen as contaminating knowledge. Keller insists, however, that some of our deepest scientific insights come from the ability to empathize with those whose behavior we study.

Some feminists applauded "connection valorizing" authors such as Chodorow (1978), Gilligan (1982), E. Keller (1985), Ruddick (1989), and Held (1993) for their insistence that social scientists include the parts of human experience traditionally assigned to women in their theories. Others thought it perverse to romanticize traditionally female characteristics such as caring, yielding, altruism, and selflessness, arguing that these are understandable but self-defeating adaptations to men's domination over women (Hoagland 1988). Another objection was to the tendency of those valorizing connection to exaggerate gender differences on this dimension. This objection was paired with a fear that exaggerations of gender differences—even if seen as environmentally created rather than innate—could be used to keep women out of powerful positions (Epstein 1988; Aries 1996).

Since the early critiques of the "separative self," feminists have also become increasingly suspicious of any "universal" notion of womanhood. Poststructuralists have argued against any universal notion of human, female, or male nature (Fraser and Nicholson 1990; Nicholson 1990; Charusheela and Zein-Elabdin, chap. 8 in this volume). Feminist theorists of color (such as Brah 2001; Collins 1990) have argued that it is often the experiences of relatively privileged white women that have been described as "the feminine" to be either rejected or valorized. For example, when one considers how insensitive white women have often been to the suffering of less privileged women they hired to clean or look after their children, one has to question whether either women's nature or social role results in empathy and caring. Just as families look less unified when men's violence toward women is recognized, women look less universally empathic when the participation of privileged white women in class, race, and national privileges is recognized.

It is something of a mantra among feminists that we should resist false dichotomies patterned on false ideas of sex differences. Julie Nelson (1992, 1996, chap. 3 in this volume) has suggested one way that we can reject the negative connotations of both separation and connection, while embracing the positive of each. She points out that traditionally female "connective" and traditionally male "separative" qualities each have both positive and negative aspects, but argues that there is a strong tendency in Western thought to see only the positive aspect of characteristics encouraged in men and only the negative aspects of those encouraged in women.

Consider, for example, the terms *hard* and *soft,* often metaphorically associated with men and women, respectively. At least in intellectual or business life, *hard* is seen as positive and *soft* as negative. But Nelson points out that it is more accurate to see *hard* as having a positive aspect, strength, and a negative aspect, rigidity, while *soft* also has a negative aspect, weakness, as well as a positive aspect, flexibility. The tendency to see the hard-soft distinction as a matter of strong versus weak and to ignore the fact that it is also a matter of flexible versus rigid is an instance of androcentric bias that keeps us seeing the good but not the bad side of male characteristics and the bad but not the good side of female characteristics. She urges a move toward nondichotomous thinking that examines how the positive characteristics associated with traditionally male and female roles can be combined because they are not really opposed to each other (Nelson 1992, 1996). Something can be strong and flexible—like a tree in the wind. Strength and flexibility are valuable in both markets and families.

Thus, while I emphasized the need to criticize the "separative" view in my chapter in *Beyond Economic Man* (England 1993), I now see the important feminist project to be formulating a view that is critical of both the separative self and its often tacit and subordinated companion, the soluble self. We need to reject the false dichotomy of individual *versus* relationship. In its place, we need empirical study of how individuation and connection combine in all spheres, and ethical theories that show the value of each. A feminist view of "individuals-in-relation" or "relational autonomy" sees merit in recognizing and reducing the extent to which women's autonomy is constrained by men's dominance, as liberal and radical feminists have emphasized. It also recognizes that complete independence and autonomy are neither possible nor desirable, and that intimacy, relationships, care, and connections are the source of much of what is valuable in human life, as communitarians and cultural feminists have emphasized. In a similar vein, Folbre (2001) gropes for a politics that combines the socialist feminist critique of class, race, national, and gender hierarchies and the liberal emphasis on self-governance with the traditionally feminine concern for nurture, care, and community, and calls it "social feminism."

Applying the Feminist Critique of Separative Self Assumptions to Economics

To apply the feminist critique of the separative side of the separative/soluble dichotomy to economics, I will show how three basic assumptions presume separative selves.

Interpersonal Utility Comparisons

Neoclassical economists assume that interpersonal utility comparisons are impossible. Since the 1930s, utility has been conceived as the satisfaction of an individual's subjective desires; this concept lacks any dimension of objective, measurable welfare that might form the basis for interpersonal comparison (Cooter and Rappoport 1984). As a result, neoclassical theory tells us that we cannot know which of two persons gained more from a given exchange, because the relevant "currency" in which gain or advantage is measured is utility, and utility is conceived as being radically subjective. Eschewing the possibility of interpersonal utility assumptions is also the consequence of seeing an individual's utility to be measured on an ordinal rather than "cardinal" scale (with equal intervals and a nonarbitrary zero point), since cardinal measurement would allow comparisons between people. This is so basic an assumption that some form of it is mentioned in most undergraduate microeconomic textbooks (Hirshleifer 1984, 476; Varian 1999, 57–58).

Using Pareto-optimality as the criterion of efficiency derives at least in part from the assumption that interpersonal utility comparisons are impossible. A distributional change is defined as Pareto-superior if at least one party gains utility and no one loses any. For example, voluntary exchange between self-interested individuals produces a Pareto-superior distribution. Each party must have felt that s/he would be made better off by the exchange than by forgoing it or s/he would not have made it. When no more Pareto-superior changes can be made through exchange, the distribution is said to be Pareto-optimal. Thus, redistribution requiring some affluent persons to lose utility for the sake of a gain by the poor cannot be Pareto-superior by definition.

How does the feminist critique of separation/connection relate to interpersonal utility comparisons? The assumption that interpersonal utility comparisons are impossible flows from assuming a separative self. To see how this is true, imagine that we started by assuming the sort of emotional connection that encourages empathy. Such empathy would facilitate making interpersonal utility comparisons, since being able to imagine how someone else feels in a given situation implies the possibility of translating between one's own and another person's metric for utility. Assuming that interpersonal utility comparisons are impossible amounts to assuming a separative self and denying the possibility of an empathic, emotionally connected self. But if we assume instead that individuals *can* make interpersonal utility comparisons, then surely we would conclude that as scholars we, too, are capable of making such comparisons. These comparisons would provide information about which of the individuals under study are likely suffer more than (i.e., have lower utility than) others. We then would view such comparisons between individuals' utility levels as practical measurement problems that we should try to surmount rather than considering them impossible a priori.

As long as we accept that utility comparisons between individuals are impossible, we find that the same principle applies to comparisons between groups. To answer questions about groups requires not only measuring utility but also averaging utilities across persons. While some applied economists study inequalities in wealth or income between groups and discuss their findings in language that (often only tacitly) implies something about unequal utility between the groups, such interpretations are in fundamental conflict with the theoretical core of neoclassical economics. Hence, generalizations such as that women in a particular society are disadvantaged relative to men are either not made by economists or not taken to imply that social arrangements may make women's average utility less than men's.

The tendency to eschew interpersonal utility comparisons is part of why positive neoclassical theories harmonize so well with conservative normative positions on distributional issues. The paradigm denies one the possibility of recognizing that those at the bottom of hierarchies average less utility than others, which would provide a basis for questioning the justice of initial unequal distribution of endowments and its consequences. The paradigm also implies that virtually all collectivistic redistribution is non-Pareto-optimal. In sum, it permits no assessments of unequal utility that otherwise might serve as grounds for advocating egalitarian redistribution; rather, it criticizes such a redistribution as inefficient (in the sense of violating Pareto optimality). To take only one example, this assumption leads one to question the merit of assistance to the large proportion of female-headed families who live in poverty. More generally, it denies us a theoretical basis for saying existing arrangements benefit some groups more than others or, specifically, men more than women.

Tastes: Exogenous and Unchanging

What the utility maximizer of economic theory will do is often indeterminate unless one knows the individual's tastes. Tastes (also called preferences) determine the amount of utility provided by different combinations of goods, services, leisure, working conditions, children, and so forth. They are an input to economic models. Economists generally do not attempt to explain the origin of these tastes. In a famous article, "De Gustabus Non Est Disputandum" (roughly translated, "there is no accounting for tastes"), George Stigler and Gary Becker (1977) argued that there is little variation in tastes between individuals and tastes change little over time, so most behavior can be explained by prices and endowments. Some economists see a role for disciplines such as sociology and psychology in explaining variations in tastes. But whether or not they believe that individuals differ in their tastes, economists typically see tastes as exogenous to their models. This implies that they will not change in response to interactions in markets.

There is no doubt that assuming fixed and exogenous rather than changing and endogenous preferences radically simplifies neoclassical models. But is the assumption reasonable? There is good reason to believe that it is not. The following questions illustrate the point: Are most individuals really so impervious to their surroundings that they can hold a job for years without their preferences being affected by the routines they get used to in this job? Are preferences never influenced by interactions with coworkers? If they are, then events in the labor market do affect tastes. Are consumer tastes never altered by interactions with neighbors? If they are, then events in the housing market (which determine the identity of one's neighbors) affect tastes. One needs to assume an unrealistic degree of emotional separation and atomism to deny the possibility of these effects of market exchanges upon tastes. A model that does not help to elucidate how tastes change through such interactions leaves out much of human experience. Further, as economists enlarge the scope of their discipline, the implausibility of the assumption becomes ever clearer. Does anyone really believe that the choice of a spouse in the "marriage market" has no effects on later tastes?

One additional problem with ignoring the endogeneity of tastes is that it obscures some of the processes through which gender inequality is perpetuated. In some of these processes, economic outcomes affect tastes. For example, according to common psychological theories of learning, also accepted by some sociologists, adults encourage gender-traditional behavior of children by explicit reinforcement and by children's modeling of adult behavior (Maccoby and Jacklin 1974; Kohlberg 1966). Imagine, then, that adult roles result in part from gender discrimination in the market. This then affects the inputs to children's socialization as they imitate the behavior of the adults around them. Indeed, Kohlberg argues that children watch what same-sex adults do, leap over what philosophers call the "is-ought" gap, and form preferences to be like same-sex adults. In this way, at the societal level, an economic process, market discrimination, affects the distribution of tastes of the next generation even if tastes are exogenous to market participation at the individual level. Or, to take an example from later in the life cycle, if schools or employers discriminate against women who start out wanting to enter "male" fields, women may not only adjust their choices but actually change their tastes to be consistent with the available options. In this example, tastes are endogenous to economic processes even at the individual level, in ways that perpetuate gender inequality. In an analogous fashion, given economic processes such as racial discrimination or inequality of opportunity by class background, economic processes may lead to race or class differences in tastes; but such differences, too, are endogenous to economic processes.

Selfishness in Markets

Neoclassical theory assumes self-interested actors. Since it says nothing explicit about what gives people satisfaction, it is not inconsistent with neoclassical assumptions for some individuals to derive satisfaction from being altruistic. That is, self-interest need not imply selfishness in the sense of failing to care for others (Friedman and Diem 1990). Nonetheless, in practice, most economists *do* assume selfishness *in markets*, as both Frank (1988, 2000), who is critical of the assumption, and Becker (1991, 277–306), an advocate, have pointed out. Sometimes auxiliary assumptions preclude altruism. An example is the assumption that utilities are independent. Since economists generally define A's altruism toward B as B's utility contributing to A's utility, altruism is precluded by the assumption that actors' utilities are independent.

The assumption that individuals are selfish is related to the separative model of the self. Emotional connection often creates empathy, altruism, and a subjective sense of social solidarity. For example, the experience of attending to the needs of a child or of mentoring a student tends to make us care more about others' well-being; that is, nurturant behavior makes us more nurturing. (Note that this is also an example of changing tastes.) Separative selves would have little basis for developing the necessary empathy to practice altruism.[5]

Most labor economists assume selfishness of employers toward employees and vice versa. If employers were altruistic toward some or all of their employees, they might pay them above-market wages, forgoing some profit. Of course, the *strategic* payment of above-market wages in "shirking" models of efficiency wages (Bulow and Summers 1986; Katz 1986) does not violate the assumption of selfishness. In these models, employers are profit maximizers and pay above-market wages only when such wages increase the productivity of workers, and thus revenue, enough to more than compensate for the costs of the higher wage.[6]

Assuming selfishness in markets fails to account for men's altruism toward other men in market behavior, altruism that may work to the disadvantage of women. When people engage in collective action, a kind of *selective* altruism may be at work (Elster 1979; Sen 1987). For example, when male employees collude in order to try to keep women out of "their" jobs, they are exhibiting within-sex altruism.

Sometimes selective within-sex altruism also exists between male employers and employees, so that employers are willing to pay male workers more than the contribution of the marginal worker to revenue product. This may be termed "pro-male altruistic discrimination" as opposed to the more common form of antifemale discrimination when women are paid less than the market-clearing wage for men. Matthew Goldberg (1982) has argued that competitive market forces do not erode this pro-male altruistic discrimination in the way that they erode antifemale discrimination.[7] The essence of his argument is that

---

5. Empathy usually encourages altruism; we are more apt to be kind to others if we "feel their pain." However, empathy can be used selfishly, although I believe this is the unusual case. The person who knows you best is the most capable of exploiting you. If A understands B's utility function well, it is more possible for A to bargain with B in a way that concedes no more than is necessary; this is the truth behind adages about the advantages of a good "poker face" that reveals little about one's feelings and preferences. For a discussion by a neoclassical economist on empathy or altruism as an endogenous taste, see Stark and Falk 1998.

6. By contrast, Akerlof's (1982, 1984) "gift exchange" model of efficiency wages does presume a sort of altruism on the part of workers and/or employers. In this sense, it is a radical departure from the usual neoclassical assumption of selfishness in markets.

7. For a nontechnical elaboration of Goldberg's argument and explanation of why economists believe market competition erodes discrimination, see England 1992, chap. 2. I have taken some liberties translating Goldberg's technical argument; his discussion is about race rather than gender discrimination, and he uses the term *nepotism* rather than *altruism*. However, he has stated in a personal

a nondiscriminator cannot buy out an altruistic discriminator for a price consistent with the present value of the business to the nondiscriminator. This is because the nonpecuniary utility the pro-male discriminator is getting from indulging his taste for altruism toward male workers makes the business worth more to the discriminator than to the nondiscriminator. By contrast, a nondiscriminator's offer to buy out an antifemale discriminator (who is hiring men for more than the wage he would have to pay women) will be compelling because the nondiscriminator can make more money than the antifemale discriminator with no sacrifice of nonpecuniary utility. If we assume the absence of altruism in markets, then we cannot recognize the possibility that this selective altruism is a source of sex discrimination that *can* endure in competitive markets. Discrimination in favor of members of one's own racial, ethnic, or national-origin group may work similarly (see Saunders and Darity, chap. 4 in this volume). Thus, recognizing selective altruism would raise questions about neoclassical economists' usual assumption that discrimination cannot endure in competitive markets.

Applying the Feminist Critique of the Soluble Self to the Economics of the Family

Even the rugged "autonomous" individuals valorized in liberal economic and political theory would seem to require a selfless altruist to take care of their dependency needs when they are very young, very old, sick, or disabled. But the broad benefits of this work, done largely by women, have remained invisible in economic and political theory until recently. It was just tacitly assumed by most economists—neoclassical, Marxist, and institutionalist—that women would provide loving care for their families and support men in their market endeavors. Of course, it was also assumed that men would, in their role as "head" of families treat women and children with love, albeit of a paternalistic variety.

Much of this remained implicit, seldom discussed, until Gary Becker's "new home economics" became a mainstream staple. Becker (1991) explicitly assumed a single family utility function in which the "head" is an altruist. From a feminist perspective, Becker's acknowledgment that production goes on in

---

communication that he considers my elaboration consistent with his argument. I refer to discrimination as altruistic (toward its beneficiaries) when employers pay a group more than marginal revenue product; if employers pay more than the going rate but less than marginal revenue product, I do not consider it altruistic.

the household and that therefore the household should be seen as part of "the economy" deserves our applause. However, Becker's assumptions about altruism and family solidarity are in need of a feminist critique. (These same criticisms apply to the more recent 1991 version of Becker's *Treatise on the Family* as well as the 1981 edition, as well as to Bernheim and Stark's 1988 discussion of altruism in the family.)

From a feminist point of view the overarching problem with Becker's work is that he fails to consider seriously that men are often *not* altruistic to their wives and children. Becker is explicit about his belief that self-interest is the correct assumption for the market, whereas altruism is more prevalent in the family (1991, 277–306). His well-known "rotten kid" theorem posits an altruistic family head who takes the utility functions of family members as arguments of "his" own utility function. He does not say that the head gives *no* weight to his own narrow self-interest, but rather that his utility function includes these preferences but also gives at least some weight to other family members' preferences (Pollak 2002). Becker argues that if the head is somewhat altruistic in this sense, then even a selfish "rotten" spouse or child will be induced to "behave" because of incentives the head sets up by redistributing away from the "rotten" family member. Commentators have pointed out, however, that the "rotten kid" theorem implicitly assumes that the family member whose altruism induces altruism in others *also* controls the resources to be distributed (Ben-Porath 1982; Pollak 1985, 2002). Otherwise the theorem does not hold; it is control over the resources that allows the head of the family to redistribute against the selfish "rotten kid" unless s/he alters behavior to be more consistent with collective family interest. Thus, the "altruist" also must be a dictator of sorts to get the result Becker wants—the ability to model the family, assuming it behaves, so as to maximize a single utility function, the utility function of the somewhat altruistic head.

Becker appears not to think that who earns the most money will affect distribution or consumption within the family. But what if the head earns most of the money needed to obtain the resources and is not so altruistic? Becker does not discuss this possibility. He does, however, discuss why he thinks men have higher earnings than women. He explains the typical (although changing) division of labor in which men specialize in market and women in household and child-rearing work in terms of its efficiency. One can certainly criticize this on the grounds that it ignores the role of tradition and market discrimination. But it is also important to look at how Becker's assumption of altruism of the person who distributes resources in the family blinds him to seeing the power men can gain over women by the access to resources that earnings provide and, thus, the disadvantages for a woman of being a homemaker (Folbre 1994;

Woolley 1996; England and Budig 1998; Kabeer 2001). To the extent that both spouses are completely altruistic, who controls distribution would not matter. But it is only on the unreasonable assumption that one or both have a completely soluble self that dissolves into the will of the other that we can imagine no conflicts of interest.

Oddly enough, the altruism of women in traditional caretaking roles does not figure much in Becker's theory. Women's altruism, at least toward children, is usually assumed by economists, but not emphasized. Indeed, the inherent dependence of the human condition is rarely discussed. As previously noted, we all need care as children and in our old age, and most of us have some periods of disability and illness during which we are dependent even during our "prime age." Even at our peak, we all benefit from love and nurturance. Where does the altruism and caring behavior that ensures this care come from? What is striking is that neither Becker nor other economists discuss this explicitly; they just seem to assume there will be enough altruism in the family to provide for dependents.

By being more explicit than other economists about altruism, Becker reveals that he actually credits the real altruism to men, despite the fact that women are socially assigned to roles like mothering where complete selflessness is encouraged![8] A cynic might say that Becker's notion of the altruism of the head (i.e., that the head's preferences give considerable weight to other family members' preferences) deflects our attention from the fact that the model is really very similar to traditional notions that assign the role of head to the man, allow him to be a dictator, and don't worry about whether this is really better for women and children or only for him. The fact that the altruist also needs to have control over distribution for his model of the family to work should alert us to the fact that it is not a model consistent with mutual altruism combined with mutuality in decision making in which, in the face of differences in preference, each spouse sometimes gets his or her way and sometimes yields to the wish of the other. A model that has such mutuality as one theoretical possibility seems to require rejection of the separative/soluble dichotomy.

But even if we believed that Becker was positing real mutual altruism among all family members, there is still an unacceptable level of dichotomous thinking. I have no problem with the notion that, on average, people are more altruistic toward family members than toward strangers. There is, however, a problem with the extreme bifurcation of the view of how humans behave in

---

8. In fact, an interesting body of recent experimental work suggests that women act more altruistically than men (Eckel and Grossman 1996a, 1996b). This does not necessarily imply innate sex differences, but may be a socially constructed preference—an endogenous taste.

the market and in the family. If economic man or woman is so altruistic in the family, might not some altruism be present in market behavior as well? Doesn't this altruism imply an ability to empathize with others that might permit making at least rough interpersonal utility comparisons? Doesn't the susceptibility of an altruist to being influenced by another's joy or pain suggest that s/he also might modify certain tastes through the process of interaction with others? If the answers to these questions are yes, as may well be the case, then the altruism assumed for the family is inconsistent with the separative self assumed for market behavior. It is simply not plausible that the altruist who displays an emotionally connective self in the family is the same person who marches out into the market selfish, entirely unable to empathize with those outside the family.

Recent Developments in Economics: A Corrective to Separative/Soluble Dichotomies?

Bargaining Models of Marriage

Suppose that economists used their usual "separative" assumptions to model behavior among spouses and between parents and children. How would a selfish individual with unchanging tastes behave within the family? When economists analyze a situation that lacks the large number of potential buyers and sellers that characterize markets, they turn to game theory, which has become increasingly popular in economics. Formal game-theoretic models of family bargaining and distribution have been offered in recent decades (Manser and Brown 1980; McElroy and Horney 1981; McElroy 1985, 1990; Chiappori 1992; Lundberg and Pollak 1993, 1994, 1996). Many of these were not developed as part of a program of gender scholarship but lead to some of the same insights developed in less formal but more substantive terms by gender scholars (England and Farkas 1986, chap. 3; Sen 1990; England and Kilbourne 1990; Folbre 1994, 1997; Woolley 1996; Agarwal 1997; England 2000a, 2000b; Kabeer 2001; England and Folbre 2002b). Both groups often characterize their contributions as inconsistent with Becker.

Whereas in a Beckerian world, the family has a single utility function and cooperates to allocate resources and each member's time efficiently in the service of this unitary utility function, in a bargaining world, resources affect whose interests prevail in decision making within the family that affects each person's utility. The idea is that, if you have more resources, you can get your way more often in terms of who does housework, how money is spent, and other issues on which spouses may disagree. *Why* might bringing money or other resources into the household give a spouse bargaining power? The game theory models that economists have applied to family bargaining answer this with the concept of "threat points" (see Lundberg and Pollak 1996 for an overview). "Divorce threat point" (also called "external threat point") models emphasize that bargaining within marriage is conducted in the shadow of the possibility of divorce. An individual's threat point is what s/he has to fall back on if the marriage dissolves. This is presumably influenced by one's own earnings, one's position in the market for a new partner, and the life skills and preferences that affect how much one enjoys being single. Utility outside marriage is also influenced by how much gender discrimination there is in the labor market, the amount of child support payments the state makes absent parents pay and how strongly this is enforced, as well as state payments to single individuals or parents. McElroy (1990) calls these factors "extrahousehold environmental parameters" and Folbre (1997) calls them "gender-specific environmental parameters." Optimizing individuals will choose whether to stay in the marriage or leave by comparing the utility they experience in the marriage to what they anticipate if they leave the marriage.

Consider a couple, A and B. The better off A would be if the marriage dissolved, the better the deal B has to provide A in the marriage to make it worthwhile for A to stay in the marriage. Individuals make concessions to their partners to keep their marriages intact if they would be worse off without the spouse than in the marriage even after having made the necessary concessions. If both spouses act this way, it follows that the better A's alternatives outside (relative to inside) the marriage, or the worse B's outside alternatives, the better a bargain A (and worse B) can strike in the marriage. Resources that one could withdraw from one's partner and/or retain for oneself if the marriage dissolved are those that increase bargaining power.

Lundberg and Pollak (1993, 1996) also discuss "internal threat point models." Here the issue is what one spouse can withhold from the other without leaving the marriage, and what that leaves the other to fall back on within the marriage. In such models, money that comes into the household through partner A gives A power because s/he could possibly fail to share some or all of the income, even without divorce or separation. Here, too, earnings should lead to some power, because they are a resource one shares or could withhold. But in this model the relevance of earnings to bargaining power does not hinge on their portability if one leaves the relationship as it does in the divorce threat model.[9]

9. Threat-point models have a similar logic to sociological exchange theory. For an overview of exchange theory, see Molm and Cook 1995 and Cook 1987. For applications to marital power, see Molm and Cook 1995, 220; and England and Farkas 1986.

Economists offer some evidence to support the bargaining view of marriage. Recent studies show that where women have more access to and control over economic resources (relative to men), more is spent on children (Thomas 1990; Alderman et al. 1995; Lundberg, Pollak, and Wales 1997).[10] This evidence is inconsistent with a view that altruism is so pervasive in the family that who controls the resources doesn't affect whose wishes prevail.

Bargaining theories allow one to see the possible disadvantages for women of a division of labor in which men specialize in market and women in household work. They imply that, to the extent men are not entirely altruistic, the result for women will be less decision-making power and a smaller share of resources going to them. Becker emphasizes that the pie is bigger with specialization because of its efficiency, but, even if this is true, there may be a trade-off for women between a bigger pie and a bigger share of a smaller pie. From a feminist point of view, it is important to have a theory that does not obscure this disadvantage to women of traditional arrangements.

Thus, while economic theory has downplayed connection and solidarity in market behavior, models of the household that use separative-self assumptions are a useful corrective for understanding the household precisely because perfect altruism does not prevail. On the other hand, they miss the considerable altruism and solidarity in the household that exists, although it was previously exaggerated. What is difficult is to devise models that recognize a role for both altruism and self-interested bargaining and still generate clear predictions.

Models of Endogenous Tastes

As discussed above, economists generally assume that tastes (preferences) are unchanging and determined exogenously. If tastes are assumed to be stable, then changes in what we choose must be due to changes in our income or the relative prices of various choices. As discussed above, this is consistent with a separative self; in this view, the self is so impervious to social influences that preferences remain uninfluenced by social networks, life experiences, and so on. Robert Pollak, a persistent mainstream critic of Becker, had earlier argued for models including endogenous preferences (Pollak 1970, 1978). (Neoclassical economists Stark and Falk [1998] also discussed empathy as an endogenous taste.) Interestingly, Becker's 1996 book, *Accounting for Tastes,* although

10. Some have challenged this conclusion, fearing omitted variable bias; factors in women's background that correlate with their resources may be correlated with how good they are as mothers. Alderman et al. (1995) concede that this is possible but argue that enough evidence has accumulated on the relationship between women's resources and children's well-being to merit shifting the burden of proof to those who claim a single household utility function.

it reprints the abovementioned famous 1977 paper with Stigler, elsewhere announces a change in position on this issue. He now argues that preferences for "specific commodities" (examples would be pears, listening to rap music, or having an intimate relationship with a particular person) can change over time in response to an individual's experiences; they are neither exogenous nor unchanging. Indeed, they may change because of one's social connections, an acknowledgment of the role of "social capital." For example, having parents or friends who play classical music may teach you to appreciate such music. Also, many things may be habit forming. Addictions are the extreme example of this, when, for example, today's choice to consume a drug affects the degree to which one prefers the drug to other goods in the future. In these ways, Becker now recognizes the existence of endogenous, changing preferences.

What Becker still sees as exogenous and unchanging is an "extended utility function," which specifies, for each individual, the way in which social connections and past consumption experiences determine how much utility will be gained from various combinations of specific commodities. This extended utility function is different from the standard economists' notion of a utility function that simply consists of one's preferences for commodities and rankings of all possible combinations and sequences thereof (see, for example, Varian 1999, chap. 4). It is more like a production function for utility functions. Simply put, in the new Becker, it is no longer what you like that is seen to be unchanging, but rather the process by which preferences are determined. There are still elements of the "separative self" concept apparent in making the utility production function impervious to social and economic influences. Yet I am not inclined to criticize him on this point because virtually every answer to the profound question of how we come to want what we want takes some portion of "human nature" as unchanging and asks how, given this, conditions affect our preferences. Becker examines questions such as how we can see all the decisions leading up to drug addiction as rational. A feminist cannot help but think of a parallel. If we put endogenous tastes together with a bargaining model (eschewed by Becker), we could hypothesize that being in a subordinate position leads to deferential behavior which, in turn, is habit forming, further reducing women's ability to "drive a hard bargain," even when their threat point improves. This would get us close to feminist notions of internalized oppression. Though Becker does not use the model of endogenous tastes in this way, it could be usefully developed to study internalized oppression.

The New Feminist Economics of Care

A third area of recent economic work I consider is from feminists within economics and related social sciences. The study of care work—tending children, nursing, doctoring, counseling, therapy, and so forth—is an excellent example of a topic that challenges all the usual dichotomies—male/female, separative/connected, selfish/altruistic, family/market. This work is increasingly done in the market, although much care is still provided in the home. It often combines altruistic motivations with working for pay. Contrary to many critiques of commodification, feminist and Marxist, the fact that care work is done in the family does not ensure that it is done entirely out of altruism, nor should we assume that moving it into the market or paying well for it takes all the real caring out of care work (Nelson 1999; Folbre and Nelson 2000; Nelson and England 2002).

How do we know whether there will be an optimal amount of genuine care, motivated by altruism, to create a good society and a productive economy (Folbre and Weisskopf 1998)? As women have better economic alternatives outside the home and in the market other than paid care work, and few men are attracted to care work, the question of whether we will have "enough" teachers, nurses, and child-care workers comes to the fore. Care work pays less than other work requiring the same amount of skill, effort, and risk (England and Folbre 1999a; England, Budig, and Folbre 2002). We should not, however, assume that this is explained by the fact that altruism is its own reward and that the low pay for this work can be explained entirely in terms of the theory of compensating differentials. It may be that the low pay results in part from the difficulties of getting all the indirect beneficiaries of this work to pay the care workers, because care work creates positive externalities and public goods (see England and Folbre 1999a, 1999b, 2000a, 2000b, 2002a, chap. 2 in this volume). That is, by increasing the capabilities of recipients, care makes its recipients into better spouses, parents, workers, and neighbors, and the benefits of this diffuse to many who never pay the care worker. (England and Folbre, chap. 2 in this volume, explore the utility of new economic institutionalist contracting models for theorizing care.)

We are a long way from an adequate theory of care, but it seems clear that the supply of and reward for care are affected by social norms encouraging altruism. We also see self-interested distributional struggles over how much of care work men and the state will take on to reduce women's traditional responsibility for care, as well as similar struggles over whose care is paid for by the state and how much state support for care work there is (O'Connor, Orloff, and Shaver 1999). Models that see all family behavior as altruistic or that deny the possibility that care workers may be motivated both by real caring *and* pecuniary motives falsely dichotomize. We need to see the self-interested agency as well as selective empathy and connection in all spheres. What is promising is that authors are explicitly trying to avoid both sides of the dichotomy in this work; what is frustrating is how hard it is to do this and still come up with firm conclusions.

Conclusion

I have argued that economists should learn from interdisciplinary feminist theory that offers models of individuals-in-relation as a corrective to traditional dichotomies of separative/soluble selves. Based on these feminist ideas, I have criticized economists' assumptions that in the market interpersonal utility comparisons are impossible, tastes are exogenous and unchanging, and individuals are selfish (i.e., utilities are independent), but that in the family altruism is the rule. The first three of these assumptions of neoclassical theory contain the "separative-self" bias that fails to recognize selective altruism, endogenous tastes, and empathy in market behavior. Economists' usual assumptions about the family go to the other extreme, seeing some actors as almost entirely altruistic or soluble. Taken together, this view glorifies and exaggerates men's autonomy outside the family while giving them credit for too much altruism within the family. This view also results in an inability to see how conventional arrangements perpetuate women's subordination to men in markets and the family.

I examined recent work in mainstream and feminist economics to see how successfully either provides a corrective to the overly "separative" view of actors in markets or the overly "soluble" view of family members. Bargaining theories of marriage bring some individual self-interest back into the family and models of endogenous tastes could, if broadly applied, show us social influences on actors in the market as well as the family, some of which perpetuate disadvantage by gender, class, and race. These contributions from mainstream economics are hopeful signs, attacking problematic assumptions one at a time. They do not, however, meet the real challenge of providing a model that includes altruism, connection, and self-interested maneuvering in both markets and families. Feminist work on the economics of care is promising in its challenge of the separative/soluble dichotomy, considering work done in families as well as markets for both love and money. Nelson (chap. 3 in this volume) extends this challenge of the separative/soluble dichotomy to the theory of firms. But we do not yet have a coherent alternative theory.

Modeling behavior when selfishness and empathy are variable and when preferences can change in response to the environment is a continuing challenge for feminist economists and other social scientists. Giving up the strong assumptions common in mainstream economic theory severely blunts the predictive power of models, even if a strong rationality assumption is retained.[11] For example, when it comes to wages and discrimination, it is harder to predict what a rational, selectively altruistic employer will do than to predict what a rational, profit-maximizing employer will do. Similarly, it is harder to predict how a rational husband who earns more than his wife will behave in a model of marriage that sees both altruism and self-interest to be present than in a model that assumes only one or the other.

Some feminists conclude that we simply need to describe reality richly, that any theorizing does violence to reality. Others believe that it takes a theory to replace a theory. My own view is that we should not give up stretching toward a comprehensive theory of human behavior and well-being even while giving up false dichotomies that have kept models simpler but also distorted them. These new models will show us both the dangers and the value in connections and in separation. They will help us understand a world where both self-interested and other-regarding motives permeate markets and families. They will help us understand the sources of inequalities and the determinants of the happiness or misery of nations, firms, and families. In my view, this is the challenge for the coming decades of work in feminist economics.

11. I have not challenged this most "sacred" neoclassical assumption of all, the rationality assumption. Some feminist philosophers argue that the concept of rationality in Western thought has been constructed to be inconsistent with anything related to traits and activities presumed to be "feminine"—nature, the body, passion, emotion—and that this has distorted the concept of rationality (Lloyd 1984; Bordo 1986; Schott 1988). Yet rationality has a rather limited meaning in neoclassical theory. The rational actor has preferences that are both transitive (if I prefer A to B and B to C, I will prefer A to C) and complete (any two outcomes can be compared), and s/he acts on the basis of correct calculations about the means that best maximize utility given these preferences (Sen 1987; Varian 1999). It is beyond my scope here to consider whether or not this neoclassical concept of rationality is relatively free from gender bias, particularly in the sense of assuming separative or soluble selves. However, even if we retain the rationality postulate, the neoclassical model needs substantial revision to make its other assumptions consistent with challenges to the separative/soluble dichotomy.

References

Agarwal, Bina. 1997. "Bargaining" and gender relations: Within and beyond the household. *Feminist Economics* 3:1–50.

Akerlof, George A. 1982. Labor contracts as partial gift exchange. *Quarterly Journal of Economics* 47:543–69.

———. 1984. Gift exchange and efficiency-wage theory: Four views. *American Economic Review* 74:19–83.

Alderman, H., P. A. Chiappori, L. Haddad, J. Hoddinott, and R. Kanbur. 1995. Unitary versus collective models of the household: Is it time to shift the burden of proof? *World Bank Research Observer* 10:1–19.

Aries, Elizabeth. 1996. *Men and women in interaction: Reconsidering the differences.* New York: Oxford University Press.

Becker, Gary S. 1991. *A treatise on the family.* Enlarged ed. Cambridge, Mass.: Harvard University Press.

———. 1996. *Accounting for tastes.* Cambridge, Mass.: Harvard University Press.

Benhabib, Seyla. 1987. The generalized and the concrete other: The Kohlberg-Gilligan controversy and feminist theory. In *Feminism as critique: On the politics of gender,* edited by Seyla Benhabib and Drucilla Cornell, 77–95. Minneapolis: University of Minnesota Press.

Ben-Ner, Avner, and Louis Putterman. 1998. *Economics, values, and organization.* Cambridge: Cambridge University Press.

Ben-Porath, Yoram. 1982. Economics and the family—match or mismatch? A review of Becker's *A treatise on the family. Journal of Economic Literature* 20:52–64.

Bernheim, B. Douglas, and Oded Stark. 1988. Altruism within the family reconsidered: Do nice guys finish last? *American Economic Review* 78:1034–45.

Bordo, Susan. 1986. The Cartesian masculinization of thought? *Signs* 11:439–56.

Brah, A. 2001. Feminist theory and women of color. In *International encyclopedia of the social and behavioral sciences,* edited by Neil J. Smelser and Paul B. Baltes, 8:5491–95. London: Elsevier.

Bulow, Jeremy I., and Lawrence H. Summers. 1986. A theory of dual labor markets with application to industrial policy, discrimination, and Keynesian unemployment. *Journal of Labor Economics* 4:376–414.

Chiappori, Pierre-André. 1992. Collective labor supply and welfare. *Journal of Political Economy* 100:437–67.

Chodorow, Nancy. 1978. *The reproduction of mothering.* Berkeley: University of California Press.

Collins, Patricia Hill. 1990. *Black feminist thought: Knowledge, consciousness, and the politics of empowerment.* Boston: Unwin Hyman.

Cook, Karen, ed. 1987. *Social exchange theory.* Newbury Park, Calif.: Sage.

Cooter, Robert, and Peter Rappoport. 1984. Were the ordinalists wrong about welfare economics? *Journal of Economic Literature* 22:507–30.

Eckel, Catherine C., and Philip Grossman. 1996a. Are women less selfish than men? Evidence from dictator experiments. Unpublished manuscript, Department of Economics, Virginia Polytechnic Institute and State University.

———. 1996b. The relative price of fairness: Gender differences in a punishment game. Unpublished manuscript, Department of Economics, Virginia Polytechnic Institute and State University.

Elster, Jon. 1979. *Ulysses and the sirens: Studies in rationality and irrationality.* Cambridge: Cambridge University Press.

England, Paula. 1992. *Comparable worth: Theory and evidence.* New York: Aldine de Gruyter.

———. 1993. The separative self: Androcentric bias in neoclassical assumptions. In *Beyond economic man: Feminist theory and economics,* edited by Marianne A. Ferber and Julie A. Nelson, 37–53. Chicago: University of Chicago Press.

———. 2000a. Conceptualizing women's empowerment in countries of the north. In *Women's empowerment and demographic processes: Moving beyond Cairo,* edited by Harriet B. Presser and Gita Sen, 15–36. Oxford: Oxford University Press.

———. 2000b. Marriage, the costs of children, and gender inequality. In *The ties that bind: Perspectives on marriage and cohabitation,* edited by L. Waite, C. Bachrach, M. Hindin, E. Thomson, and A. Thornton, 320–42. New York: Aldine de Gruyter.

England, Paula, and Michelle Budig. 1998. Gary Becker on the family: His genius, impact, and blind spots. In *Required reading: Sociology's most influential books,* edited by Dan Clawson. Amherst: University of Massachusetts Press.

England, Paula, Michelle Budig, and Nancy Folbre. 2002. The wages of virtue: The relative pay of care work. *Social Problems* 49 (4): 455–73.

England, Paula, and George Farkas. 1986. *Households, employment, and gender: A social, economic, and demographic view.* New York: Aldine de Gruyter.

England, Paula, and Nancy Folbre. 1999a. The cost of caring. In *Emotional labor in the service economy,* edited by Ronnie J. Steinberg and Deborah M. Figart, 39–51. Annals of the American Academy of Political and Social Science 561. Thousand Oaks, Calif.: Sage.

———. 1999b. Who should pay for the kids? In *The silent crisis in U.S. child care,* edited by Suzanne W. Helburn, 194–209. Annals of the American Academy of Political and Social Science 563. Thousand Oaks, Calif.: Sage.

———. 2000a. Capitalism and the erosion of care. In *Unconventional wisdom: Alternative perspectives on the new economy,* edited by Jeff Madrick, 29–48. New York: Century Foundation.

———. 2000b. Reconceptualizing human capital. In *The management of durable relations,* edited by Werner Raub and Jeroen Weesie, 126–28. Amsterdam: Thela Thesis Publishers.

———. 2002a. Care, inequality, and policy. In *Child care and inequality: Re-thinking carework for children and youth,* edited by F. Cancian, D. Kurz, S. London, R. Reviere, and M. Tuominen, 133–44. New York: Routledge.

———. 2002b. Involving dads: Parental bargaining and family well-being. In *Handbook of father involvement: Multidisciplinary perspectives,* edited by Catherine S. Tamis-LeMonda and Natasha Cabrera, 387–408. Mahwah, N.J.: Erlbaum Associates.

England, Paula, and Barbara Stanek Kilbourne. 1990. Markets, marriages, and other mates: The problem of power. In *Beyond the marketplace: Rethinking economy and society,* edited by Roger Friedland and A. F. Robertson, 163–88. New York: Aldine de Gruyter.

Epstein, Cynthia Fuchs. 1988. Deceptive distinctions: Sex, gender, and the social order. New Haven, Conn.: Yale University Press.

Ferber, Marianne A., and Julie A. Nelson, eds. 1993. *Beyond economic man: Feminist theory and economics.* Chicago: University of Chicago Press.

Folbre, Nancy. 1994. *Who pays for the kids? Gender and the structures of constraint.* New York: Routledge.

———. 1997. Gender coalitions: Extrafamily influences on intrafamily inequality. In *Intrahousehold resource allocation in developing countries: Models, methods, and policy,* edited by Lawrence Haddad, John Hoddinott, and Harold Alderman, 263–74. Baltimore: Johns Hopkins University Press.

———. 2001. *The invisible heart: Economics and family values.* New York: New Press.

Folbre, Nancy, and Heidi Hartmann. 1988. The rhetoric of self-interest: Ideology and gender in economic theory. In *The consequences of economic rhetoric,* edited by Arjo Klamer, Donald N. McCloskey, and Robert M. Solow, 184–203. New York: Cambridge University Press.

Folbre, Nancy, and Julie Nelson. 2000. For love or money—or both? *Journal of Economic Perspectives* 14:123–40.

Folbre, Nancy, and Thomas E. Weisskopf. 1998. Did father know best: Families, markets, and the supply of caring labor. In *Economics, values, and organization,* edited by Avner Ben-Ner and Louis Putterman, 171–205. Cambridge: Cambridge University Press.

Frank, Robert. 1988. *Passions within reason: The strategic role of the emotions.* New York: Norton.

———. 2000. *Microeconomics and behavior.* New York: McGraw-Hill.

Fraser, Nancy, and Linda J. Nicholson. 1990. Social criticism without philosophy: An encounter between feminism and postmodernism. In *Feminism/postmodernism,* edited by Linda J. Nicholson, 19–38. New York: Routledge.

Friedman, Debra, and Carol Diem. 1990. Comments on England and Kilbourne. *Rationality and Society* 2:517–21.

Gilligan, Carol. 1982. *In a different voice: Psychological theory and women's development.* Cambridge, Mass.: Harvard University Press.

Goldberg, Matthew S. 1982. Discrimination, nepotism, and long-run wage differentials. *Quarterly Journal of Economics* 97:308–19.

Granovetter, Mark. 1985. Economic action and social structure: The problem of embeddedness. *American Journal of Sociology* 91:481–510.

———. 1988. The sociological and economic approaches to labor market analysis: A social structural view. In *Industries, firms, and jobs: Sociological and economic approaches,* edited by George Farkas and Paula England, 187–216. New York: Plenum.

Hahnel, Robin, and Michael Albert. 1990. *Quiet revolution in welfare economics.* Princeton, N.J.: Princeton University Press.

Hausman, Daniel M., and Michael S. McPherson. 1993. Taking ethics seriously: Economics and contemporary moral philosophy. *Journal of Economic Literature* 31:671–731.

Held, Virginia. 1993. *Feminist morality: Transforming culture, society, and politics.* Chicago: University of Chicago Press.

Hirshleifer, Jack. 1984. *Price theory and applications.* 3d ed. Englewood Cliffs, N.J.: Prentice-Hall.

Hoagland, Sarah. 1988. *Lesbian ethics: Toward new value.* Palo Alto, Calif.: Institute of Lesbian Studies.

Hogarth, Robin M., and Melvin W. Reder, eds. 1987. *Rational choice: The contrast between economics and psychology.* Chicago: University of Chicago Press.

Jaggar, Allison. 1983. *Feminist politics and human nature.* Totowa, N.J.: Rowan & Allanheld.

Kabeer, Naila. 2001. Family bargaining. In *International encyclopedia of the social and behavioral sciences,* edited by Neil J. Smelser and Paul B. Baltes, 8:5315–19. London: Elsevier.

Katz, Lawrence. 1986. Efficiency wage theories: A partial evaluation. *Macroeconomic annual.* Cambridge, Mass.: National Bureau of Economic Research.

Keller, Catherine. 1986. *From a broken web: Separation, sexism, and self.* Boston: Beacon Press.

Keller, Evelyn Fox. 1983. *A feeling for the organism: The life and work of Barbara McClintock.* New York: Freeman.

———. 1985. *Reflections on gender and science.* New Haven, Conn.: Yale University Press.

Kohlberg, Lawrence. 1966. A cognitive developmental analysis of children's sex-role concepts and attitudes. In *The development of sex differences,* edited by E. E. Maccoby, 82–173. Stanford, Calif.: Stanford University Press.

Lloyd, Genevieve. 1984. *The man of reason: "Male" and "female" in Western philosophy.* Minneapolis: University of Minnesota Press.

Lundberg, Shelly, and Robert A. Pollak. 1993. Separate spheres bargaining and the marriage market. *Journal of Political Economy* 101:988–1010.

———. 1994. Noncooperative bargaining models of marriage. *American Economic Review* 84:132–37.

———. 1996. Bargaining and distribution in marriage. *Journal of Economic Perspectives* 10:139–58.

Lundberg, Shelly J., Robert A. Pollak, and Terence J. Wales. 1997. Do husbands and wives pool their resources? Evidence from the U.K. child benefit. *Journal of Human Resources* 32:463–80.

Maccoby, Eleanor Emmons, and Carol Nagy Jacklin. 1974. *The psychology of sex differences.* Stanford, Calif.: Stanford University Press.

Mackenzie, Catriona, and Natalie Stoljar, eds. 2000. *Relational autonomy: Feminist perspectives on autonomy, agency, and the social self.* New York: Oxford University Press.

Mansbridge, Jane, ed. 1990. *Beyond self-interest.* Chicago: University of Chicago Press.

Manser, Marilyn, and Murray Brown. 1980. Marriage and household decision-making: A bargaining analysis. *International Economic Review* 21:31–44.

McElroy, Marjorie B. 1985. The joint determination of household membership and market work: The case of young men. *Journal of Labor Economics* 3:293–316.

———. 1990. The empirical content of Nash-bargained household behavior. *Journal of Human Resources* 25:559–83.

McElroy, Marjorie B., and Mary J. Horney. 1981. Nash-bargained household decisions: Toward a generalization of the theory of demand. *International Economic Review* 22:333–49.

Molm, Linda, and Karen Cook. 1995. Social exchange and exchange networks. In *Sociological perspectives on social psychology,* edited by Karen Cook, Gary Fine, and James House, 209–35. Needham Heights, Mass.: Allyn & Bacon.

Nelson, Julie A. 1992. Gender, metaphor, and the definition of economics. *Economics and Philosophy* 8:103–25.

———. 1995. Feminism and economics. *Journal of Economic Perspectives* 9 (2): 131–48.

———. 1996. *Feminism, objectivity, and economics.* New York: Routledge.

———. 1997. Feminism, ecology, and the philosophy of economics. *Ecological Economics* 20:155–62.

———. 1999. Of markets and martyrs: Is it OK to pay well for care? *Feminist Economics* 5 (3): 43–59.

Nelson, Julie A., and Paula England. 2002. Feminist philosophies of love and work. Introduction to *Feminist philosophies of love and work,* special issue of *Hypatia* 17 (2): 1–18.

Nicholson, Linda, ed. 1990. *Feminism/postmodernism.* New York: Routledge.

Nussbaum, Martha. 1995. Introduction to *Women, culture, and development: A study of human capabilities,* edited by Martha Nussbaum and Jonathan Glover, 1–15. Oxford: Oxford University Press.

O'Connor, Julia S., Ann Shola Orloff, and Sheila Shaver. 1999. *States, markets, families: Gender, liberalism, and social policy in Australia, Canada, Great Britain, and the United States.* London: Cambridge University Press.

Pollak, Robert A. 1970. Habit formation and dynamic demand functions. *Journal of Political Economy* 78:745–63.

———. 1976. Interdependent preferences. *American Economic Review* 66:309–20.

———. 1978. Endogenous tastes in demand and welfare analysis. *American Economic Review* 68:374–79.

———. 1985. A transaction cost approach to families and households. *Journal of Economic Literature* 23:581–608.

———. 1988. Tied transfers and paternalistic preferences. *American Economic Review* 78:240–44.

———. 2002. Gary Becker's contributions to family and household economics. Unpublished manuscript, Department of Economics, Washington University.

Pollak, Robert A., and Susan Cotts Watkins. 1993. Cultural and economic approaches to fertility: Proper marriage or mésalliance? *Population and Development Review* 19:467–96.

Reid, Margaret. 1934. *Economics of household production.* New York: Wiley.

Ruddick, Sarah. 1989. *Maternal thinking: Towards a politics of peace.* Boston: Beacon Press.

Schott, Robin May. 1988. *Cognition and eros: A critique of the Kantian paradigm.* Boston: Beacon Press.

Sen, Amartya. 1970. *Collective choice and social welfare.* San Francisco: Holden-Day.

———. 1982. *Choice, welfare, and measurement.* Cambridge, Mass.: MIT Press.

———. 1987. *On ethics and economics.* New York: Basil Blackwell.

———. 1990. Gender and cooperative conflicts. In *Persistent inequalities: Women and world development,* edited by Irene Tinker. New York: Oxford University Press.

Sober, Elliott, and David Sloan Wilson. 1998. *Unto others: The evolution and psychology of unselfish behavior.* Cambridge, Mass.: Harvard University Press.

Stark, Oded, and Ita Falk. 1998. Transfers, empathy formation, and reverse transfers. *American Economic Review* 88:271–76.

Steinberg, Ronnie. 2001. Comparable worth in gender studies. In *International encyclopedia of the social and behavioral sciences*, edited by Neil J. Smelser and Paul B. Baltes, 4:2293–397. London: Elsevier.

Stigler, George, and Gary Becker. 1977. De gustabus non est disputandum. *American Economic Review* 67:76–90.

Thomas, Duncan. 1990. Intra-household resource allocation: An inferential approach. *Journal of Human Resources* 25:635–64.

Varian, Hal R. 1999. *Intermediate microeconomics: A modern approach*. 5th ed. New York: Norton.

Warren, Karen J. 2001. Feminist theory: Ecofeminist and cultural feminist. In *International encyclopedia of the social and behavioral sciences*, edited by Neil J. Smelser and Paul B. Baltes, 8:5495–99. London: Elsevier.

Woolley, Frances. 1996. Getting the better of Becker. *Feminist Economics* 2:114–20.

Yi, Yun-Ae. 1996. Margaret G. Reid: Life and achievements. *Feminist Economics* 2:17–36.

2

Contracting for Care

. . . Paula England and Nancy Folbre

Women's traditional responsibility for the unpaid work of caring for dependents has contributed to their economic dependence on men and disadvantaged them in the labor market. Mothers earn substantially less than other women over their lifetime and face a significant risk of poverty in the event of nonmarriage or divorce (Budig and England 2001; Davies, Joshi, and Peronaci 2000; Waldfogel 1997; Joshi 1990). More care work is now being done for pay, mostly by women who earn less than they would in other jobs requiring the same education and experience (England, Budig, and Folbre 2001; England and Folbre 1999). Although many of those whose jobs involve providing care services are poorly paid, the cost of care services relative to other goods and services is rising. Sometimes those who need care cannot afford it. The federal government is setting limits on public assistance to mothers at home caring for their children and is seeking to contain medical care costs, especially for the elderly. The quality of care services for dependents such as children and the elderly seems uneven and in some cases unacceptably low. In short, the "care sector" of our economy suffers from a number of serious problems.

What has caused these problems? Many economists argue that care services and other jobs filled by women are underpaid because of an *over*supply of labor to these fields. Both explicit

The research for this chapter was funded in part by the MacArthur Foundation's Research Network on the Family and the Economy.

discrimination and gender role socialization limit women's access to employment and crowd them into traditionally female jobs (Bergmann 1981, 1986; Jacobsen 1994; Blau, Ferber, and Winkler 1998). Research on comparable worth suggests that cultural bias also comes into play and that employers tend to devalue jobs that are filled by women and to set lower pay scales for them (England 1992). All these factors help explain why care work is poorly rewarded. In our opinion, however, they do not provide a complete explanation. Furthermore, they shed little light on the other problems outlined above.

In this essay, we argue that care work itself has distinctive characteristics that help explain the economic vulnerability of those who provide it. High-quality care often requires long-term commitments or "contracts" characterized by emotional connection, moral obligation, and intrinsic motivation. Whether such contracts take the form of implicit agreements governed largely by social norms or explicit agreements between employers and employees, they are difficult to specify and enforce. Yet they are especially important for the well-being of dependents such as children, the sick, and the elderly, who are seldom in a position to renegotiate them.

Our analysis explicitly links feminist theory with "new institutionalist" approaches within economic theory. Most of the interdisciplinary feminist literature on care engages with economic theory primarily to criticize it (see, e.g., Himmelweit 1999; Kabeer 2001; Staveren 2001; Held 2002). This is hardly surprising, since most economists assume that individuals are "rational," self-interested calculators who respond primarily to changes in prices and incomes. Most economists also focus on transactions in an impersonal spot market without long-term contractual obligations. One could hardly ask for a theory less appropriate to an analysis of care work, which has important emotional and altruistic dimensions and is shaped by values and social norms (see England, chap. 1 in this volume). Care work tends to be personal in nature, and it often takes place within relatively long-term relationships.

Mainstream economics remains largely unconcerned with such issues. This mainstream is, however, becoming slightly more diffuse, with the emergence of new side streams and undercurrents deploying concepts such as "transactions costs," "implicit contracts," "endogenous tastes," and "reciprocity" (Williamson 1985; Pollak 1985; Stiglitz 1987; Akerlof 1982; Bowles and Gintis 1998). For shorthand, we refer to this literature as the "new institutionalist economics" and define it quite broadly. Though still largely based on traditional assumptions, new institutionalist approaches generally emphasize the ways that values, norms, and preferences help coordinate individual decisions. They often use the term *contract* as a metaphor to help explain the evolution of nonmarket institutions and long-term relationships. We believe this metaphor—in spite of its limitations—offers some important economic insights into the social orga-nization of care. We also believe that the language of contracts provides a way of explaining feminist concerns that could help redirect mainstream economic discourse.

A contract implies a binding commitment that may restrict future choices. Yet individuals presumably choose to enter into—or at least to conform to—both explicit and implicit contracts. Thus, the contract metaphor seems to pro-vide an appealing way of preserving the element of individual choice even while explaining limits on it. Some kinds of contracts, however, are more difficult to design and enforce than others. We argue that contracts for care are especially susceptible to three problems: (1) individuals cannot fully participate in the formulation of contracts that have an impact on them; (2) care contracts are difficult to monitor and to enforce; and (3) individuals themselves are modified by the contracts into which they enter. These contracting problems contribute not only to gender inequality, but also to low pay, poor quality of services, and insufficient supply of high quality labor in paid care work. They point to the need for serious efforts to rethink and redesign the social organization of care.

Feminist Conceptualizations of Care

A rich body of feminist literature criticizes lack of attention to care within the Western intellectual tradition and emphasizes both its centrality in women's lives and its importance to society as a whole. Much of this literature highlights the distinctive characteristics of care as an activity that conspicuously violates the standard assumptions made regarding the motivation of "rational economic man"—dispassionate pursuit of narrow self-interest (Staveren 2001). No binary opposition between "care" and "noncare" is implied here, but rather location along a continuum. Care tends to have particularly salient emotional dimen-sions, and it often involves strong moral obligations. As such, it is a highly gendered concept, one that tends to be located more within the feminine than the masculine realm (Nelson 1996).

Often the word *care* itself is used to describe a motive or a moral imper-ative (Noddings 1984; Tronto 1987; Gordon, Benner, and Noddings 1996). In a similar spirit, some social scientists use the phrase "caring labor" to call attention to the fact that caring motives imply emotional connection between the giver and receiver of care. Kari Waerness (1987) and Arnaug Leira (1994) emphasize the ways caring labor departs from traditional economistic defini-tions of work as an activity performed despite its intrinsic disutility, simply in order to earn money. Both Jean Gardiner (1997) and Sue Himmelweit (1999) argue that equating family care with "work" obscures its personal and emotional dimensions and that paid care retains its personal quality to the extent that it resists "complete commodification."

In other words, caregivers are not motivated purely by pecuniary rewards. Emily Abel and Margaret Nelson (1990, 4) put it this way: "Caregiving is an activity encompassing both instrumental tasks and affective relations. Despite the classic Parsonian distinction between these two modes of behavior, caregivers are expected to provide love as well as labor." Likewise, Francesca Cancian and Stacy Oliker (2000, 2) define caring as a combination of feelings and actions that "provide responsively for an individual's personal needs or well-being, in a face-to-face relationship." In the same spirit, Nancy Folbre has previously defined caring labor as work that provides services based on sustained personal (usually face-to-face) interaction and is motivated (at least in part) by concern about the recipient's welfare (Folbre 1995; Folbre and Weisskopf 1998).

Other feminist scholars define care in terms of the task done or services rendered. Thus, for instance, Mary Daly (2001) defines care as all activities that benefit dependents, such as the ill, dependent elderly, and young children; and Diemut Bubeck (1995, 183) defines care as "meeting a need that those in need could not possibly meet themselves." Deborah Ward (1993) uses the term more broadly for many needs of individuals met by the family and the community but outside the market. Despite their emphasis on outcomes, all these writers also emphasize the role that gendered social norms play in shaping the motives for providing care.

Empirical researchers cannot easily verify or measure motives and therefore tend to focus on other characteristics of care work. In our own recent research, we define caring labor as work providing face-to-face services that develop the capabilities of the recipient (England, Budig, and Folbre 2001). *Capabilities* refers to health, skills, or proclivities that are useful to the individuals themselves or to others. These include physical and mental health, and physical, cognitive, and emotional skills, such as self-discipline, empathy, and care. Such care services are provided by parents, other family members, friends, and volunteers, but also by people who are paid, such as teachers, nurses, childcare workers, elder-care workers, therapists, and others. We show that being employed in such jobs leads to a wage penalty, net of education, years of experience, and a number of job characteristics, such as sex composition, skill demands, industry, whether the workers are unionized, and whether they are self-employed or work for government, and so forth.

Preliminary estimates suggest that care services, defined in terms of the type of work performed, account for a significant portion of all unpaid and paid work within the United States today. Time budget studies show that about one-half of total work hours take place outside the market economy, and a substantial share of this work involves the care of family members. Furthermore, about one-fifth of the paid labor force in 1998 was employed in industries providing care: hospitals, other health services, educational services, and social services (Folbre and Nelson 2000). Women devote considerably more time to family care than men do, and within the paid labor force, women remain concentrated in occupations and industries involving care (Folbre and Nelson 2000; England, Budig, and Folbre 2001). The ways in which these care services are organized have particularly significant implications for female workers, as well as for the welfare of the children, the sick, the elderly, and others in special need of care. One of the most important dimensions of their organization concerns the nature of the contracts that define the mutual rights and responsibilities of workers, managers, supervisors, owners, and clients.

Many recent discussions of feminist public policy concern the appropriate role of the family, the market, and the state in the provision of care (Meyer, Herd, and Michel 2000; Ungerson 2000; England and Folbre 2002). For instance, should feminists support paid family leave from work that would enable parents to spend more time caring for infants, or should they support public subsidies for child care outside the home, or both (Bergmann 2000)? These institutional contexts matter in large part because their contractual arrangements vary substantially, with implications for the quantity and quality of care supplied as well as both the level and distribution of costs and compensation.

Contracts

The new institutionalist economics explores the economic logic of long-term commitments in both firms and families, asking two questions of particular relevance to the social organization of care. Why do contracts emerge in the first place, when individuals could make more flexible decisions by avoiding long-term commitments? Why do contracts take implicit as well as explicit forms? Little, if any of this literature addresses feminist concerns and therefore has often elicited strong negative responses from feminist theorists. Nonetheless, it offers some potentially important insights. While many authors writing under the new institutionalist economics umbrella believe that all contracts are efficient, some emphasize the role of distributional struggle (Bowles and Gintis 1998; Hirshleifer 2001). We believe this emphasis on distributional struggle can and should be extended to analysis of the ways in which specific contractual arrangements both reflect and shape differences in the relative power of men and women.

As mentioned above, we use the term *contracts* to refer to agreements or understandings between two or more parties concerning mutual expectations or obligations. In other words, we define the term more broadly than legal scholars such as Margaret Brinig (2000). Unlike simple exchanges of goods and services in spot markets, contracts imply binding commitments over a period of time. Some contracts are explicit agreements, written or verbal, as, for instance, "If you agree to take care of my child for five hours, I will pay you $20." Even explicit agreements often have informal or implicit dimensions. For instance, it might be understood that taking care of the child requires more than simply providing supervision and food.

Contracts take place in a legal context that generally defines their scope. Most legal traditions place restrictions on allowable contracts. For instance, persons are not allowed to sell themselves or their children into slavery. Some contracts are standardized by law. For instance, in the United States, the state where two persons marry stipulates many important features of the contract governing their economic obligations to one another and their ownership of property. Some laws essentially take the place of contracts. For instance, parental responsibility to children is not based on any signed agreement, but it resembles one. Parents who fail to provide for the basic well-being of their children can be punished, even jailed, or lose their parental rights. In England, between 1871 and the advent of Old Age Pensions in the early twentieth century, the state attempted to require adult children to support their parents, and, to help enforce this, they began treating the elderly like other paupers, requiring them to live in the workhouse to get any relief (Quadagno 1982, chap. 4; Orloff 1993, 119).

Similarly, the responsibilities that an individual citizen owes to the state, including payment of taxes, are not specified in an explicit contract, but nonetheless represent an enforceable obligation. The rights and responsibilities of citizens are partly specified in the Constitution of the United States, which also establishes the principle that an individual must, under most conditions, yield to laws established by majority rule.

The "social contract" is often construed even more broadly to refer not just to laws, but also to expectations of reciprocity. These expectations are often strongly influenced by gender and age. For instance, no current U.S. law stipulates that adults must provide support or care for their parents, yet, despite the absence of a current law, our society considers this an obligation based on reciprocity: they took care of you when you were a dependent child, hence you should take care of them when they are dependent elderly. Similarly, many gender norms embody a particular version of reciprocal exchange: men should provide income and women should provide care.

Because contracts represent commitments with some power to bind, they limit individual choice. Thus, the very existence of contracts poses a challenge to traditional neoclassical economic theory. For example, why do individuals form the long-term relationships known as "firms" to engage in business enterprise when they could, theoretically, just buy and sell the labor and other inputs they need on the spot? In a classic article, Ronald Coase (1937) argues that contracts between employer and employee are more efficient than spot markets because they economize on the costs of obtaining information and conducting transactions. Oliver Williamson (1985) builds upon Coase to argue that firms also use long-term relationships with other firms (such as input suppliers) to lower transactions costs.

Similarly, much of the new institutionalist literature on families argues that they represent an efficient means of organizing the care of dependents (Ben-Porath 1980; Pollak 1985). It has been suggested that monogamy, a specific form of marriage contract, emerged in Western Europe because it led to better outcomes for children than other arrangements (Macdonald 1995). Gary Becker's *Treatise on the Family* (1991) includes considerable speculation on why families have changed over time as the economic benefits of gender specialization have declined. Becker, in particular, describes individual decisions to marry and raise children as essentially similar to decisions about buying or selling commodities, a description most feminists find offensive (Bergmann 1995). However, one need not agree with Beckerian assumptions to acknowledge that both firms and families are characterized by contractual elements with important implications for individual incentives and economic efficiency.

The factors affecting the emergence of specific types of contracts are also related to costs and benefits. Explicit or formal employment contracts are expensive to specify and to monitor, creating an incentive to develop implicit or informal agreements that are reinforced by higher wages or returns to seniority (England and Farkas 1986). To the extent that workers are self-interested and find leisure preferable to work, they will have an incentive to shirk. At the same time, modern methods of team production make it difficult to assess individual productivity. Direct monitoring in the form of surveillance or supervision is costly. An alternative strategy is to increase the cost of job loss by paying an "efficiency" wage that is higher than one that would be generated by the forces of supply and demand alone (Akerlof 1982; England 1992, chap. 2). Higher wage costs can be counterbalanced by higher effort, which in turn leads to higher output per worker (Stiglitz 1987). Similarly, virtually all businesses offer returns to seniority that essentially "overpay" older workers relative to younger ones, both to encourage worker effort and to allow the firm to capture the advantages of firm-specific experience (Lazear 1990).

In a significant departure from traditional economic assumptions, many social scientists argue that trust and reciprocity in the form of "social capital" can help enforce implicit contracts (Putnam 2000; La Porta et al. 1997). Even *Business Week* goes so far as to argue that economic prosperity depends on an "intricate web of relationships, norms of behavior, values, obligations, and information channels. . . . The essential qualities of social capital, as opposed to physical or human capital, are that it reflects a community or group and that it impinges on individuals regardless of their independent choices" (Pennar 1997, 153; see also Nelson, chap. 3 in this volume). Samuel Bowles and Herbert Gintis (1998) review experimental evidence showing that people are often willing to sacrifice income in order to punish those who do not conform to norms of reciprocity. George Akerlof (1982) goes beyond concepts of trust and reciprocity to suggest that employers may try to encourage the development of affection and loyalty by paying a higher wage. Robert Frank (1988) explains a number of other ways in which emotions can play a strategic role in lowering monitoring and information costs. These are observations that have obvious relevance to the provision of care.

Feminist theorists might be more receptive to arguments about explicit and implicit contracts if these were less closely linked to traditional assumptions presuming economic efficiency. Most of the institutionalist literature offers little insight into social inequalities based on nation, race, class, or gender, ignoring the ways in which powerful groups may use collective action to design contractual arrangements that allow them to maintain control or to extract a surplus (Folbre 1994b). A widely accepted explanation of the emergence of capitalist firms, for instance, suggests that they simply provide a more efficient set of incentives than worker-owned enterprises (Alchian and Demsetz 1972; Hart 1995). Similarly, most economists working within the Beckerian tradition simply assume that the gender division of labor is an efficient one that has no important distributional consequences for men and women.

It is important to challenge these assumptions by moving beyond definitions of efficiency that hold the distribution of income fixed (e.g., the Paretian criterion that no one can be made better off without making someone else worse off). Most contractual arrangements tend to benefit one group more than another, and hierarchical arrangements often create conflicts of interest that can lead to inefficient outcomes. For instance, capitalist firms may provide efficient incentives for residual claimants (owners) but not for wage earners (Bowles 1985). Similarly, patriarchal property rights that promote efficient "management" may also contribute to other effects that are inefficient as well as unfair. For instance, Elissa Braunstein and Nancy Folbre (2001) argue that traditional patriarchal property rights forced women to "overspecialize" in childbearing and child rearing, reducing the overall level of economic efficiency. They argue that some forms of economic development created incentives for men to allow more flexibility in the gender division of labor, which contributed to women's empowerment.

In general, analysis of the shifting costs and benefits of different contractual arrangements could help inform strategic efforts to overturn those that are unfair or exploitative. Successful application of the insights of the new institutional economics to the care sector, however, will depend on explicit consideration of the distinctive characteristics of care work.

Contracting Problems

To illustrate the metaphor of implicit contract, we propose an informal long-term agreement between new institutionalist economists and feminist theorists that could benefit both groups. Institutionalist economists should acknowledge that the provision of care is an economically crucial activity that does not conform to their typical assumptions (as pointed out in this chapter's first section). Feminist theorists should acknowledge that the metaphor of contract does not necessarily require acceptance of that traditionally stylized paragon of efficiency known as "economic man" (as pointed out in this chapter's second section). In this section we offer feminist theorists several examples of problems in the care sector that can be interpreted as contracting problems. At the same time, we emphasize that these problems are not only more serious than most institutionalist economists concede, but also have particularly adverse consequences for women and dependents (as well as men who provide a significant amount of care).

Missing and Incomplete Markets

Although contracts are, in some respects, a substitute for spot markets, explicit contracts often rely on marketlike processes—in particular, the ability to strike a deal. Economists acknowledge a problem of "missing markets" that emerges when individuals willing to pay for a good or service are unable to make arrangements to obtain it. Another case of missing markets arises when the consumption of public goods cannot be easily restricted to those who pay for them. In both cases, the result is a less than optimal provision of the good or service in question in the economy as a whole. This category of problems has obvious relevance to the provision of care.

Becker (1991) offers a tongue-in-cheek example of markets that are missing because of lack of agency. Imagine children who have not been but would like to be conceived, contracting with their (possible) parents to bring them into the world in exchange for some later payback. Obviously, the agents who could strike this deal do not exist. Although he acknowledges this problem, Becker fails to fully consider its implications. Many children already born suffer from inadequate love, food, or medical care. Because they are children, however, they cannot contract for better care.

Frank Knight (1921, 374–75) put it this way: "We live in a world where individuals are born naked, destitute, helpless, ignorant, and untrained, and must spend a third of their lives acquiring the prerequisites of a free contractual existence." Like Becker, however, Knight draws a sharp distinction between dependence and independence based entirely on age. Most people experience periods of dependency not only as children, but also during periods of illness or crisis and in old age. Dependency exists on a continuum, and even many healthy working-age adults lack the cognitive or emotional skills needed to take care of themselves without any help from others. Dependency may also have economic causes, as when individuals lack resources as a result of forces beyond their control—layoffs, bank failures, terrorism, or war. Further, it is precisely when we need care the most that we are least able to contract with others to meet our needs (England and Folbre 2002).

Another example of a missing market involves externalities, or spillovers from private transactions that impinge on individuals who are not party to them. As a classic treatment by Ronald Coase (1960) emphasizes, individuals theoretically have the power to seek a contractual remedy. In principle, someone affected by a negative externality can sue for damages. In practice, however, their ability to do so is limited when the effects are diffuse and difficult to measure (as, for instance, when air quality is reduced by a number of different sources of pollution with different effects on different people).

Economists have devoted little attention to social (as opposed to physical) externalities, but a range of evidence suggests that care produces outcomes that have the "nonexcludability" aspect of public goods—that is, once produced, there is no way to get people to pay the producer for them. Care work that develops recipients' capabilities has potential spillover effects on all those likely to come into contact with those individuals, whether as friends, neighbors, intimate partners, or fellow workers (England and Folbre 1999; Wax 1999a, 1999b). Sociologist James Coleman (1988) focuses on averted social costs, noting that children raised in unstable or uncaring environments, such as a succession of short-term foster care homes, are far more likely than others to impose costs on society through crime. Care services almost certainly increase the quantity and quality of what Robert Putnam (2000) and others term "social capital."

The provision of care services to children also results in positive fiscal externalities, or savings to taxpayers. Pension systems based on "pay-as-you-go" financing redistribute income from the working-age population to the elderly without regard for differences in the level of resources the elderly had committed to child rearing in earlier years (George 1993; Folbre 1994a). Yet elderly individuals with living children are often less likely than others to require publicly subsidized nursing home care (Wolf 1999). In April 2001 the German Constitutional Court ruled that childless workers were free riding on the efforts of parents, and should pay higher rates for social insurance ("No German Children?" 2001). Recognition of such fiscal externalities provides the rationale for the family allowance systems in effect in most Northwestern European countries.

Monitoring and Enforcement Problems

The quality of care services is especially difficult to measure. Sometimes, the person receiving the service is not competent to judge its quality. This is especially clear with children and adults whose capacities are impaired as a result of illness. Employers of care workers can monitor physical abuse and technical incompetence. Theoretically, video cameras could be placed in all child-care centers, schools, and nursing homes. Of course, there is the obvious difficulty that watching video monitors is time consuming and that installing them would erode morale of workers under surveillance. But there is also the problem that more subtle emotional aspects of care, such as warmth, nurturance, reassurance, and the sense of "being cared for" are difficult to monitor. Furthermore, care skills have a significant person-specific and situation-specific component that makes them very different from a manufacturing or clerical assembly line. Finally, education, health services, and nursing home care are generally provided through third-party payment systems such as the government or an insurance company. These institutions often limit the providers that can be used, restricting the right of consumers to "shop around" and find providers that provide high-quality care.

Given that the quality of care is hard to assess, why are care workers not among those who generally receive an "efficiency wage" that elicits higher effort in response to higher pay? One reason may be that the logic of efficiency wages hinges on the assumption that average output per worker can be measured, even if individual effort cannot. As for quality, consumers will pay more if they can be sure their product is of higher quality. In the case of care services, however, "outputs" as well as "inputs" are difficult to assess.

Even competent adult consumers may not be the best judges of quality when purchasing services designed to increase their capabilities rather than merely provide immediate pleasure. Clearly, care that makes a recipient "feel good" is not always the best form of care. A teacher's job is to educate students, not necessarily to make them happy. A therapist's job is to help people learn to cope with their problems, not always to cheer them up. Furthermore, the capabilities at stake are often complicated. Standardized tests measure teachers' success in improving students' test scores, but not their success in motivating children to become lifelong learners, or fostering important emotional skills such as self-control and empathy. Yet evidence suggests that motivation and emotional skills are as vital to success as cognitive skills (Goleman 1995). Likewise, nurses' ability to insert a needle can be easily tested, but their ability to reassure and comfort a patient cannot be easily judged.

In mental health, child care, and education, as well as many other industries within the care sector, skepticism about the link between higher expenditures and improved outcomes fuels resistance to increased spending. The difficulty of measuring treatment efficacy helps explain the declining health insurance coverage of mental illness (American Psychological Association 1997; USDHHS 1999). Both parents and developmental psychologists express considerable disagreement regarding the best form of child care for infants (Phillips and Adams 2001; Sylvester 2001). While some economists insist that increased expenditures are a necessary, though not sufficient, condition for improving educational outcomes (Card and Krueger 1992), others insist that it is largely irrelevant (Hanushek 1996).

Combined with the third-party payment structures that are typical of care for dependents, these information problems reduce the consumer sovereignty that is usually considered necessary for market efficiency. They may also contribute to low pay for care workers. Measurement of care outcomes could probably be improved. Nonetheless, the inherent difficulties of measuring and monitoring both inputs and outputs help explain why the care sector relies heavily on intrinsic motives rather than extrinsic rewards.

Endogenous Preferences

A third category of contracting problems with significant implications for care activities has been less well explored by economists: the transformative effect of care itself. (See England, chap. 1 in this volume, for a broader discussion of endogenous preferences.) Care workers may become attached to care recipients in ways that make it difficult for them to withhold their services in order to demand more remuneration for them. The emotional content of care services reduces the flexibility of both providers and recipients of care, affecting the way either group perceives their needs and wants. In the more technical vocabulary of neoclassical theory, preferences for care provision are often partially endogenous.

Performance of care may increase commitment to provide it. Sociological evidence of the impact of jobs on workers comes from the research of Melvin Kohn and others, showing that individuals in jobs requiring more intellectual skill get successively "smarter" (Kohn and Schooler 1983). Similarly, in jobs requiring care, individuals may become more caring. Also, as mentioned before, economist George Akerlof (1982) suggests that employees may "acquire sentiment" for employers or coworkers. In care work, however, employees often acquire sentiment for their clients. Child-care workers become attached to the toddlers they see every day. Nurses empathize with their patients. Teachers worry about their students. The fact that these emotional bonds are important to the development and health of the care recipients helps explain why high turnover rates in child care and elder care are worrisome.

At the same time, these emotional bonds put care workers in a vulnerable position, discouraging them from demanding higher wages or changes in working conditions that might have adverse effects on care recipients. We might call the workers "prisoners of love"; a kind of emotional "hostage effect" comes into play. Owners, employers, and managers are less likely to come into direct contact with clients or patients than are care workers. Therefore, they can generally engage in cost-cutting strategies without "feeling" their consequences. In fact, they can even be confident that adverse effects of their decisions on clients will be reduced by workers' willingness to make personal sacrifices to maintain high quality care. For instance, workers may respond to cutbacks in staffing levels by intensifying their effort or agreeing to work overtime. In this situation, the "acquisition of sentiment" paradoxically contributes to a worsening of working conditions and very likely care quality as well. Giving workers more voice in managerial decisions through institutional mechanisms such as trade unions could turn their sentiment to better advantage for their clients as well as themselves.

One could argue that workers who reveal a preference for providing a care service receive a compensating differential for lower pay—their sacrifice is rewarded by "psychic income"—the appreciation of the care recipient. This is probably true to some extent. But this rationalization unravels if the preference is not exogenously given, but develops as a result of particular circumstances. As with other models of "addiction," workers may not know ahead of time to what extent they may become vulnerable to the acquisition of costly preferences (Orphanides and Zeroos 1995). Whether "hostage" logic applies more to care than to other kinds of work is an empirical question. Nonetheless, it could help explain the persistence of a gendered division of labor, to the extent that cultural norms encouraging women to take responsibility for care are reinforced by the actual experience of providing it.

Both economists and psychologists have contributed to a growing literature on the effects of intrinsic motivation—willingness to do a task even with little or no extrinsic reward, or to provide a high level of effort despite lack of pecuniary incentive. Some studies find that offering payment for volunteer activities or civic participation can have the opposite of the intended effect—they reduce labor supply or effort, leading to a "crowding out" effect (Eisenberger and Cameron 1996; Deci, Koestner, and Ryan 1999). However, much depends on particular circumstances. Many of the experiments discussed in this literature focus on the effect of crossing the highly charged symbolic divide between things done for no money at all versus those done for money, rather than on the effects of increases in pay, which are more relevant to the organization of paid care services.

Furthermore, the effects of extrinsic rewards are strongly affected by the form they take. The experimental studies suggest that extrinsic rewards that are seen as "controlling" tend to reduce intrinsic motivation for a task, while those that are seen as "acknowledging" increase intrinsic motivation. Rewards called "controlling" in this literature are those coupled with close supervision or other processes that raise questions about the recipients' abilities and threaten their self-esteem. "Acknowledging" rewards are those that send the message that the recipient is trusted, respected, and appreciated (Frey 1998; Frey and Goette 1999; Frey and Jegen 2001). Applying this insight to the care sector, we might expect that linking teachers' pay to students' scores on standardized tests or paying nurses a premium for reducing the lengths of patient hospital stays might reduce intrinsic motivation, because they suggest that we don't trust these professionals to do the right thing without careful measurement of outputs. On the other hand, honoring the outstanding "teacher of the year" or the "nursing team of the week" with a pay bonus might enhance such intrinsic motivation.

Conclusion

Since women take responsibility for a disproportionate share of care work, a better understanding of the logic of its social organization is crucial to a better understanding of gender inequality. Furthermore, human society cannot flourish without an adequate supply of care, which helps us develop our capabilities and provides comfort and meaning in our lives. The Western intellectual tradition has traditionally assumed that women naturally provide care for others, especially dependents. But the provision of care has always been in substantial part socially constructed and susceptible to economic pressures affecting both its quantity and quality. A better understanding of these pressures could contribute to the development of a society in which all human beings can flourish.

The contracting problems described in this chapter deserve more attention from feminist theorists. At the same time, they demonstrate why economists need to pay more attention to feminist theory. The traditional masculine emphasis on individual choice, rational choice, and measurable results has deflected attention from the provision of care services that involve social obligation, emotional commitment, and important but often intangible outcomes. As we shift from a regime that was based largely on implicit contracts within the family to more explicit contracts within paid employment, the costs of care become more visible.

Some of the implications of this shift were hinted at by the economist William Baumol (1967) when he coined the phrase "cost disease of the service sector." He argued that the service sector of the economy was more resistant to productivity-enhancing technical change than manufacturing and was therefore likely to experience rising relative prices. In retrospect, Baumol was wrong to lump all services together. Retail, banking, and insurance services have reaped the benefit of innovations in information technology, leading to significant cost reductions. Care services, however, are inherently labor intensive: they require face-to-face, hands-on contact. Their relative price will almost certainly continue to rise even if wages of care workers remain low (Donath 2000).

Both the weakening of social obligations imposed on women and the expansion of female employment opportunities contribute to increases in the cost of care services. It seems inappropriate, however, to describe this process as a "disease." Rather, we should resist several unhealthy ways of responding to higher prices: demanding that women assume disproportionate responsibility for unpaid care, skimping on pay, lowering quality standards, or reducing public support for those who cannot afford adequate care on their own. A better understanding of contracting problems could help us design better ways of increasing the quantity and quality of care services. It could also move us toward a more equitable distribution of their costs.

References

Abel, Emily K., and Margaret K. Nelson. 1990. Circles of care: An introductory essay. In *Circles of care: Work and identity in women's lives,* edited by Emily K. Abel and Margaret K. Nelson, 4–34. Albany: SUNY Press.

Akerlof, George. 1982. Labor contracts as partial gift exchange. *Quarterly Journal of Economics* 97:543–70.

Alchian, Armen A., and Harold Demsetz. 1972. Production, information costs, and economic organization. *American Economic Review* 62:777–95.

American Psychological Association. 1997. Ending discrimination in health insurance. Accessed May 14, 2001, at www.apa.org/practice/paper/.

Baumol, William J. 1967. Macroeconomics of unbalanced growth: The anatomy of urban crisis. *American Economic Review* 57:415–26.

Becker, Gary. 1991. *A treatise on the family.* Enlarged ed. Cambridge, Mass.: Harvard University Press.

Ben-Porath, Yoram. 1980. The F-connection: Families, friends, and firms and the organization of exchange. *Population and Development Review* 6:1–30.

Bergmann, Barbara. 1981. The economic risks of being a housewife. *American Economic Review* 7:8–86.

———. 1986. *The economic emergence of women.* New York: Basic Books.

———. 1995. Becker's theory of the family: Preposterous conclusions. *Feminist Economics* 1:141–50.

———. 2000. Subsidizing child care by mothers at home. *Feminist Economics* 6:77–88.

Blau, Francine D., Marianne A. Ferber, and Anne E. Winkler. 1998. *The economics of women, men, and work.* 3d ed. Upper Saddle River, N.J.: Prentice-Hall.

Bowles, Samuel. 1985. The production process in a competitive economy. *American Economic Review* 77:16–36.

Bowles, Samuel, and Herbert Gintis. 1998. The evolution of strong reciprocity. Santa Fe Institute Working Paper no. 98-08-073E. Santa Fe, New Mexico.

Braunstein, Elissa, and Nancy Folbre. 2001. To honor and obey: The patriarch as residual claimt. *Feminist Economics* 7:25–44.

Brinig, Margaret F. 2000. *From contract to covenant: Beyond the law and economics of the family.* Cambridge, Mass.: Harvard University Press.

Bubeck, Diemut. 1995. *Care, gender, justice.* Oxford: Clarendon Press.

Budig, Michelle, and Paula England. 2001. The wage penalty for motherhood. *American Sociological Review* 66:204–25.

Cancian, Francesca M., and Stacy J. Oliker. 2000. *Caring and gender.* Thousand Oaks, Calif.: Pine Forge Press.

Card, David, and Alan B. Krueger. 1992. Does school quality matter? Returns to education and the characteristics of public schools in the United States. *Journal of Political Economy* 100 (1): 1–40.

Coase, Ronald. 1937. The nature of the firm. *Economica* 4:386–405.

———. 1960. The problem of social cost. *Journal of Law and Economics* 3:1 44.

Coleman, James. 1988. Social capital in the creation of human capital. *American Journal of Sociology* 84:S95—S120.

Daly, Mary. 2001. Alternative ways of compensating for care in Western Europe. Unpublished manuscript, International Labour Organization, Geneva.

Davies, Hugh, Heather Joshi, and Romana Peronaci. 2000. Forgone income and motherhood: What do recent British data tell us? *Population Studies* 54 (3): 293–305.

Deci, Edward L., Richard Koestner, and Richard M. Ryan. 1999. A meta-analytic review of experiments examining the effects of extrinsic rewards on intrinsic motivation. *Psychological Bulletin* 125:627–68.

Donath, Susan. 2000. The other economy: A suggestion for a distinctively feminist economics. *Feminist Economics* 6:115–23.

Eisenberger, Robert, and Judy Cameron. 1996. Detrimental effects of reward: Reality or myth. *American Psychologist* 51 (11): 1153–66.

England, Paula. 1992. *Comparable worth: Theories and evidence*. New York: Aldine de Gruyter.

England, Paula, Michelle Budig, and Nancy Folbre. 2001. Wages of virtue: The relative pay of care work. Unpublished manuscript, Department of Sociology, Northwestern University.

England, Paula, and George Farkas. 1986. *Households, employment, and gender: A social, economic, and demographic view*. New York: Aldine Publishers.

England, Paula, and Nancy Folbre. 1999. The cost of caring. In *Emotional labor in the service economy*, edited by Ronnie J. Steinberg and Deborah M. Figart, 39–51. Annals of the American Academy of Political and Social Science 561. Thousand Oaks, Calif.: Sage.

———. 2002. Care, inequality, and policy. In *Child care and inequality: Re-thinking carework for children and youth*, edited by Francesca Cancian, Demie Kurz, Andrew London, Rebecca Reviere, and Mary Tuominen, 133–44. New York: Routledge.

Folbre, Nancy. 1994a. Children as public goods. *American Economic Review* 84 (2): 86–90.

———. 1994b. *Who pays for the kids? Gender and the structures of constraint*. New York: Routledge.

———. 1995. Holding hands at midnight: The paradox of caring labor. *Feminist Economics* 1:73–92.

Folbre, Nancy, and Julie Nelson. 2000. For love or money—or both? *Journal of Economic Perspectives* 14:123–40.

Folbre, Nancy, and Thomas Weisskopf. 1998. Did father know best? Families, markets, and the supply of caring labor. In *Economics, values, and organization*, edited by Avner Ben-Ner and Louis Putterman, 171–205. Cambridge: Cambridge University Press.

Frank, Robert. 1988. *Passions within reason: The strategic role of the emotions*. New York: Norton.

Frey, Bruno S. 1998. Institutions and morale: The crowding-out effect. In *Economics, values, and organization*, edited by Avner Ben-Ner and Louis Putterman, 437–60. Cambridge: Cambridge University Press.

Frey, Bruno S., and Lorenz Goette. 1999. Does pay motivate volunteers? Unpublished manuscript, Institute for Empirical Research in Economics, University of Zurich.

Frey, Bruno S., and Reto Jegen. 2001. Motivation crowding theory: A survey of empirical evidence. *Journal of Economic Surveys* 15 (5): 589–611.

Gardiner, Jean. 1997. *Gender, care, and economics*. Basingstoke, U.K.: Macmillan.

George, Rolf. 1993. On the external benefits of children. In *Kindred matters: Rethinking the philosophy of the family*, edited by Diana Tietjens Meyers, Kenneth Kipnis, and Cornelius Murphy Jr., 209–17. Ithaca, N.Y.: Cornell University Press.

Goleman, Daniel. 1995. *Emotional intelligence*. New York: Bantam.

Gordon, Suzanne, Patricia Benner, and Nel Noddings, eds. 1996. *Caregiving: Readings in knowledge, practice, ethics, and politics*. Philadelphia: University of Pennsylvania Press.

Hanushek, Eric. 1996. School resources and student success. In *Does money matter? The effect of school resources on student achievement and adult success*, edited by Gary Burtless, 43–73. Washington, D.C.: Brookings Institution Press.

Hart, Oliver. 1995. *Firms, contracts, and financial structure*. Oxford: Clarendon Press.

Held, Virginia. 2002. Care and the extension of markets. *Hypatia* 17 (2): 19–33.

Himmelweit, Susan. 1999. Caring labor. In *Emotional labor in the service economy*, edited by Ronnie J. Steinberg and Deborah M. Figart, 27–38. Annals of the American Academy of Political and Social Science 561. Thousand Oaks, Calif.: Sage.

Hirshleifer, Jack. 2001. *The dark side of the force: Economic foundations of conflict theory*. Cambridge: Cambridge University Press.

Jacobsen, Joyce P. 1994. *The economics of gender*. Cambridge, Mass.: Blackwell.

Joshi, Heather. 1990. The cash opportunity cost of childbearing: An approach to estimation using British evidence. *Population Studies* 44 (1): 41–60.

Kabeer, Naila. 2001. Family bargaining. In *International encyclopedia of the social and behavioral sciences*, edited by Neil J. Smelser and Paul B. Baltes, 8:5314–19. London: Elsevier.

Knight, Frank. 1921. *Risk, uncertainty, and profit*. Boston: Houghton Mifflin.

Knight, Jack. 1992. *Institutions and social conflict*. Cambridge: Cambridge University Press.

Kohn, Melvin L., and Carmi Schooler. 1983. *Work and personality: An inquiry into the impact of social stratification*. Norwood, N.J.: Ablex.

La Porta, Rafael, Florencio Lopez-de-Silanes, Andrei Schleifer, and Robert W. Vishny. 1997. Trust in large organizations. *American Economic Review* 87:333–39.

Lazear, E. 1990. Pensions and deferred benefits as strategic compensation. In *The Economics of Human Resource Management*, edited by Daniel J. Mitchell, J. B. Zaidi, and A. Mahmood, 109–26. Cambridge, Mass.: Blackwell.

Leira, Arnaug. 1994. Concepts of caring: Loving, thinking, and doing. *Social Service Review* 68:185–201.

Macdonald, Kevin. 1995. The establishment and maintenance of socially imposed monogamy in Western Europe. *Politics and the Life Sciences* 14 (1): 3–23.

Meyer, Madonna Harrington, Pam Herd, and Sonya Michel. 2000. Introduction to *Care work: Gender, labor, and the welfare state*. Edited by Madonna Harrington Meyer, 1–4. New York: Routledge.

Nelson, Julie. 1996. *Feminism, objectivity, and economics*. New York: Routledge.

Noddings, Nel. 1984. *Caring: A feminine approach to ethics and moral education*. Berkeley: University of California Press.

No German children? Then pay up. 2001. *Economist*, April 7, 54.

Orloff, Ann. 1993. *The politics of pensions: A comparative analysis of Britain, Canada, and the United States, 1880–1940*. Madison: University of Wisconsin Press.

Orphanides, Athanasios, and David Zeroos. 1995. Rational addiction with learning and regret. *Journal of Political Economy* 4:740–52.

Pennar, Karen. 1997. The ties that lead to prosperity. *Business Week*, December 15, 153–55.

Phillips, Deborah, and Gina Adams. 2001. Child care and our youngest children. *Future of Children* 11 (1): 35–51.

Pollak, Robert A. 1985. A transaction cost approach to families and households. *Journal of Economic Literature* 23:581–608.

Putnam, Robert. 2000. *Bowling alone: The collapse and revival of American community*. New York: Simon & Schuster.

Quadagno, Jill S. 1982. *Aging in early industrial society: Work, family, and social policy in nineteenth-century England*. New York: Academic Press.

Staveren, Irene van. 2001. *The values of economics: An Aristotelian perspective*. New York: Routledge.

Stiglitz, J. E. 1987. The causes and consequences of the dependence of quality on price. *Journal of Economic Literature* 25:1–48.

Sylvester, Kathleen. 2001. Caring for our youngest: Public attitudes in the United States. *Future of Children* 11 (1): 53–61.

Tronto, Joan. 1987. Beyond gender difference to a theory of care. *Signs: Journal of Women in Culture and Society* 12 (4): 644–63.

Ungerson, Claire. 2000. Cash in care. In *Care work: Gender, labor, and the welfare state*, edited by Madonna Harrington Meyer, 68–88. New York: Routledge.

USDHHS (United States Department of Health and Human Services). 1999. Executive summary of *Mental health: A report of the surgeon general*. Rockville, Md.: U.S. Department of Health and Human Services, Center for Mental Health Services, National Institutes of Health, National Institute of Mental Health.

Waerness, Kari. 1987. On the rationality of caring. In *Women and the State*, edited by A. S. Sassoon, 207–34. London: Hutchinson.

Waldfogel, Jane. 1997. The effect of children on women's wages. *American Sociological Review* 62:209–17.

Ward, Deborah. 1993. The kin care trap: The unpaid labor of long-term care. *Socialist Review* 23 (1): 83–106.

Wax, Amy. 1999a. Caring enough: Sex roles, work, and taxing women. *Villanova Law Review* 44 (3): 495–523.

————. 1999b. Is there a caring crisis? *Yale Journal of Regulation* 16 (2): 327–58.

Williamson, O. 1985. *The economic institutions of capitalism: Firms, markets, relational contracting.* New York: Free Press.

Wolf, Douglas A. 1999. The family as provider of long-term care: Efficiency, equity, and externalities. *Journal of Aging and Health* 11 (3): 360–82.

3

Separative and Soluble Firms: Androcentric Bias and Business Ethics

. . . Julie A. Nelson

In chapter 1 in this volume, Paula England examines neoclassical economic assumptions about the individual agent. Drawing on feminist work in psychology, political philosophy, and the philosophy of science concerning the roles of separation and connection in defining human identity, England discusses the biases implicit in assuming that agents are entirely autonomous and self-interested, on the one hand, or lacking in any independent will or agency, on the other.[1] This chapter extends England's analysis to more aggregate levels, considering questions of contemporary business organization.

On the one hand, business firms are often thought of—by mainstream economists and feminist scholars alike—as distinctly bounded entities, whose only concern is the maximization of profits. This is the image of the active, autonomous,

I thank Andrew Stern and Becky Branch for excellent research assistance, and participants in New York Society for Women in Philosophy (particularly Amy Baehr) and the 2001 conference of the International Association for Feminist Economics in Oslo, Norway, for their helpful comments. This work was supported by a fellowship from the Center for the Study of Values in Public Life at Harvard Divinity School.

1. Feminist discussions of issues of separation and connection began by seriously challenging the notion of human individuals as fundamentally autonomous and self-interested. Feminists pointed out that this view of "economic man" ignores precisely those activities and attributes that are traditionally assigned to women. While "economic man" is seen as autonomous, self-interested, rational, and in control, women have traditionally been seen as helpmeets for their spouses, nurturing, dependent, emotional, and closer to nature. The image of the "separative" man is in fact complemented and supported by the image of the "soluble" woman. For earlier works in this area, see, e.g., Keller 1986; England 1993; and Nelson 1996.

"separative" firm. Meanwhile—and not entirely consistently—business firms are also sometimes thought to be forced, inexorably, into particular actions by the dictates of competitive market forces. According to the image of the passive, dependent, "soluble" firm, businesses are driven by forces beyond their control. The purpose of this essay is to explore the implications of feminist discussion of modes of relationality that go beyond the separative/soluble dichotomy for the study of contemporary economic organization among and within firms.

Images of Firms in Popular Thought, Economics, and Feminist Scholarship

The images of firms as separative, soluble, or both have considerable academic and popular currency. The image of firms as asocial, amoral, discrete, and mechanical entities, for example, has been aided by the famous pronouncement of Milton Friedman: "Few trends could so thoroughly undermine the very foundations of our free society as the acceptance by corporate officials of a social responsibility other than to make as much money for their stockholders as possible" (1982, 133). The idea that modern economies, in turn, are grand systems composed of such profit-maximizing firms, coordinated by impersonal market forces (the "invisible hand"), has been popular since Adam Smith.

The fullest development of the separative/soluble firm assumptions is, of course, in basic neoclassical microeconomic theory, where a firm is defined as an economic unit that maximizes profits. Exactly what this unit is, in terms of people and internal organization, goes unspecified in the simplest theories. At the same time, in the case of perfectly competitive markets with many firms, the firm's relation to the external world is envisioned as entirely passive (since each is assumed to be a "price taker"). This is the model first taught to economics undergraduates, further elaborated at the start of graduate theory courses, and accepted as the default assumption in much economic research. Whether newer developments in the economic theory of the firm constitute significant improvements will be discussed later in this essay.

Ironically, given the critical stance of feminist theory toward the image of the masculinist, autonomous, individual *self* found in law, literature, political science, economics, and elsewhere, the assumption that *firms* and *markets* are fundamentally nonrelational has not been challenged by most contemporary feminist theorists. For example, political theorist Nancy Fraser writes about "relatively autonomous markets" that "follow a logic of their own" and about how "under capitalist conditions . . . the economic dimension becomes relatively decoupled from the cultural dimension, as marketized arenas, in which strategic action predominates, are differentiated from non-marketized arenas, in which value-regulated interaction predominates" (2000, 111, 118). Feminist philosopher Virginia Held repeats this common assumption when she writes, "Once an . . . activity has been taken over by the market, anything other than economic gain is unlikely to be its highest priority, since a corporation's responsibility to its shareholders leads it to try to maximize economic gain" (2002, 27). It is taken as a truism that firms and markets are amoral and nonrelational. To see that something else may be possible requires exploring the roots of separative/soluble thinking and alternatives to it.

The Limited Relationships in Separative/Soluble Thinking

Thinking about human selfhood in a dualistic, separative/soluble way severely limits our way of conceiving possible relationships. The image of the individual human forms the basis for conceptualizing possibilities of how people and organizations interact. If the only options for individuals are to be either separative, and therefore radically individual and active, or soluble, and therefore totally self-less and passive, then interactions can take only three forms:

1. *Separative-separative (arm's length):* When separative selves interact with other separative selves, such interactions must be purely external. The action of one party cannot have any effect on the other's inviolable constitution.
2. *Soluble-soluble (merger):* When soluble selves interact with other soluble selves, the relation must be one of complete merger. The individuals must be completely melded into one unit.
3. *Separative-soluble (domination):* When a separative self interacts with one or more soluble selves, the result is a strict hierarchy. The soluble selves take orders from and support (albeit invisibly) the separative self, who is perceived as autonomous, active, and in control.

Feminist critics have noted, in particular, the way in which the separative-separative possibility has been incorporated into traditional images of "citizens" and "economic actors." Romanticized notions of families acting as harmonious wholes are based in the soluble-soluble image. The patriarchal family—in which the husband is envisioned as household "head," while his wife remains invisible and submissive—is the example of hierarchy most fully elaborated in existing feminist theory.

It may be that human cognition and psychology makes it easier for us to think in terms of such simple extremes than in terms of greater complexity. This would help explain the splitting of individuality and relatedness, or agency and receptivity, in many other contexts as well. Economist James Duesenberry once wrote, "Economics is all about how people make choices. Sociology is all about why they don't have any choices to make" (1960, 233), highlighting how each discipline took one side of the separative (active)/soluble (passive) dualism. Or, to borrow some of theologian Martin Buber's phrases, the model of the separative self avoids dealing with relations to the world because in it "the world . . . [is] . . . embedded in the I, and . . . there is really no world at all," while the soluble self model avoids it by imagining "the I . . . embedded in the world, and there is really no I at all" (1958, 71–72).

Getting beyond separative/soluble thinking, then, is not just a matter of being critical about gender roles. It challenges deeply held and wide-ranging assumptions about how the world works.

An Alternative: "Individuals-in-Relation"

I created a small tool to make it easier to envision a more sophisticated way of thinking, which I called a gender/value compass (Nelson 1996). In figure 1, the characteristics of selves as separate from others are to the left; these are culturally coded (in Western, "Enlightenment" thought) as masculine. To the right are characteristics of selves as connected, culturally coded as feminine.

It must be stressed that these characteristics are a matter of gender, that is, of factors that are *culturally and cognitively* associated with sex. Too often, the point that men *and* women are both individual *and* related gets bowdlerized into "men are individual" and "women are related"—a tendency particularly pronounced in many later interpretations of Gilligan's (1982) work. What is highlighted here is how a full notion of human identity has been artificially split along gender-coded lines; the argument is in no way the "essentialist" one that would claim these as necessary characteristics of actual women and men. The upper cells represent characteristics that can be positively valued, while the lower cells represent harmful corruptions of the properties above them.

Breaking out of separative/soluble thinking into thinking about individuals-in-relation opens up a whole new range of possibilities. The way that we are shaped as physical bodies and by family, socialization, and culture can be respected at the same time that individual uniqueness and ability to reflect and act need not be denied. Thinking about forms of relationship beyond the three

Figure 1. The gender/value compass

	M+ individual	and	F+ related
	M− separative		F− soluble

possibilities mentioned earlier (arm's length, merger, or domination) becomes possible.

The individuals-in-relation idea receives considerable support from certain strains of psychological research. Based on the fact that we all start out as infants, and on insights from considerable research in child development, we know that developing a sense of self involves a complicated struggle and never-ending tension between individuation and relation (e.g., Chodorow 1978; Benjamin 1988; Winnicott 1996). To put it in simple terms, a person who is smothered by relation, and so has an insufficient sense of self, ends up overly malleable, codependent, in the extreme a doormat. This person, lacking a sense of her (or his) unique individuality, acts as a "soluble" self.

Individuals who are not effectively attached in relation, on the other hand, act as though they were "separative." Such people exist in a profoundly lonely world. The recent adoption of the name "Post-Autistic Economics" by a group of dissident French economics students is poignant, because the difficulty many autistic persons have in joining in social relations mirrors the irrelevance of relations in the model of *Homo economicus*. The frustration of such aloneness may be manifested in a need to relate through domination and control, or in extreme cases the violence of a sadist or sociopath (Benjamin 1988).

By culturally splitting off separation and connection into separate paths for men and women (or dominant races, ethnicities, etc. and submissive ones)— into "doer" and "done-to"—individual pathologies are echoed at higher levels of social organization.

On the other hand, the positive complementarity achieved by combining individuality and relation, illustrated in the top half of the diagram, suggests that this need not be so. What is lost in limiting the conceptual apparatus to that of separative/soluble organization is any sense of the possibility of authentic, cocreative, individual-respecting relationship. In taking individuality to the extreme of separativeness and connectedness to the extreme of solubility, this apparatus denies that people (or organizations) can be both individual and related at the same time. It denies that they can be related—can influence each other and affect each other in profound ways—while remaining unique individuals. Only individuals-in-relation can support real interactions characterized by integrity, respect, and mutuality.

Feminist theorists (among others) have explored the possibility of such relationships of individual-affirming mutuality at the level of relatively intimate social groupings, especially among family members and social peers. This essay explores the possibility of such relationships in contemporary *business* life.

A Typology of Assumptions about Firms

Separative/soluble thinking has strongly influenced notions of the behavior of firms at two levels. First, looking at firms from the point of view of the larger economy and environment, it is clear that a business is often thought to be (1) *separative*, inasmuch as a firm is seen as profoundly individual—a unit clearly distinguishable from its natural and social environments; (2) *soluble*, inasmuch as the "dictates" of law or competitive market pressures are often portrayed as inexorably forcing it to move in certain directions, implicitly denying the firm any real agency or autonomy.

Furthermore, if we look at what is assumed to go on *inside* the firm, we see that the relations among actors such as shareholders, managers, and workers are often thought to be (1) *separative-separative*, when people who make up the firm are themselves considered to be self-interested, autonomous agents; (2) *soluble-soluble*, when all are assumed to be united in pursuit of a common goal (usually the maximization of value to shareholders); (3) *separative-soluble*, when organizational issues are expressed simply as problems of designing the appropriate hierarchies of control. What is missing, clearly, in all of these is any notion that firms might be active, connected, evolving organizations, or that they or the people within them have the capacity of acting in engaged, meaningful, and responsible ways.

As mentioned above, conventional economists and many writers in the humanities seem to limit their thinking about firms to the separative/soluble options. Other researchers and scholars, however, have developed very different models of business behavior. Looking at actual conduct within and among firms—*without the presupposition that these must represent only coldly impersonal, merged, or hierarchical interactions*—many have found evidence of rather rich and complex economic phenomena. The remainder of this essay draws upon literatures in management and organizational behavior (disciplines usually housed in business schools), law and legal studies, economic sociology (a social science), and business ethics (often a joint venture between philosophy and business) to bring to light and analyze individuals-in-relation behavior within and among firms. Much of this literature questions the notions that firms must be thought of as separative and/or soluble.

What Is a Firm?

Is the Firm "Separative"—An Autonomous Unit?

As already noted, the firm, envisioned as separative, is defined as a distinct organizational entity, which has the sole purpose of maximizing profits for the shareholders. "It" is merely an organizational extension of the will of its owners and therefore acts to maximize returns.

Responsibilities of corporations to parties other than their shareholders was, however, a hot topic in the 1930s. It surged again in the 1980s, framed in the terminology of "shareholders" and "stakeholders," following a formulation of the problem by the influential business administration scholar R. Edward Freeman (1984). He questioned whether it is the purpose of a corporation to provide profits for its shareholders or whether its actions should also take into account the interests of others who have a stake in the firm.

One theoretical justification for the stakeholder view, phrased in somewhat economistic language, comes from the insight that shareholders are only one among many groups whose "investments" make up a company. Edward S. Adams and John H. Matheson (2000) argue, in a law journal, that managers and employees have invested "human capital" in the firm. Suppliers, customers, creditors, and local communities may have made accommodations on the assumption that the corporation will continue as a going concern. Legally, "the modern trend in state law is to view the corporation as a 'nexus of contracts'" (1096).

Mark Granovetter, a leader in the field of economic sociology, suggests we should recognize that "economic action . . . is embedded in ongoing networks of personal relationships" and that "economic institutions . . . do not arise automatically in some form made inevitable by external circumstances; rather, they are 'socially constructed'" (1992, 25). Michael Best and Jane Humphries (2001) discuss how the idea of firms as embedded, complex organizations has been developed—and then neglected—in economic thought over recent decades. Taking into account the relations that make up a corporation leads to a model of the firm as a social organization, complex and dynamic. The firm isn't something that just *is,* and then acts. It is *made up of* the actions and interrelations of managers, workers, shareholders, customers, suppliers, local communities, activists, legislators, and regulators. In short, a firm is individuals-in-relation.

A firm is also profoundly interknit with the sustenance and change of the natural environment. Just as some feminist theory stresses that people are physically embodied (as well as socially embedded), movements toward "green investing" recognize that the same is true of firms; they, too, have a physical constitution, and a reciprocal relationship with the natural world. Firms are not independent of the influence of natural disasters, ecological degradation, or ecological improvement, and their actions in turn affect the ecological balance.

Of course, acceptance of a more organic, individuals-in-relation model of the firm is not without its detractors. William Dimma, for example, claims that the popularity of the stakeholder view is based on its "emotional appeal" and that its implementation "thrust[s] directors and management into a fuzzy, shapeless world" (1997, 33). Perceiving firms in this mode requires recognizing the presence of characteristics such as emotion and ambiguity, which have, indeed, historically been considered feminine and "fuzzy," as the separative/soluble discussion earlier pointed out. An individuals-in-relation model may seem to take away the power of directors to actively and rationally direct the activities of the (supposedly) unitary firm.

Is the Firm "Soluble"—Driven by Law and/or Markets?

Side by side with the model of the firm as a free, unencumbered rational actor are theories which deny firms much in the way of independent action at all. Firms are often thought of as so tightly constrained by law or market competition to maximize profits that they simply have no discretion to take into account ethical, stakeholder, or environmental considerations. Seen as without options, they are seen as "soluble" and passive vis-à-vis some larger power.

Perhaps the most cited legal case concerning corporations' obligations regarding profits is *Dodge v. Ford*, decided in Michigan in 1919 (see, e.g., Dimma 1997). Henry Ford, majority shareholder in Ford Motor Company, had decided that instead of issuing special dividends to shareholders, he would use available funds to expand capacity and employment and make cars cheaper so they could be purchased by families lower down the income scale. Minority shareholder Dodge sued. The Michigan court found for the plaintiff, stating that if Ford wanted to pursue altruistic goals, "he should do it with his own money, not the corporation's" (quoted in Dimma 1997). This ruling is clearly based on the assumption that a corporation exists to make profits for its shareholders and should not use profits for other purposes. While often cited as the legal underpinning of corporate capitalism, this case is, however, only one snapshot, and an outdated one, from a long-running story of legal controversy.

In the United States, corporations are granted charters by the fifty states, and the states have the authority to specify what can be required in return. In clear contradiction to the usual interpretation of the Ford case, legal scholars note that in contemporary law "each state implicitly recognizes that a broader group of interests may be considered" and "*no* state corporation code in existence specifies that the directors of a corporation owe a fiduciary duty *solely* to the shareholders" (Adams and Matheson 2000, 1088; emphasis added). Further, in thirty-two states, "constituency statutes" exist which explicitly transform the obligations of corporate directors by expanding the groups to which boards of directors are accountable (Adams and Matheson 2000, 1085; see also Business Roundtable 1997).[2] Nor are ethical considerations always considered out of bounds: according to the American Law Institute (1994), "corporate decisions are not infrequently made on the basis of ethical considerations even when doing so would not enhance corporate profit or shareholder gain. Such behavior is not only appropriate, but desirable." Harvard Business School professor Lynn Sharp Paine (2002) argues that moral and social responsibility is increasingly being recognized as an essential part of that nature of corporate institutions.

A further argument may, however, be brought up. The Market, it is often claimed, exerts inexorable pressures that will keep firms in line with unyielding economic laws. Competitive pressures and increasing globalization of financial, input, and product markets will simply run out of business any corporations that pay attention to anything other than wealth maximization for shareholders. Economists Bengt Holstrom and Steven N. Kaplan (2001), for example, claim that market discipline will drive firms back into shareholder-interest-only governance. In light of such market pressures, David Korten, a critic of corporate capitalism, sees no hope for corporate social responsibility (1995, 212–13).

When held as a fundamental belief (as it usually is), there is little that one can say to directly refute this, as it deals with unverifiable predictions about the future and untestable attributions of causality. One can, however, examine existing evidence and the assumptions involved.

The evidence suggests that running with some "slack," rather than at the competitive razor's edge, may be normal for many organizations and that acting on ethical and social concerns may even help increase long-term profitability. Also, the idea that competition mechanically determines a "market wage" is

2. For example, in Minnesota, the groups in whose interests the directors may act are listed in the statute as "the corporation's employees, customers, suppliers, and creditors, the economy of the state and nation, community and societal considerations, and the long-term as well as short-term interests of the corporation and its shareholders" (cited in Adams and Matheson 2000, 1087).

undermined by research suggesting that wages for the same job in the same geographic area may vary by 20 percent or more, with the variation depending on, among other things, the firm's financial health and concern with worker morale (Krueger 2001). Business scholars James Collins and Jerry Porras reported in their influential book, *Built to Last: Successful Habits of Visionary Companies*, that " 'maximizing shareholder wealth' or 'profit maximization,' " was *not* "the dominant driving force or primary objective" of the "visionary" companies they studied (1994, 8). Yet these companies were all leaders in their fields, in existence for at least fifty years.

At the theoretical level, the inexorable-pressures story assumes that market competition is a stronger force than all other forces that affect human organization. Perhaps considering how this assumption plays out in another context will raise more doubt about its validity. According to some economists, market forces will lead to automatic correction of race and sex discrimination. Since discriminatory practices lead employers to fail to hire the most productive workers available at the lowest possible wage, this story goes, competitive pressures will drive discriminators out of business. Therefore, changes in social attitudes, or laws and agencies to protect employment rights, are unnecessary to get rid of discrimination. Rather, the increased exposure of noncompetitive enterprises such as "government, public institutions, and regulated monopolies" to competitive pressure is the "greatest weapon in preventing discrimination" (Polachek 1995, 74). Do we really believe that market pressures are *that* all-powerful? Might not tradition, culture, religion, education, kinship, politics, gender, and ethnic identities, loyalties of all sorts, and ethical concerns also be forces to reckon with, in explaining human organization? Can't such forces sometimes be intransigent and fight back, as well? It is a peculiar theory that chooses only one of a great variety of forces and asserts that it alone is ultimately powerful.

It would be more realistic to replace the notion of an all-powerful Market, to which "soluble" firms can only submit, by an image of markets (as well as firms and individuals) as socially embedded. In a volume on business ethics, Sandra B. Rosenthal and Rogene A. Buchholz present such an image: "The economic system is fully woven into the fabric of society as only one dimension, inseparable from others, of the sociocultural matrix in which we act out our day-to-day behavior. . . . 'the economic system,' far from being a reality engulfing the social, is a product of the fallacy of giving a supposedly independent status to a discriminable dimension of the fullness of existence, an existence which is inherently social and value laden in all sorts of ways" (2000, 122). Marta B. Calás and Linda Smircich write, "The Market does not exist now, and it probably never did" (1997, 73; capitalization in original). A more adequate view of markets (small *m*, plural) would recognize the socially and ethically significant ways in which concrete organizations interact in actual, complex economies.[3]

Even if profit maximization should indeed eventually take over as the sole concern of business, would this prove the inexorability of competitive market dynamics? Or would it prove the opposite notion: that people's beliefs about economic dynamics are important in the construction of economic institutions and can indeed become self-fulfilling prophecies?

Inside the Firm

In basic neoclassical theory, relations in the interior of a firm are characterized as *soluble-soluble*: the firm is just thought of as a unit, and it is simply presumed that all parts of it will work smoothly toward the goal of profit maximization. Few economists would now claim that this is a tenable view (even though it still guides much teaching and research that is not specifically focused on within-firm behavior).

Further developments within or close to the economic mainstream do take internal relations of firms into account to a greater extent. Internal relations within firms are the focus of much "new institutionalist" theorizing (e.g., Williamson 1991), as well as the study of information asymmetries and principal-agent questions.[4] In such theories, the problem is usually framed as that of how firms can maintain a hierarchy of control when the self-interest of managers and workers distracts them from the firm's purpose of maximizing profits for shareholders. How to get those lower down in the hierarchy to actually follow orders—to act "solubly" vis-à-vis the interests of "the firm"—is treated in standard economics as a technical problem of writing a clever-enough contract, so that conformance with directives from above will be in the self-interest of the (presumably) opportunistic agents.[5]

3. J. K. Gibson-Graham (1996) argues for a similar decentering of the notion of an all-powerful "capitalism," but from a Marxist perspective.

4. "Old" institutional economics and some variants of "evolutionary" economics, on the other hand, have more in common with alternative approaches that will be discussed below. A full discussion of this point would take this chapter too far afield, but an extensive description of contemporary "old" institutionalism can be found in Hodgson 1998. Also, Jennings (1993) and Nelson (2003) discuss its relation to feminist thought.

5. See England and Folbre (chap. 2 in this volume) for a somewhat different, and expanded, view of contracting.

While these theories of internal relations do go beyond the simple model, it must be noted that the range of motivations and relations implied is still exceedingly restricted. The only motivations considered are those of self-interest and opportunism, and the relations incorporated are limited to either impersonal contract (*separative-separative*) or hierarchy, domination, and control (*separative-soluble*). Even when, as in recent literature on "social norms," it may be allowed that actual human behavior within organizations often diverges from that which would be predicted by the narrowest rational-choice models (Ostrom 2000; Fehr and Gächter 2000), the approach tends to be to explain such "anomalies" as a more complicated form of individual utility maximization.[6]

This limitation of possible relationships to either contract or control rules out of court the idea that values, group identity, mutuality, nonhierarchical structures, or ethics—*not* merely derived as some variant of self-interest—could play a role within and among contemporary business organizations. The wider literature challenges this view.

Are Managers and Workers "Separative"—Autonomous Agents?

An individuals-in-relation view challenges the notion that managers and workers are separative agents, interested only in their own economic gain and held together only by arm's length agreements. Empirical research indicates that real humans do not simply leave their needs for social relations, their values, their loyalties, and their creativity at the workplace door. Economic sociologists Karin Knorr Cetina and Urs Bruegger (2002), for example, have examined foreign exchange trading. Even here, in what would seem to be a classic case of an impersonal auction market, the traders created "virtual societies" in which trust, reputation, and social repartee were integral to carrying on economic transactions. Viviana Zelizer (1994, forthcoming), another economic sociologist, has examined how forms of money take on social meaning in ways that often reinforce, rather than impersonalize and destroy, relations of intimacy.

---

6. For example, Ben-Ner and Putterman (1998) suggest a program of examining interactions and reciprocity within organizations in a dynamic, evolutionary setting, based on core assumptions of self-interested agents (19, 52, 53, 56) and a methodology of constrained optimization (58) and game theory. Similarly, Manski (2000) demands that economic social interactions be formally analyzed in terms of equilibrium outcomes arising from individual optimizing choices. If, in some cases, certain social norms cannot be explained as helpful coordination mechanisms for self-interested *human agents*, then believers in the self-interest-and-optimization approach can fall back on analysis at the level of self-interested *genes* (e.g., Ben-Ner and Putterman 1998, 28).

Few employees of organizations of any size—including universities—can have failed to notice the recent waves of attention to "corporate culture," "vision statements," "Total Quality Management," and so on. While now available in many different flavors—and applied both by the dedicated and by the patently insincere—such management strategies tend to share the insight that people work better when they are supported, empowered, and allowed to draw on their own creativity than when they are consistently treated as potential shirkers who have to be brought under control. As Collins and Porras reported, "People still have a fundamental human need to belong to something they can feel proud of. They have a fundamental need for guiding values and sense of purpose . . . a fundamental need for connection with other people. . . . employees will demand operating autonomy while also demanding that the organization they're connected to *stand* for something" (1994, 228; emphasis in original). These authors had matched eighteen "visionary" companies with eighteen "successful-but-second-rank" companies, and they came to the conclusion that what distinguished the groups was the existence of corporate "core values," how deeply these were believed, and how consistently they were lived (8). They see people as needing to belong, as well as needing to have some autonomy. In their analysis, then, one sees individuality and relation kept in balance. Not constrained by the assumption that behavior must follow separative/soluble lines, these business analysts are open to seeing something much richer occurring in the companies they studied.

Collins and Porras's analysis also notes both people's material interest and the importance of their other values. For example, they quote David Packard (of Hewlett-Packard) as saying, "Profit . . . is not the proper end and aim of management—it is what makes all of the proper ends and aims possible," with the proper aim being to "make a contribution to society" (1994, 56). Nobel Laureate economist Amartya Sen (1998) points out that, far from being an extraneous addition, values are part and parcel of all economic thinking. He writes that while "moral sentiments" tend to appear to conventional economists as something "mushy and soft . . . we should not fall into the trap of presuming that the assumption of pure self-interest is, in any sense, more 'elementary' than assuming other values. Moral or social concerns can be just as basic and elementary" (viii, xii). If one assumes that individuals are self-interested and that firms maximize profits, this is not an objective description of a value-neutral reality, but rather selectively highlights some values from among many that individuals and organizations may in fact hold.

Of course, the fact that the "visionary" firms have values beyond profit-maximization does not guarantee that these are values everyone would endorse. For example, one of the "visionary" firms in Collins and Porras's study was

Philip Morris, among whose corporate core values was a passionate defense of individuals' freedom of choice to smoke (1994, 85). Likewise, ambitions for nonmaterial self-aggrandizement have been noted to be among the interests that motivate some managers and workers. Thus, Granovetter argues that "the pursuit of economic goals is typically accompanied by that of such noneconomic ones as sociability, approval, status, and power" (1992, 25).

While the literatures from economic sociology and organizational behavior do not explicitly exclude non-self-interested values from analysis (the way the economics literature does), the "mushier" and more relational values still seem to be downplayed. Granovetter, for example, neglects to mention care, concern, or search for meaning as possible motivators. Similarly, Nitin Nohria writes about actors using "their prominence to push others into doing things" and "constantly trying to wrest control for themselves or blocking others from taking control" (1992, 6, 7). This emphasis on control and conflict and the omission of care and collaboration suggest that there may be a tendency in these fields as well to concentrate on more masculine-typed values, neglecting the traditionally more feminine-typed ones, even in the face of evidence to the contrary.[7]

Are Lower-Level Workers "Soluble"—Controlled by Hierarchies?

Within the limited options offered by a separative/soluble framework, the only alternative to organizing people by impersonal market exchange is to order them by hierarchy, in which one person agrees to follow the orders of another (see Williamson 1991). When the conceptual framework is widened to include individuals-in-relation, more forms of interactions can be taken into account. Nohria notes that, in contrast to conventional economic theory, his field of organizational behavior recognizes that "organizations are networks of recurring relationships," rather than merely "markets-and-hierarchies" (1992, 4, 12).[8] Worker attitudes, modes of communication, affiliation, and creativity

---

7. In the same volume as Granovetter's piece, White (1992) takes a mathematical approach to organizational behavior, emphasizing agency, control, rationality, gamings, countergamings, and hierarchy—much like the economics literature discussed earlier.

8. The term *network* has also been used within economics to indicate ties formed by parties in noncooperative games, as discussed above (e.g., Bala and Goyal 2000). Closer to the organizational theory literature is the work of economist Michael J. Piore (1992), in that he recognizes the importance of external and internal connections. However, his focus is narrowly on knowledge, technology, and explaining economic growth. While some cases of investigation of actual social ties do exist within the economics literature (e.g., Kelly and O Grada 2000), these are rare and to my knowledge have not been applied to intrafirm relations.

become visible when one considers businesses as networks of interrelated actors, rather than envisioning them as structures controlled from the top. Further, leadership is imagined differently in firms seen as communities or webs. Effective leaders are seen as those who understand the complexities of such intricate and dynamic systems and who work with others in a responsive and collaborative manner.

Surprisingly, while R. Edward Freeman's 1984 book on the stakeholder concept touched off widespread discussion, the fact that this concept was revised, ten years later, *with explicit reference to feminist theory* (Wicks, Gilbert, and Freeman 1994), seems to have gone unnoticed by feminist ethicists and economists. Contrasting hierarchies of control and networks of relation, Andrew Wicks, Daniel Gilbert, and R. Edward Freeman noted that in a hierarchical order, "Things that disrupt order or promise change and complexity are seen as a threat to the self, and the reaction is to seek control" (480). In a web of relation, on the other hand, "there is less fear. . . . The sense of interdependence arising from feminist thought makes the world appear less alien and artificial and more of . . . a fellow traveler whose fate is bounded up with one's own" (485). Robert C. Solomon's analysis of the "individual-in-the-organization" (1997, 151) and the role of caring (168) also takes a feminist-informed, individuals-in-relation view of firms' internal organization.

Conclusion

The image of the "separative firm"—of businesses as unitary (or, at most, as hierarchically organized) entities, concerned only with maximizing profits—while popular among mainstream economists and many critics alike, is severely flawed. Likewise flawed is the image of the "soluble firm," at the mercy of market forces. This chapter has used both feminist theory concerning separation and connection, and empirical evidence from law, social science, and business to outline a view of firms—and the markets they are embedded in—as webs of individuals-in-relations of social and ethical consequence.

Conventional economists may, of course, argue that these insights are all well and good for scholars in other fields, but that the "separative" model is still all that is needed in economics. Ignoring the significance of relations and values within corporations, however, leads to inadequate analysis and guidance, for three reasons.

First, models of firms that neglect these cannot explain many of the important economic phenomena of our time. For example, while mainstream economists were busy modeling financial markets in terms of rational choice and economic organizations as hierarchies of control, a single securities trader, Nick Leeson, lost $2 billion of Barings Bank's money, bringing it down and precipitating the Asian financial crisis of 1995. As analysts have commented (e.g., Hunt and Heinrich 1996), part of the problem was with organizational values, and another part was with how relations were carried out within the firm and between the firm and regulators. The 2002 U.S. stock market plunge precipitated by the Enron, WorldCom, and other ethical scandals is another case in point.

Second, the assumption that firms maximize profits has been shown to be more ideology than fact. Legal struggles over corporate governance and responsibilities are as old as the legal definition of corporations themselves.

Third, thinking of firms as asocial and amoral takes them off the hook concerning moral responsibility and leaves the people working for them split down the middle. Problems of injustice, inhumane working conditions, and environmental damage are exacerbated when the institutions most in charge are seen as not responsible. People working for corporations are left trying to accommodate two lives, one of entirely instrumental economic action and another of personal responsibility and meaning, within the confines of the one life each actually has.

In our day-to-day work, economists' standard tools based on the separative/soluble assumptions need not be entirely discarded, since organizations with relations approximating hierarchical control and values heavily tilted toward maximization of profit do exist. These tools, however, should be seen as only part of a larger, more adequate toolbox. Insisting on the use of *only* these concepts amounts to a serious bias, with gendered roots.

Feminists and other critics on the left might want to reexamine their assumptions about capitalism as well, to see if they have in fact believed too readily certain claims about firms and markets. It would be unwise, of course, to ignore the incentives arising from competitive structures or the way in which national and global institutions are affecting the balance of power between corporations and governments. But actual firms and markets—entities that involve real, living people who form complex economic (and social) relationships— may only have a passing resemblance to "the corporation" and "the market," as abstractly conceived. Shifting from a separative to an individuals-in-relation view of firms and markets emphasizes that both are human constructions that are actively shaped by human efforts. They may be formed with respect and mutuality in ways that are welfare-enhancing and sustainable, as well as with greed and domination in ways that are oppressive and ultimately self-defeating. To treat firms and markets as disputed territory, rather than lost ground, in regard to liberatory strategies opens areas of activism that antimarket rhetoric would foreclose.[9]

It may be more intellectually comfortable to measure contemporary economies against some simpler ideal—the "free market," the after-the-revolution just society, or the cooperative commune purged of the impurities of money—but such comparisons tend to direct the energy of intelligent people away from where we are in terms of economic organization and economic justice, here and now . . . and from where we are going.

9. It would also bridge some of the divide between the academic left and the rest of the world. Models of action that take seriously both markets and ethics include organizations of firms such as Business for Social Responsibility, alliances of industry and advocacy groups like the Forest Stewardship Council, and alternative marketing networks like TransFair USA.

References

Adams, Edward S., and John H. Matheson. 2000. A statutory model for corporate constituency concerns. *Emory Law Journal* 49:1085–135.

American Law Institute. 1994. *Principles of corporate governance: Analysis and recommendations.* Excerpted in *Managerial duties and business law,* Harvard Business School publication no. 9–395-244, July 1995.

Bala, Venkatesh, and Sanjeev Goyal. 2000. A noncooperative model of network formation. *Econometrica* 68:1181–229.

Benjamin, Jessica. 1988. *The bonds of love: Psychoanalysis, feminism, and the problem of domination.* New York: Pantheon.

Ben-Ner, Avner, and Louis Putterman. 1998. Values and institutions in economic analysis. In *Economics, values, and organization,* edited by Avner Ben-Ner and Louis Putterman, 3–69. Cambridge: Cambridge University Press.

Best, Michael, and Jane Humphries. 2001. Edith Penrose: A feminist economist? Working paper, University of Massachusetts, Lowell, and Oxford University.

Buber, Martin. 1958. *I and thou.* New York: Scribner's.

Business Roundtable. 1997. Statement on corporate governance. Accessed August 7, 2001, at www.brtable.org/pdf/11.pdf.

Calás, Marta B., and Linda Smircich. 1997. ¿Predicando la moral en calzoncillos? Feminist inquiries into business ethics. In *Women's studies and business ethics: Toward a new conversation,* edited by Andrea Larson and R. Edward Freeman, 50–79. New York and Oxford: Oxford University Press.

Cetina, Karin Knorr, and Urs Bruegger. 2002. Global microstructures. The virtual societies of financial markets. *American Journal of Sociology* 107 (4): 905–50.

Chodorow, Nancy Julia. 1978. *The reproduction of mothering: Psychoanalysis and the sociology of gender.* Berkeley: University of California Press.

Collins, James C., and Jerry I. Porras. 1994. *Built to last: Successful habits of visionary companies.* New York: HarperBusiness.

Dimma, William A. 1997. Putting shareholders first. *Ivey Business Quarterly* 62 (1): 33.

Duesenberry, James S. 1960. Comment. In *Demographic and economic change in developed countries,* 231–34. Report of the National Bureau of Economic Research. Princeton, N.J.: Princeton University Press.

England, Paula. 1993. The separative self: Androcentric bias in neoclassical assumptions. In *Beyond economic man*, edited by Marianne A. Ferber and Julie Nelson, 37–53. Chicago: University of Chicago Press.

Fehr, Ernst, and Simon Gächter. 2000. Fairness and retaliation: The economics of reciprocity. *Journal of Economics Perspectives* 14:159–81.

Fraser, Nancy. 2000. Rethinking recognition. *New Left Review* 3:107–20.

Freeman, R. Edward. 1984. *Strategic management: A stakeholder approach.* Boston: Pittman.

Friedman, Milton. 1982. *Capitalism and freedom.* Chicago: University of Chicago Press.

Gibson-Graham, J. K. 1996. *The end of capitalism (as we knew it).* Cambridge, Mass.: Blackwell.

Gilligan, Carol. 1982. *In a different voice: Psychological theory and women's development.* Cambridge, Mass.: Harvard University Press.

Granovetter, Mark. 1992. Problems of explanation in economic sociology. In *Networks and organizations: Structure, form, and action*, edited by Nitin Nohria and Robert G. Eccles, 25–56. Boston: Harvard Business School Press.

Held, Virginia. 2002. Care and the extension of markets. In *Feminist philosophies of love and work*, edited by Julie A. Nelson and Paula England, special issue of *Hypatia* 17 (2): 19–33.

Hodgson, Geoffrey M. 1998. The approach of institutionalist economics. *Journal of Economic Literature* 36:166–92.

Holstrom, Bengt, and Steven N. Kaplan. 2001. Corporate governance and merger activity in the United States. *Journal of Economic Perspectives* 15:121–44.

Hunt, Luke, and Karen Heinrich. 1996. *Barings lost: Nick Leeson and the collapse of Barings plc.* Singapore: Reed Academic Publishing Asia.

Jennings, Ann L. 1993. Public or private? Institutional economics and feminism. In *Beyond economic man*, edited by Marianne A. Ferber and Julie A. Nelson, 111–29. Chicago: University of Chicago Press.

Keller, Catherine. 1986. *From a broken web: Separation, sexism, and self.* Boston: Beacon Press.

Kelly, Morgan, and Cormac O Grada. 2000. Market contagion: Evidence from the panics of 1854 and 1857. *American Economic Review* 90:1110–24.

Korten, David. 1995. *When corporations rule the world.* Bloomfield, Conn.: Kumarian Press and Berrett-Koehler Publishers.

Krueger, Alan B. 2001. Economic scene. *New York Times*, April 26, C22.

Manski, Charles F. 2000. Economic analysis of social interactions. *Journal of Economic Perspectives* 4 (3): 115–36.

Nelson, Julie A. 1996. *Feminism, objectivity, and economics.* London: Routledge.

———. 2003. Confronting the science/value split: Feminist economics, institutionalism, pragmatism and process thought. *Cambridge Journal of Economics* 27:49–64.

Nohria, Nitin. 1992. Is a network perspective a useful way of studying organizations? Introduction to *Networks and organizations: Structure, form, and action*, edited by Nitin Nohria and Robert G. Eccles, 1–22. Boston: Harvard Business School Press.

Ostrom, Elinor. 2000. Collective action and the evolution of social norms. *Journal of Economic Perspectives* 14:137–58.

Paine, Lynn Sharp. 2002. *Value shift: Merging social and financial imperatives to achieve superior performance.* New York: McGraw-Hill.

Piore, Michael J. 1992. Fragments of a cognitive theory of technological change and organizational structure. In *Networks and organizations: Structure, form, and action*, edited by Nitin Nohria and Robert G. Eccles, 430–44. Boston: Harvard Business School Press.

Polachek, Solomon W. 1995. Human capital and the gender earnings gap: A response to feminist critiques. In *Out of the margin: Feminist perspectives on economic theory*, edited by Edith Kuiper et al., 61–79. London: Routledge.

Rosenthal, Sandra B., and Rogene A. Buchholz. 2000. *Rethinking business ethics: A pragmatic approach.* New York: Oxford University Press.

Sen, Amartya. 1998. Foreword to *Economics, Values, and Organization*, edited by Avner Ben-Ner and Louis Putterman, vii–xiii. Cambridge: Cambridge University Press.

Solomon, Robert C. 1997. Competition, care, and compassion: Toward a nonchauvinist view of the corporation. In *Women's studies and business ethics: Toward a new conversation*, edited by Andrea Larson and R. Edward Freeman, 144–73. New York: Oxford University Press.

White, Harrison C. 1992. Agency as control in formal networks. In *Networks and organizations: Structure, form, and action*, edited by Nitin Nohria and Robert G. Eccles, 92–117. Boston: Harvard Business School Press.

Wicks, Andrew C., Daniel R. Gilbert Jr., and R. Edward Freeman. 1994. A feminist reinterpretation of the stakeholder concept. *Business Ethics Quarterly* 4:475–97.

Williamson, Oliver E. 1991. Introduction to *The nature of the firm: Origins, evolution, and development*, edited by Oliver E. Williamson and Sidney G. Winter, 3–17. New York: Oxford University Press.

Winnicott, D. W. 1996. *Thinking about children*. New York: Addison-Wesley.

Zelizer, Viviana A. 1994. *The social meaning of money*. New York: Basic Books.

———. Forthcoming. Circuits of commerce. In *Self, social structure, and beliefs: Explorations in the sociological thought of Neil Smelser*, edited by Jeffrey Alexander, Gary T. Marx, and Christine Williams. Berkeley: University of California Press.

4

Feminist Theory and Racial Economic Inequality

. . . Lisa Saunders and William Darity Jr.

> In the process of human learning an individual or group in-
> culcates concepts, values, customs, or views that result in a
> particular way of perceiving or evaluating data, communicating
> ideas, and regulating behavior.
>
> Vernon Dixon, "The Diunital Approach
> to Economics: A Black Perspective"

Traditional economic theories about racism attribute unequal treatment by race to premarket events, exogenous preferences, or information asymmetries. Such theories are inadequate for the task of explaining racial inequality in economic opportunities and status. The concepts, customs, and values that they foster bias scholars' perceptions of data, constrain their ability to communicate ideas, and influence their behavior toward policy analysis as well as their attitudes toward groups different from their own.

The persistence of inequality and discrimination by race is an indication that there are material incentives for the construction of racial categories and boundaries. An examination of such incentives is necessary to better understand racial norms and their persistence over time and across economic conditions. Critical to this approach is recognition that those who initiate the construction of racial lines do so to establish and maintain group-linked privileges, often concretely economic ones. Thus, they apportion to themselves wealth, status, and control over the "other." When racial boundaries are breached, given the locus of power, it is the dominant group that usually chooses the conditions and place where the break occurs. An example would be the sexual breach of the Southern slavocracy, leading to the emergence of "mulatto" children, often the products of the rape of enslaved black women by the men of the white master class. This chapter considers whether the further development of economic theory about race and racial inequality might be enhanced by incorporating the point of view of feminist theory.[1]

As discussed in the introduction to this volume, feminist theory informs us that sex and gender are distinct concepts. *Sex* refers to female or male human biological status. *Gender* refers to behaviors that are linked to practices culturally designated as masculine or feminine. Thus, in some communities a man (in a biological/sex sense) is not a "man" (in a cultural/gender sense) if he performs housework, and a woman (in a biological/sex sense) is not a "woman" (in a cultural/gender sense) if she participates in contact sports. Therefore, sex is (to a great extent) fixed, while gender is more fluid. Discrimination can operate both on the basis of distinctions that are rooted in biological differences (sex) and cultural expectations of persons who differ biologically (gender).

The distinction made by feminist theory between sex and gender is suggestive of an important distinction in an identity-focused and race-conscious economic theory, the distinction between race and racism. Race is a social category that divides human beings into groups based on either appearance or ancestry or both. Racism is the mobilization of the categories to establish a *hierarchy* of superiority and inferiority across the groups with attendant privileges and shackles for those ranked high and those ranked low, respectively.

Race, unlike sex, has the quality of a fiction about it because there is an arbitrariness to human markers of intergroup distinction, for example, skin shade, hair texture, hair color, parentage, and so on. Today, physical anthropologists have all but given up the project of identifying racial types on the basis of DNA-centered characteristics. But racism certainly is not a fiction. It is practiced in a wide range of contexts: in the subjugation of the Buraku in Japan; in the genocidal violence in Rwanda, Burundi, and the former Yugoslavia; in the subordination of the Catholics by the Protestants in Northern Ireland; in the degradation of the Dalits in India by higher caste Hindus, and on and on.

---

1. Social divisions in the United States are often based on one or more of the following dimensions: age, color, disability, gender, race, religion, nationality, sexual orientation, and size. We would argue that taking account of race and gender alone in an analysis of social divisions in the United States would be incomplete, and individuals should be taken into consideration in their entirety. However, in this chapter, the economic analysis of discrimination by race and, to some extent, gender received our full attention.

Consequently we need an economic theory that is "race conscious" to genuinely understand our world. And race consciousness is necessary to prescribe *remedies* for group-based inequality and injustices. We cannot ignore race if we are to address the effects of racism. Hence, the goal is not to develop a framework of analysis that is race neutral or "color-blind." Rather, the goal is to develop a framework of analysis that can enable us to achieve a race-just society.

Feminist theory suggests that race-based discrimination bears more resemblance to gender-based discrimination than sex-based discrimination, for the foundations of racial identities are as culturally rooted as gender. Does a feminist viewpoint necessarily improve our ability to examine and address racial inequality? To what extent would its methods differ from those of traditional economics? Would it open us to a wider range of questions not considered by economists who view the world through conventional lenses? Specifically, we address the question whether such an approach is likely to illuminate the processes whereby socially constructed racial differentiation generates inequality.

Neoclassical Theory about Racism and Inequality

When neoclassical economists theorize about inequality based upon race, they traditionally explain it in the context of labor markets operating imperfectly.[2] Disparate treatment in hiring and pay is assumed to result from premarket events, exogenous preferences (unchecked by labor market competition), employers having inadequate information about the qualifications of potential employees, or all of these.

Ways in which particular interactions in institutions, including labor markets, reduce or raise inequalities and many other considerations of fairness often go unexamined, as do the historical and institutional origins of social division. In the United States those origins would include slavery, Jim Crow practices in

---

2. Though quite severe, inequality of outcomes other than in hiring and pay receive little attention. Current Population Survey data show that in 2000 Hispanics earned only 67 percent and blacks earned 80 percent of the median weekly earnings of whites. There is no doubt that labor market earnings inequality is a problem requiring analytical focus. However, other types of severe and persistent inequality receive little attention from economists. Chiteji and Stafford (1999) cite findings of a black/white ratio of mean wealth ranging from 0.17 to 0.25 and median wealth ratios ranging from 0.08 to 0.13, depending on data source and definition of "family wealth." The Census Bureau reported in 1999 that 26.1 percent of blacks and 25.9 percent of Hispanics lived at income levels below the poverty line, while for whites the rate was 8.2 percent. Moreover, the former groups experience mortgage lending discrimination, as documented in a 1999 Urban Institute report (see Fix and Struyk 1993; Ackerman et al. 2000).

the South, the provision of inferior schools, and the denial of the capacity to accumulate property for black Americans. Scholars who wish to take up such questions from the vantage point of economics frequently are advised to pursue these matters in another of the social sciences.[3]

Economics thus is characterized as a disciplinary space that greatly privileges endless theorizing about auctions and auction markets over issues of race and gender. The vast majority of economists view a thorough examination of racial inequality as beyond the scope of the discipline or an unwelcome interruption to the normal flow of economic research. We contend that a more comprehensive examination of racial discrimination and disparity is very much a subject for economics and its inclusion within the thematic hub of the field is well worth the effort.

Economists have been trained to concentrate disproportionately on the efficiency, and not the equity, aspects of economic behavior. Moreover, if an economist embraces the Pareto principle, s/he cannot rank which among allocations is most efficient. Rational actors, informed about specific costs and benefits, are motivated by self-interest. Differences in individuals' motivations and constraints can be and sometimes are accommodated by traditional models. Yet the other ways of knowing and choosing among options are ignored, especially if they conflict with the traditional behavioral assumptions in the models. Model building requires abstraction from many details of reality. What we wish to consider, however, is how the particular choice of abstractions can undermine a theory's efficacy for explaining social division and intergroup inequality.

Neoclassical economists normally assume that profit-maximizing participants in markets will not continue to indulge in prejudicial behavior that leads to disparate treatment and rewards for workers when there are no substantive differences in productivity. Therefore, discrimination in labor markets is not sustainable, and observed, measurable gaps in economic outcomes are attributed to factors that operate prior to the market. Thus, workers from a racial group that receives lower pay must have an average productivity deficit relative to workers from a higher paid group that fully explains the gap. One of the more popular stories making the rounds now is the claim that the black-white gap in labor market outcomes can be explained by black cognitive skill deficiencies.[4]

3. For another discussion of attempts to include institutions and history in economic analysis, see Blank and Reimers, chap. 7 in this volume.

4. The standard reference making this claim has become Neal and Johnson 1996. There are several studies that challenge this assertion that frequently are simply ignored by proponents of the cognitive-skills-deficit position. One of these is Rodgers and Spriggs's 1996 study that addresses racial

Further, in the neoclassical paradigm, sources of racial *preferences* typically are not examined but are treated as a given—just as one would have a taste for tomato soup over onion soup. Thus, the way in which customs, habits, and beliefs are socially formed is ignored, but their existence and influences on behavior are assumed to be instrumental in determining outcomes.[5]

For example, Vernon Dixon (1971) has argued that individualism, a value deeply embedded in the American cultural matrix, permeates the discipline of economics. With individualism as a silently understood norm, neoclassicists generally assume the independence and autonomy of each person's utility function. This leaves beyond view actions produced via social interdependence and interaction, in other words, learning what it means to be "white" or to be "black," learning "one's place" in society. In fact, standard economics leaves other ways of knowing, doing, and deciding largely outside of theoretical activity.[6]

Concerning decision makers who treat equally qualified applicants differently, neoclassicists argue that this is rational either if information is costly or, more generally, if markets are imperfect. If information is costly, it is rational, they argue, for employers to make decisions about individual hires on the basis of group averages. Employers in markets that are imperfect, for example a single-employer market, may rationally entertain her/his personal racial preference in hiring and pay decisions. Similarly, an employer's decision to accommodate outright bigotry on the part of white (or male) customers or employees is theorized to be rational as long as it is profitable.

As noted above, many economists argue that labor market discrimination has been exaggerated due to inadequate measures or controls for productivity differences among job applicants. By treating race and gender discrimination as an outcome of rational choices or of market failure of some type, neoclassical economics constructs a narrative that renders discriminatory behavior less tangible, more inconsequential, and ultimately justifiable. Indeed, from this perspective, racist practices are not grounded in racism.

Thus, the agency of many groups exists beyond the purview of economics as conventionally practiced, apart from the few instances when economists treat

---

differences in processes that generate measurable differences in cognitive skills by race. Another is the work of Goldsmith, Veum, and Darity (2000a) that demonstrates strong remaining discriminatory differentials, even after taking into account the same measures of cognitive skills used by Neal and Johnson, when psychological capital also is considered.

5. For further discussion of preference formation, see England, chap. 1 in this volume; and Blank and Reimers, chap. 7 in this volume.

6. Perhaps with the exception of a small clique of quasi-maverick mathematical economists connected with the Santa Fe Institute who are explicitly concerned about neighborhood and contagion effects.

groups as legitimately reducible to the joint product of the individual group members. The role of the social existence of one's group in shaping an individual's actions is bypassed at the very moment when tastes and preferences are treated as exogenous or solely the product of an individual's personal and asocial development.

Paula England (1993, chap. 1 in this volume) describes a separative self that is embodied in the individualism and exogenous, unchanging preferences that dominate neoclassical economics and an associated long-standing prohibition against interpersonal comparisons of happiness or satisfaction. It is this prohibition in neoclassical economics, she argues, that leaves the analysis of inequality and disadvantage at the margins of economic thought.

The Origin and Function of Racial Norms

The construction of race as a category provides a mechanism to produce oppression.[7] However, the precise motivations of individual economic actors are multidimensional. Race and gender oppression operate differently from one another in some cases and similarly in others, but they necessarily operate in tandem. Whether either holds more sway in determining an outcome is situational.

For example, when an employer, landlord, loan officer, or other person similarly situated, makes choices about individuals, s/he forms impressions based on all that s/he thinks s/he knows about the individuals. There is strong evidence that such decisions are likely to be influenced not only by the individual's formal qualifications, but by what the decision maker believes about which group the individual belongs to and his/her perception of the group. Thus, the final decision (about hiring, pay, promotion, layoffs, housing, loans) is based on both formal and informal assessments.

Qualitative studies often provide insight into the racial norms subscribed to and acted upon by some employers and the reactions of some workers. For example, Browne and Kennelly (1999) examined the perceptions of employers for clues about whether unequal treatment is motivated by "closure." Closure is a concept developed in sociology that describes group and individual behaviors intended to preserve one's own group's privileges. Comparing the interview responses of employers in the Atlanta, Georgia, area with employee profiles, the authors found that the responses of white male employers to (open-ended)

---

7. When the subordinate group takes on and modifies the imposed identity as an instrument of pride, identity can become an instrument of resistance.

questions about their workers were rather uniform, and they were often incorrect. The employers volunteered comments that emphasized differences in the personal and performance characteristics of women from men and of blacks from whites. They appeared to hold stereotypical notions about their workers.

These employers overestimated the share of all women who had young children living at home and the share of black women who were single mothers. They overestimated the time lost by women for child care and underestimated it for men. They made remarks regarding women with children that were more positive and sympathetic when referring to white women than when referring to black women.[8] Employers volunteered comments that were less favorable or sympathetic when referring to black men than when referring to black women.

Understanding Race and Gender Interactions

The employers' responses above suggest that their attitudes toward women and any resulting gender discrimination are racialized and that simultaneously their racial attitudes and race-based prejudices are gendered. Employer remarks in this study alone demonstrate the importance of incorporating feminist analysis into the study of racial discrimination and the analysis of race into the study of gender discrimination.[9]

In principle, it would appear to be straightforward to argue that white females necessarily only face gender discrimination, while black women face both gender and racial discrimination. Hence, the level of discrimination faced by black women ought to be higher, and it should be possible to net out the pure effects of racial discrimination on black female earnings by subtracting the effects of gender discrimination on white female earnings.

This assumes, however, that the discriminatory effects of race and gender layer in a straightforward additive fashion. In all likelihood, they do not. In addition, there is also an empirical anomaly. Most statistical endeavors to detect the presence of labor market discrimination in the United States, specifically against black women vis-à-vis white women, do not find evidence of it.[10]

8. A different study cites sympathetic comments by white male executives whose wives or daughters have professional careers (Zetlin 1999). Some of the executives that the author interviewed stated that their own attitudes and behaviors toward female managers improved as they learned of the disadvantages faced by their wives or daughters. Some of the men actually initiated support programs for women. It is unclear whether or to what extent such modifications in behavior are extended to female managers who are not white.

9. Evelyn Nakano Glenn (1985) wrote about this some time ago.

10. An exception to the general finding in statistical work of a lack of discrimination against black women is Marlene Kim's (2002) recent work using 2000 Current Population Survey (CPS) data.

However, to conclude that black women do not face racial discrimination would be wrong. In striking contrast with the statistical research referred to above are the direct tests of the presence of discrimination. In such audit studies, trained actors are supplied with identical résumés and coached in interviewing. The black and white actors then apply for the same jobs, noting the actions of the interviewers and measuring how far they advance in the hiring process. These tests tend to find substantial discrimination against black women when paired with white women at all stages of the hiring process: they are less likely to be invited to interview, less likely to be offered the job, less likely to be told about unadvertised advancement opportunities, and, if offered the job, more likely to be offered a lower wage (Bendick, Jackson, and Reinoso 1997). How might we reconcile these contradictory findings?

The statistical studies usually control for the workers' occupational sector, sometimes at a very broad level, sometimes at a more detailed level, so that they ultimately accept wage disparities among occupational categories as given. These gaps remain substantial for black men but appear to be even greater for women, both black and white. Conrad (2001) demonstrates that even into the 1990s, college-educated black women are found concentrated in low-wage occupations. This may be the result of mechanisms that assign women, both black and white, to jobs that are gender-typed and assign black women to jobs that are both gender- and race-typed, with accompanying lower pay (Simms and Malveaux 1986). If this is the case, wage regressions specified to control for occupational category may mitigate detection of racial discrimination among women. Hamilton and Darity (2002) found evidence that such crowding led to black-white wage differences among men. In a footnote to their study, they explained that a comparison of black and white women revealed differences in the types of jobs that black women obtained. However, this job variation was not correlated with occupational wage differences between black and white women.

Independently, Hamilton had the insight that the failure to find wage discrimination against black women arises from the failure to control for motivation (personal e-mail communication). He drew that conclusion from a substantial body of work by Goldsmith, Veum, and Darity (2000b and elsewhere) using the National Longitudinal Study of Youth data, where, when motivation is included as a right-hand-side variable, they find evidence of discrimination against black women in wages. Differences in familial and community responsibilities may create in black women greater motivation to work than in white

---

Kim raises the question as to why her results using the CPS differ from results generated using the 1980 and 1990 decennial censuses but offers no answer.

women with similar measured human capital. If audit studies send out applicants who are matched in motivation, we would expect them to detect employer discrimination. A statistical analysis that does not control for racial differences in motivation, on the other hand, is likely to confound residuals due to familial pressures and those due to discrimination, thereby underestimating discrimination. Without a vision that is sensitive to the different but interactive effects of race and gender on economic outcomes, we would not see the differences in patterns of discrimination nor be impelled to ask how we might explain them. We would not know that antidiscrimination measures might need to be tailored to adjust for the different ways in which underpayment is executed for black women and men.

Women disagree about the extent to which their interactions in the labor market are based on color or gender. Higginbotham and Weber (1999) examine professional-managerial worker attitudes and reactions to their labor-force experiences. They examine interviews of Memphis area female workers and find similarities and differences in the ways that black and white women perceive the treatment they received on the job. Both groups emphasized group experiences of discrimination and deemphasized individual experiences. While both groups were quite aware of barriers to advancement and listed some obstacles that were similar, "black women experience more and different forms of discriminatory treatment in the workplace than do white women" (350). Black women said they frequently observed racial differences in treatment, while most white women said they never observed racial discrimination against women of any race.

Exclusion based on race and gender may operate similarly in some respects and differently in others; also, they may operate independently or in conjunction with one another, depending upon the specific interaction under examination. Yet neoclassical labor economists apply the same methods to different forms of oppression. This suggests that they assume employers use identical exclusionary strategies for all racial groups and that they use these same strategies for exclusion by gender, regardless of race (or class, sexual orientation, etc.). Instead, it is quite likely that employers actually make decisions according to their assessments and biases unique to each group and situation. Thus, exclusion often operates differently across racial groups and across time, economic conditions, and so forth.[11] Certainly, the women in the Memphis

---

11. See, e.g., Darity and Deshpande 2000 for a discussion of recent changes in racial inequality in several different countries and Darity 1989, which provides examples of differences in the economic opportunities among immigrant Americans, even when they are from the same racial groups. See also England, Christopher, and Reid 1999 and Cintrón-Velez 1999.

survey perceived, and probably experienced, both similar and different types of exclusion. To the extent that there are important differences in the ways that race and gender operate to include and exclude people, it is essential to know what these differences are, how they interact, and how they affect outcomes. At the same time, as demonstrated above, theorizing in either-or terms about race and gender puts limits on economic analysis.

Until recently, much of the published research on racial employment and wage inequality has focused on black men, excluding black women as well as men and women in other racial groups. Similarly, economic research on women, until recently, has primarily examined the employment, earnings, and family experiences of white women.

Labor markets certainly do function to include and exclude workers from occupations by race and gender, to the greater disadvantage of some groups than others. The actual forms that group disadvantages take vary by region and over time, as does the disadvantages' severity.[12] Thus, it is certainly understandable that much can be learned about a specific group from such a singular focus. We would argue, however, that not very much would be learned about racial or gender inequality. When separating out an individual group results in the claim that one category (e.g., race or gender) has the greatest effect on economic opportunity, then other dimensions of discrimination may be overlooked, suppressed, or subordinated.

Higginbotham and Weber (1999) described the failure of white women in their survey to acknowledge the racial problems that black women observed as a barrier to cooperation between the two groups. They argued that this lack of acknowledgment both created "potential obstacles for their black coworkers" and reduced "the potential for white women to work in coalitions with black colleagues against racial injustice in the workplace." They concluded that "Only through comparative studies that document the meaning of race to white and black women can the foundation for such coalitions be assessed" (349–50). Comparative studies could be quite useful to economists studying the gendered nature of racial inequality and the racial nature of gender inequality.[13]

Theorizing Feminism and Antiracism

An important lesson we might also take from Higginbotham and Weber is the possibility for powerful coalitions among scholars who abandon the singularity

---

12. See Amott and Matthaei 1996 for an excellent multiracial economic history of women in the United States.

13. See, e.g., Reskin 1998 on affirmative action.

of race or gender or any one, essential, basis for oppression. Though there is no one path to either feminist or antiracist scholarship, they have much in common. Researchers in both schools struggle against the hegemony in the discipline that categorizes their theories as marginal and renegade. Scholars of both take a variety of approaches, conceptualizing theories from another perspective than that of the mainstream, using traditional and nontraditional methods, and formulating new insights for policy.

Many economists have sought to understand what are the economic incentives for and consequences of treating people differently according to racial identity. Scholars who consider unequal and unfair treatment to be a logical outcome of long-established social norms examine the development and persistence of such norms. While much of this research has been done in disciplines other than economics,[14] many economists have pursued an understanding of racial norms as well.[15]

To be valuable to all women, a feminist examination of inequality of economic opportunity would need to contain a racial analysis.[16] Unfortunately, this is not yet the case in most feminist scholarship in economics. When Dixon writes, "White people have found it possible to relate to black people by recognizing them and denying them at one and the same time" (1971, 30), he is explaining that the ability to relate represents a contradiction for whites who think in black and white, who see blacks as not white, as other. He goes on to say that they resolve the conflict by making all that is white universal and authoritative (see also Charusheela and Zein-Elabdin, chap. 8 in this volume). There is a potential for this conflict among feminists who examine the lives of people of color. The notion that fighting sexism is part and parcel of fighting oppression against other groups (or at least oppression against the women in those other groups) creates a dilemma for feminists generally and for feminists of color in particular. White feminists could easily relate to women of color as women and "deny them at one and the same time" by ignoring the role that race plays in what happens to them and by making all that is antisexist (according to them) universal and authoritative. If the feminist model of exploitation by gender is based solely on the experiences specific to white women, it will be of limited use for addressing the disadvantages accruing to women of color. We

14. See, especially, Browne and Kennelly 1999; Higginbotham and Weber 1999; and Reskin 1998.

15. See Darity 1989; Williams 1993; Matthaei 1996; Darity, Mason, and Stewart 2000; King and Easton 2000; and Spriggs and Williams 2000.

16. For our purposes, we define feminist scholarship as an epistemology dedicated to the elimination of inequitable treatment of women. Of course, there are other definitions of feminism; for an overview, see Nelson 1993.

think that would be unfortunate, because feminism can be informed by and help to inform antiracist economics.[17]

By the same token, antiracist scholars can little afford to ignore feminism. Many, if not most, of the interactions women of color have with others are at least partly a function of gender. An inclusive antiracist economic theory about racial inequality would, therefore, also have to be feminist and acknowledge the gendered nature of discrimination against women and men of color.

An adequate feminist analysis of racial inequality is a racialized analysis of economic inequality by gender and requires complex analytical tools, some of which are more frequently practiced outside the neoclassical economics paradigm. Such a theory would need to allow that individuals vary within groups as well as across groups, in terms of what they value and how their lives unfold. It would take into account selfish and unselfish, economic and noneconomic incentives. It would treat institutional racism as a category of exclusion that may be addressed as concerted group behavior or as an indirect outcome of persistent and widespread individual behaviors with multidimensional motivations. While, as already suggested, race and gender oppression operate differently in some cases and similarly in others, they operate in tandem. How they interact and influence behavior and economic conditions over time would be part and parcel of the racialized feminist analysis.

While new research shows great promise for a better understanding of racism's effect on economic outcomes, it seems a bit scattered. (To date, there has been no concerted effort by similarly predisposed scholars.) It is, we think, not as well informed as it might be by the work that has been done in other disciplines. However, many interesting questions have come to our attention, and many worthy scholars are intent on finding the answers. Among these questions, quite a number are rather basic, but complex: Where do racial norms come from? How do they change? Are they always gender specific? Under what economic and institutional conditions are racial norms reinforced or diminished? What kinds of policies can be designed to increase the cost of racial norms, including bigotry and prejudice? How do other types of oppression (homophobia, religious bigotry, etc.) interact with racism?

Conclusion

In *Beyond Economic Man*, Williams argues for the "racializing of our (feminist) theorizing of gender," because, after all, economic ideas grew up in a postcolonial culture, where scientists declared race a legitimate categorization for

---

17. See Williams 1993 and Matthaei 1996.

human beings (1993, 144–45). We agree with her that racializing feminist analysis is long overdue. Ten years later the need remains urgent; and we argue for that and much more.

In this chapter we have described the ways in which we believe the basic structure of economic theory marginalizes racial inequality and how specific empirical research strategies trivialize and sometimes fail to recognize how racial discrimination operates. We argue that feminist and antiracist scholars can mutually benefit by recognizing and applying, wherever possible, the basic principle that economic outcomes differ within and across racial groups in gender-specific ways and within and across gender groups in race-specific ways. We demonstrate this, using findings from quantitative and qualitative research. We recommend that economists report findings and adapt more complex methods and ideas, including those from other disciplines, wherever it facilitates their investigation into the race- and gender-specific nature of economic inequality.

References

Ackerman, Frank, Neva Goodwin, Laurie Dougherty, and Kevin Gallagher. 2000. *The political economy of inequality*. Washington, D.C.: Island Press.

Amott, Teresa, and Julie Matthaei. 1996. *Race, gender, and work: A multicultural history of women in the United States*. 2d ed. Boston: South End Press.

Bendick, Mark Jr., Charles W. Jackson, and Victor A. Reinoso. 1997. Measuring employment discrimination through controlled experiments. In *African-Americans and post-industrial labor markets*, edited by James B. Stewart, 77–100. New Brunswick, N.J.: Transaction Publishers.

Browne, Irene, and Ivy Kennelly. 1999. Stereotypes and realities: Images of black women in the labor market. In *Latinas and African American women at work*, edited by Irene Browne, 302–26. New York: Russell Sage Foundation.

Chiteji, Ngina, and Frank Stafford. 1999. Portfolio choices of parents and their children as young adults: Asset accumulation by African-American families. *American Economic Review* 89 (2): 377–80.

Cintrón-Velez, Aixa. 1999. Generational paths into and out of work: Personal narratives, of Puerto Rican women in New York. In *Latinas and African American women at work*, edited by Irene Browne, 207–43. New York: Russell Sage Foundation.

Conrad, Cecilia. 2001. Racial trends in labor market access and wages: Women. In *America becoming: Racial trends and their consequences*, vol. 2., edited by Neil J. Smelser, William J. Wilson, and Faith Mitchell, 124–51. Washington, D.C.: National Research Council.

Darity, William, Jr. 1989. What's left of the economic theory of discrimination? In *The question of discrimination: Racial inequality in the U.S. labor market*, edited by S. Shulman and William Darity Jr., 335–74. Middletown, Conn.: Wesleyan University Press.

Darity, William, Jr., and Ashwini Deshpande. 2000. Tracing the divide: Inter-group disparity across countries. *Eastern Economic Journal* 26 (1): 75–85.

Darity, William, Jr., Patrick Mason, and James Stewart. 2000. The economics of identity: The origin and persistence of racial norms. Unpublished manuscript.

Dixon, Vernon J. 1971. Introduction; Two approaches to black-white relations; and The diunital approach to economics: A black perspective. In *Beyond black or white: An alternate America*, edited by Vernon Dixon and Badi Foster, 1–6, 23–66, and 83–94. Boston: Little Brown.

England, Paula. 1993. The separative self: Androcentric bias in neoclassical assumptions. In *Beyond economic man: Feminist theory and economics,* edited by Marianne A. Ferber and Julie A. Nelson, 37–53. Chicago: University of Chicago Press.

England, Paula, Karen Christopher, and Lori Reid. 1999. Gender, race, ethnicity, and wages. In *Latinas and African American women at work,* edited by Irene Browne, 139–82. New York: Russell Sage Foundation.

Fix, Michael, and Raymond J. Struyk. 1993. *Clear and convincing evidence: Measurement of discrimination in America.* Washington, D.C.: Urban Institute Press.

Glenn, Evelyn Nakano. 1985. Racial ethnic women's labor: The intersection of race, gender, and class oppression. *Review of Radical Political Economy* 17 (3): 86–108.

Goldsmith, Arthur H., Jonathan R. Veum, and William Darity Jr. 2000a. Working hard for the money? Efficiency wages and worker effort. *Journal of Economic Psychology* 21:351–85.

———. 2000b. Motivation and labor market outcomes. *Research in Labor Economics* 19:109–47.

Hamilton, Darrick, and William Darity Jr. 2002. Crowded out? The racial composition of American occupations. Unpublished manuscript.

Higginbotham, Elizabeth, and Lynn Weber. 1999. Perceptions of workplace discrimination among black and white professional-managerial women. In *Latinas and African American women at work,* 327–51. New York: Russell Sage Foundation.

Kim, Marlene. 2002. Has the race penalty disappeared for black women in the United States? *Feminist Economics* 8 (2): 115–24.

King, Mary C., and Todd Easton. 2000. Should black women and men live in the same place? An intermetropolitan assessment of relative labor market success. *Review of Black Political Economy* 27 (3): 9–34.

Matthaei, Julie. 1996. Why feminist, Marxist, and anti-racist economists should be feminist-Marxist-anti-racist economists. *Feminist Economics* 2 (1): 22–42.

Neal, Derek, and William Johnson. 1996. Black-white differences in wages: The role of pre-market factors. *Journal of Political Economy* 104:869–95.

Nelson, Julie A. 1993. The study of choice or the study of provisioning? Gender and the definition of economics. In *Beyond economic man: Feminist theory and economics,* edited by Marianne A. Ferber and Julie A. Nelson, 23–36. Chicago: University of Chicago Press.

Reskin, Barbara F. 1998. *The realities of affirmative action in employment.* Washington, D.C.: American Sociological Association.

Rodgers, William, III, and William Spriggs. 1996. What does the AFQT really measure: Race, wages, schooling, and the AFQT score. *Review of Black Political Economy* 24 (4): 13–46.

Simms, Margaret, and Julianne Malveaux. 1986. *Slipping through the cracks: The status of black women.* New Brunswick, N.J.: Transaction Books.

Spriggs, William E., and Rhonda M. Williams. 2000. What do we need to know about African American unemployment? In *Prosperity for all?* edited by Robert Cherry and William Rodgers, 188–207. New York: Russell Sage Foundation.

Turner, Margery Austin, and Felicity Skidmore, eds. 1999. *Mortgage lending discrimination: A review of existing evidence.* Washington, D.C.: Urban Institute Press.

Williams, Rhonda M. 1993. Race, deconstruction, and the emergent agenda of feminist economic theory. In *Beyond economic man: Feminist theory and economics,* edited by Marianne Ferber and Julie Nelson, 144–53. Chicago: University of Chicago Press.

Zetlin, Minda. 1999. Behind closed doors: Male executives discuss the glass ceiling. *Women's Times,* September.

5

Economic Rationality and Globalization: A Feminist Perspective

. . . Lourdes Benería

During the past fifteen years, feminist theory has made important contributions that have deeply transformed many disciplines. Belatedly and perhaps to a lesser extent, it has also had an impact on economics. As demonstrated by the success of *Beyond Economic Man*, feminist economics has raised much interest among those who have been questioning conventional economic analysis. Their questions range from traditional economics' often androcentric assumptions to its tendency to focus on efficiency, growth, and the maximization of gains and wealth rather than on the enhancement of human development and well-being.

In *Beyond Economic Man*, the authors brought attention to the fact that gender and the academic discipline of economics are not immutable, naturally occurring phenomena, but rather are socially constructed. This chapter argues that the project of honing the critique and constructing alternative models could benefit from an extension of feminist analysis to the social construction of *markets*. This concern is all the more pressing since

This chapter has been updated and shortened from a paper published in *Feminist Economics* 5, no. 3 (fall 1999): 61–83. Its basic arguments have been presented at different forums and are part of a book in preparation on gender and the global economy, for which the author has received help from the MacArthur Foundation, the Radcliffe Public Policy Institute, and the Woodrow Wilson Center for International Research. I want to thank Gunseli Berik, Savitri Bisnath, Maria Floro, Nancy Folbre, Philip McMichael, and Kathy Rankin for their comments on earlier versions of this work. Many thanks also to Marianne Ferber and Julie Nelson for their comments and editorial help.

markets have been expanding and have become ever more integrated on a global scale, while increasingly more aspects of daily life are commodified and larger segments of the world's population are engaged in market-oriented work.

The next section focuses on Karl Polanyi's analysis of the social and political construction of markets and of "market society" during the nineteenth and early twentieth centuries in Europe. Following that, I discuss the extent to which this type of analysis can be applied to the formation of global markets in the late twentieth century. The next section argues that this transformation had, and continues to have, gender dimensions and points out the tension between the assumptions of economic rationality associated with market behavior and the real-life experiences of women and men. I then extend this analysis to the effects on women of globalization and the feminization of the labor force. The final section argues that economists need to change the predominant approaches in orthodox neoclassical models to one that puts humans first, an agenda in which feminist economics can play an important role.

The Social Construction of Markets

This section questions the extent to which social organization is the result of economic organization or vice versa—as well as the extent to which the expansion of markets is a natural process, resulting from the growth of economic activity and gains in productivity and efficiency associated with the expansion of markets. One of the most thorough and influential discussions of these questions can be found in Karl Polanyi's *The Great Transformation*. Written during the Second World War by this Polish social scientist, then living in the United States, it was first published in 1944. In it, Polanyi provides an analysis of the construction and growth of the self-regulated market and of laissez-faire capitalism during the Industrial Revolution up to the early part of the twentieth century.

Polanyi's analysis centers on the profound change in human behavior represented by market-oriented choices and decisions in which gain replaced subsistence as the main purpose of economic activity. Given current trends in which the pursuit of gain and profit appear to be the primary goal in our societies, his argument that gain and profit had never before played such an important role in human activity is especially relevant. Critical of Adam Smith's suggestion that the social division of labor depends upon the existence of markets and upon a human propensity to "truck and barter," Polanyi argued that the division of labor in earlier societies depended on differences inherent in the facts of sex, geography, and individual endowment and that instead it was ensured through reciprocity and redistribution in an economic system that was "a mere function of social organization," in other words, at the service of social life. Capitalism, on the other hand, evolved in the opposite direction, leading to the hegemony of an economic system that determines social organization. In other words, the economic has primacy over the social.

For Polanyi, a crucial point in this gradual transformation toward the predominance of "the economic" was the shift from "isolated markets into a [self-regulated] market economy." Contrary to conventional wisdom, he saw this change not as "the natural outcome of the spreading of markets" (57) but as the result of "an enormous increase in continuous, centrally organized and controlled interventionism" through legislative initiatives and other means. In England these included the enclosure laws and the "bureaucratic control involved in the administration of the New Poor Laws" (140). Polanyi also mentions the enormous increase in the administrative functions of the state—newly endowed with a central bureaucracy—the strengthening of private property, and the enforcement of contracts in market exchange and other transactions. In his words, "The gearing of markets into a self-regulating system of tremendous power was not the result of any inherent tendency of markets toward excrescence, but rather the effect of highly artificial stimulants administered to the body social in order to meet a situation which was created by the no less artificial phenomenon of the machine" (57). Thus, Polanyi argued that laissez-faire liberalism was actually "the product of deliberate state action" and that "all these strongholds of government interference were erected with a view to the organizing of some simple [market] freedom." Likewise, he described the formation of a competitive national labor market in eighteenth- and nineteenth-century England as the result of a series of policies that dislocated labor and forced the new laboring classes to work for low wages.

This was the foundation on which economic liberalism was built. For Polanyi, the 1920s was the zenith of this regime, with the emphasis on "sound budgets and sound currencies" justifying all necessary social costs. He was in many ways a prophet of contemporary dogma: "The repayment of foreign loans and the return to stable currencies were recognized as the touchstones of rationality in politics; and no private suffering, no infringement of sovereignty, was deemed too great a sacrifice for the recovery of monetary integrity" (142). In the thirties, on the other hand, these absolutes were called into question, with international debts repudiated and the tenets of economic liberalism disregarded "by the wealthiest and most respectable" (142).

The profound change brought about by the gradual construction of a market society led to equally profound changes in human behavior and particularly to the prevalence of economic man. As Polanyi stated, "a market economy can only exist in a market society," where appropriate changes in norms and behavior enable the market to function. This includes the expectation that human beings behave so as to achieve maximum gains: the entrepreneur seeks to maximize profit, the employee seeks to maximize earnings, and the consumer seeks to maximize utility and material well-being, all of it from an individualistic perspective. Adam Smith linked this selfish pursuit of individual gain to the maximization of the wealth of nations as a result of the operation of the invisible hand of the market, and he saw no contradiction between the two. Orthodox economists today continue to rely on this basic link.

Economic rationality has been a basic tenet of neoclassical economic theory. It is assumed to be the norm in human behavior and the way to ensure the smooth functioning of the competitive market. Under this assumption, the market is viewed as leading to the most efficient allocation of given resources. Feminist economists have, however, pointed out that this assumption excludes behavior based on other types of motivation, such as altruism,[1] empathy for others, love, the pursuit of art and beauty for their own sake, reciprocity, and care; selfless behavior is viewed as confined to the nonmarket sector, such as the family. To be sure, there have been efforts to incorporate what Folbre (1994) calls "imperfectly rational somewhat economic persons" or institutions in the analysis. Such actors pursue their self-interest in ways not neatly adjusted to clear-cut definitions of economic rationality and "selfishness," and their actions include complex mixtures of behavior that are more realistic, albeit more difficult to model. As she points out, these models undermine any strong claims about the inherent efficiency of a market economy. They are also helpful in developing alternatives to the assumption that economic rationality is the norm. A growing number of experiments regarding personal preferences show that individuals respond to a variety of factors other than self-interest. We will return to this issue in a later section.

The Construction of National and Global Markets

> Capitalism without bankruptcy is like Christianity without hell.

The above quote is a comment attributed to Westerners in a *New York Times* article on the Asian financial crisis which argues that corporations in Asia failed in record numbers but without disappearing from the market (WuDunn 1998),

---

1. Gary Becker's analysis of altruism in the family is a notable exception, but it has been criticized by feminist economists for its unrealistic and patriarchal assumptions (Folbre 1994; Bergmann 1995).

in other words, without "going to hell." It raises an important question about the nature of markets and of capitalism. As the twenty-first century unfolds, many parallels can be traced between the social construction of national market economies analyzed by Polanyi for nineteenth-century Europe, and the expansion and deepening of markets across the globe during the last decades of the twentieth century. To be sure, a debate exists about the extent to which globalization represents a new trend. For example, various authors have pointed out that, comparable to current levels, high levels of globalization were reached during earlier historical periods—such as at the beginning of the twentieth century and before World War I. Yet the intensification of integrative processes among countries during the past thirty years—for example the increasingly rapid movement of goods and communications—has been unprecedented. The financial sector has led in the trend toward transcending national boundaries. Trade liberalization and the internationalization of production have accelerated the global integration of markets, and numerous governments have played an active role in globalizing national economies and their countries' social, political, and cultural life. This time, however, the construction of global markets has taken place mainly through the interventions of international institutions, such as regional free-trade areas and common markets, the growth of multinational corporations, international organizations such as the World Bank and the International Monetary Fund (IMF), as well as the international influence of powerful governments and other actors, such as private banks. Below are examples of such dynamics.

First, nation-states have enacted deregulation schemes in financial, goods, and labor markets. Although the degree of deregulation varies, the tendency to "free" markets from intervention has become an integral part of neoliberal policies in high- and low-income countries. Not surprisingly, in high-income countries, this has aroused opposition from groups such as trade unions and labor in general—including women's groups—that have lost economic and social power as a result of these policies and have objected to the deep cuts in social services and to the dismantling of the welfare state. In low-income countries, protests against neoliberal policies have been varied and numerous.

Second, the formation of transnational entities such as the European Union, the North American Free Trade Association, Mercosur, and others have contributed to the globalization of markets, as would the proposed Free Trade of the Americas Association. The strong push in this direction has been in response to powerful interests and actors likely to benefit from such schemes.[2]

2. To be sure, economic interests are not the only driving forces behind such schemes. In the European Community, for example, political objectives of unification have been very important, from

In addition, globalization has been furthered by governments acting as agents, as they did, for instance, in the Uruguay Round of trade negotiations that led to the replacement of the General Agreement on Tariffs and Trade (GATT) by the World Trade Organization (WTO) in 1995. These negotiations largely responded to the initiatives of high-income countries and of global interests expecting to benefit from trade liberalization and freer markets (Vernon 1988; Epstein, Graham, and Nembhard 1990; Arrighi 1994). Similarly, high-income countries have influenced the integration of the previously centrally planned economies into international organizations and global markets (Kotz 1995; Sachs 1997; Haney 2000).

Third, national policies leading to a higher degree of globalization have often been inspired, and at times dictated, from the outside, particularly in developing countries. One example is that of the structural adjustment policies (SAPs) adopted by a large number of countries since the early 1980s. SAPs represent a profound deepening of the market in the countries affected. They have resulted in deep economic restructuring of their economies and have required a high dose of belt tightening for a large proportion of the population. These programs, representing agreements between debtor and creditor countries, commercial banks, and international organizations such as the IMF and the World Bank have generally been unpopular because of the harsh conditions imposed in order to negotiate new loans.[3] These harsh conditions have encompassed developing the right environment for the expansion of markets, including government budget cuts, privatization programs, deregulation, trade liberalization, easing of controls on foreign investment, and shifts from import substitution to export promotion policies. Such measures have facilitated further integration of these countries into the global economy.

These policies have increased the freedom of many economic actors and brought about a great leap forward in the construction of national and global markets but have done so—à la Polanyi—by deliberate state intervention, imposed from the top down. As O'Grady (1997) put it in the *Wall Street Journal*

---

its early stages, as a way to overcome historic tensions among nations. Nonetheless, trade liberalization and economic integration were largely driven by financial and industrial interests. For specific examples, see Epstein, Graham, and Nembhard 1990.

3. The literature on the social costs of structural adjustment is abundant. See, e.g., Cornia, Jolly, and Stewart 1987; Frieden 1991; Elson 1992; Sahn, Dorosh, and Younger 1994; Sparr 1994; Çağatay, Elson, and Grown 1996; Floro and Schaefer 1998; Azis 2001. The opposition to SAPs, which have been instrumental in introducing market deregulation, has been quite loud in developing countries, led by a variety of social groups and activist organizations representing a large proportion of the population adversely affected. Many international forums have also reflected such opposition (Afshar and Dennis 1992; Aslanbeigui, Pressman, and Summerfield 1994; Friedmann, Abers, and Autler 1996; UNDP 1999; Bello, Bullard, and Malhotra 2001).

for the case of Argentina, "the reforms were largely accomplished by the political will of a presidential strongman who invoked executive decrees over 1,000 times." In fact, in Latin America, the only country that consulted its citizens about privatization was Uruguay, and its vote was negative. In most of the countries of the former Soviet Union, the shock therapy of structural adjustment was imposed with great haste by the newly formed governments. As a result of the transition from centrally planned to market economies, the corresponding policies were implemented simultaneously with drastic economic and institutional restructuring and profound changes in political and social relations.

At the same time, the expansion of markets, associated with the intensification of "modernization" across the globe, has been accompanied by triumphant (re)statements and affirmations of the norms associated with economic rationality. They must be seen as part of the process of constructing market society. We have witnessed this process in multiple forms, ranging from the importance placed on productivity, efficiency, and financial rewards, to shifts in values and attitudes, such as a new emphasis on individualism and competitive behavior, together with ready acceptance of social inequalities and greed.[4]

At the global level, these developments have been symbolized by the spirit of the "Davos Man," whose influence in the global marketplace, according to the neoliberal weekly *The Economist*, has replaced that of the "Chatham House Man."[5] In this view, the Davos Man includes businessmen, bankers, officials, and intellectuals who "hold university degrees, work with words and numbers, speak some English and share beliefs in individualism, market economics and democracy. They control many of the world's governments, and the bulk of its economic and military capabilities." The Davos Man does not "butter up the politicians; it is the other way around." Written as a critique of Samuel Huntington's thesis in *The Clash of Civilizations and the Remaking of the World Order*, the praise of Davos Man by the *Economist* was also an ode to the contemporary global version of economic man: The Davos Man, symbolizing rational economic man gone global, is expected, through the magic powers of the market, to bring people and cultures together.

4. The evidence supporting this shift has been overwhelming. As an article in the *New York Times* put it, "with the growth of free markets generally accepted around the world, debates focus less on whether greed is good or bad than on specific checks on excess: on when or which superpayments may be deserved" (Hacker 1997). For a typical view of the preeminence of productivity, see "The Future of the State" 1997.

5. The reference is to the annual meeting in Davos, Switzerland, of "people who run the world" and to the elegant Chatham House of the Royal Institute of International Affairs in London where "diplomats have mulled the strange ways of abroad" for "nearly 80 years" ("In Praise of the Davos Man" 1997).

The article in the *Economist* further suggests that an integral part of this discourse is the survival of the fittest: hence the view that bankruptcy is a necessary punishment for those who do not perform efficiently and according to the dictates of the market. The hegemonic assumption of orthodox economics that the "feeble" must be eliminated rather than "transformed" or helped to avoid massive layoffs and human suffering is not questioned. It typically reflects the centrality of efficiency over that of people and social goals.

What this view of the world does not recognize is that the commercialization of everyday life and of all sectors of the economy generates dynamics and values that some individuals and members of some cultures are likely to find repulsive and contrary to deeply held values. As Polanyi anticipated, we have witnessed the tendency for society to become "an accessory to the economic system" rather than the other way around. The logic of the market often clashes with the logic of collectivity predominant in traditional societies.

The shift toward the predominance of this orthodox discourse has been particularly dramatic in the countries of the former Soviet Union. The transition to market economies has been carried out with a great deal of state intervention, often guided by outside forces and teams of advisers from the capitalist world (Kotz 1995; Sachs 1991, 1997; Haney 2000). Unlike Polanyi's description of the earlier market formation in Europe, this transition has developed within the context of a globalized neoliberal model and, therefore, in some respects resembles those observed in the Third World. The abuses associated with the search for individual economic gain and rapid accumulation of wealth from the newly created markets in these countries has been criticized even by some who have been involved in the process (Soros 1998).

Gender and the Market

The fact that markets have been socially constructed has important gender-related implications, for links to the market have been historically different for men and women, with consequences for their choices and behavior. A large proportion of the population engages in unpaid production, only indirectly linked to the market. Women are disproportionately concentrated in this type of work, which includes agricultural family labor and working in family businesses, domestic work, and volunteer work. According to the UNDP's "rough estimates," if unpaid activities were valued at prevailing wages, they would amount to $16 trillion or about 70 percent of total world output ($23 trillion). Of this, $11 trillion, or almost 69 percent, represent women's work (UNDP 1995). To be sure, it is difficult to compare paid and unpaid work, because without the competitive pressures of the market, productivity levels might be very different.[6] Nonetheless, these estimates provide a rough indication of the contribution of unremunerated activities to human welfare, and they complement more specific studies illustrating the importance and diversity of women's unpaid work (Barrig 1996; Friedmann, Abers, and Autler 1996).

Thus, to a large extent, men and women have been positioned differently with respect to both market transformations and the linkages between gender and nature. While the market has been associated with public life and "maleness," women have been viewed as closer to nature—often in essentialist ways rather than as a result of historical constructions. This in turn has affected the meaning of gender (Gilligan 1982; Bem 1993; Butler 1993) and our notions of the market (McCloskey 1993; Strassmann 1993). For these reasons, the notion of the social construction of markets needs to be expanded to incorporate gender dimensions.

Given that the sphere of unpaid work is not equally subject to the norms and competitive pressures of the market as is paid work, it can respond to motivations other than gain, such as love and altruism, or to other norms of behavior, such as duty and religious beliefs and practices. Historically, these motivations have affected women and men differently, a subject often discussed in the feminist literature. This literature includes an extensive discussion about women's concentration in caring, nurturing, and service work, whether paid or unpaid. Without falling into essentialist arguments about gender-related motivations and keeping in mind the multiple differences across countries, cultures, and time periods, we can conclude from the literature that there are variations in norms, values, and behavior related to gender (England 1993, chap. 1 in this volume; Seguino, Stevens, and Lutz 1996).

Although data such as those collected by the UNDP clearly show the current predominance of women in unpaid work and of men in paid activities, neither is the exclusive domain of one sex. In earlier societies, the principles of reciprocity and distribution did not necessarily function according to the rules of market rationality. Instead, tradition, religion, kinship, and community played an important role in shaping norms and values. In subsistence economies, production is not geared to the market, and family labor is motivated primarily by needs. Similarly, in market economies, behavior following norms of solidarity and work/leisure choices that do not necessarily pursue gain

---

6. The task is not an impossible one. Folbre (1982) has argued that some comparability exists between domestic and market work because household production is under pressure to achieve at least a survival level of productivity. Beyond this, during the past two decades much progress has been made toward more accurate measurement and greater understanding of unpaid work (Benería 1999; ILO 1998; Daly 2001).

or follow the dictates of efficiency, competition, and productivity associated with economic rationality have by no means disappeared. This is indicated, among other things, by the large numbers of volunteer workers and of those engaged by choice in poorly remunerated work that is inherently rewarding. In the case of volunteer work, commonly carried out at the community level, the motives often are associated with a sense of collective well-being, empathy for others, political commitment, or the pursuit of beauty and creativity, irrespective of its market value.

Feminist economists have written a good deal about the extent to which economic rationality may not be as prevalent as assumed in mainstream economics (e.g., England, chap. 1 in this volume). As a result, they have emphasized the need to develop alternative models based on assumptions of cooperation, empathy, and concern for collective well-being (Strober 1994, chap. 6 in this volume; Folbre 2001). In so doing, they join other scholars who have also questioned neoclassical assumptions predicated upon the Hobbesian view of self-interested individuals. They argue that the numerous exceptions to this rule suggest that behavior responds to a complex set of often contradictory tendencies (Marwell and Ames 1981; Frank, Golovich, and Regan 1993) as well as to different emotional states (Lawler and Thye 1999). Thus, neoclassical assumptions appear to contradict "real-life experiments in which collective action and empathetic, connected economic decision-making are observed" (Seguino, Stevens, and Lutz 1996). Furthermore, a number of authors have pointed out that such behavior is in many circumstances found to be more prevalent among women than men (Guyer 1980; Gilligan 1982; Benería and Roldán 1987).

Likewise, in a study comparing the behavior of economists and noneconomists, Seguino, Stevens, and Lutz suggested that women are "more likely to exhibit constitutive desires and empathetic or connected behavior in contributing to public goods than do males" (1996, 15). Experiments have shown that many alternatives exist to the traditional model that assumes only self-interest motivates individual preferences and ignores altruism, fairness, and reciprocity (Croson 1999). Other authors have emphasized the extent to which social codes and identities are constructed "at the deepest cognitive levels through social interaction"—therefore questioning the validity of static assumptions about tastes and preferences of conventional economic models (Cornwall 1997). As product developers and advertising agencies know, social codes and individual preferences are subject to social constructions and exogenous interference that result in dynamic and continuous change. In the same way, Gagnier (2000) has shown how literary and other cultural critics may contribute to economic knowledge by showing how people come to "choose" what they do and how tastes are developed and constrained. All of this points to the need to construct models of human behavior different from those based on mere economic maximization.

The claim of feminist economists that models of free individual choice are not adequate to analyze issues of dependence/interdependence, tradition, and power is of particular relevance for cultures in which individualistic, market-oriented behavior is more the exception than the norm. Feminists have pointed out that neoclassical analysis is based on a "separative-self model," in which utility is viewed as subjective and unrelated to that of other people. This model is linked to the assumption that individual behavior is selfish since "emotional connection often creates empathy, altruism, and a subjective sense of social solidarity" (England 1993). The model is gender biased because it downplays the traits of interdependence and emotion that are so much a part of being human—yet so often associated with or encouraged only in women. In addition, to the extent that this model typifies Western individualism, it also has a Western bias and is foreign to societies with more collective forms of action and decision making (see also Charusheela and Zein-Elabdin, chap. 8 in this volume). Neoclassical economics has had little to say about these alternative modes of behavior and their significance for social organization.

Gender and Globalization

The extension and deepening of markets across the globe raises many questions about their effects on individual behavior and, more specifically, on the behavior of women. The questions are numerous. Are gender norms changing as women are entering the labor market in increasing numbers as a result of globalization and market expansion? Furthermore, what is the effect on women as the importance of their paid labor increases relative to that of unpaid work? Does this imply that they are increasingly adopting the norms of economic rationality à la "economic man"? Are they becoming more individualistic and selfish and less nurturing? Is market behavior undermining "women's ways of seeing and doing"? Are gender identities being reconstituted?

The answer to these questions is not clear. To begin with, a nonessentialist view of gender differences implies that social change influences gender (re)constructions; as women become continuous participants in the market, it is likely that this will influence their motives and aspirations, so that they will adopt patterns of behavior traditionally observed more frequently among men. Based on casual observation, this may already be happening. However, areas of ambiguity, tensions, and contradictions remain, as discussed below.

Many studies have documented women's role in processes of industrialization and production for global markets in a variety of countries.[7] During the past quarter-century, we have witnessed the rapid formation of a female labor force across the globe, especially in the service sector and in production for export, even in countries where women's participation in paid work was traditionally low and not socially acceptable (Hein 1986; Ong 1987; Pyle 1990; Feldman 1992; Kabeer 2000). The feminist movement has contributed to this trend by emphasizing the need for women to increase their financial autonomy, bargaining power, and control over their lives.

These tendencies are clearly not uniform across the globe. For example, in the countries of the former Soviet Union, the post-1989 period has created contradictory tendencies. Here, women previously had very high labor-force participation rates, but have suffered disproportionately from the social costs of the transition, including unemployment, gender discrimination, and reinforcement of patriarchal norms. The transition has, for the most part, reduced women's employment opportunities and has relegated some of them to temporary and low-pay jobs (Bridger, Kay, and Pinnick 1996; Moghadam 1999; Haney 2000). At the same time, the new market forces have generated demand for women's cheap labor, particularly in labor-intensive production for global markets. A report by the World Bank (1996) concludes that, so far at least, the transition has left women in these economies not freer, but more constrained than before.

Several authors have pointed out that the transition has exacerbated "latent and manifest patriarchal attitudes," increasing women's vulnerability both culturally and economically (Bridger, Kay, and Pinnick 1996; Moghadam 1999). They note that the initial rounds of democratic elections in Russia virtually wiped women off the political map and that their re-emergence is painfully slow. Also, in some of the Central Asian republics, new restrictions on women's lives have been imposed, such as not appearing in public without a male or an older woman, not wearing pants, and not driving cars (Tohidi 1999). It is not yet clear how soon and to what extent the market and "modernization" will break down these patriarchal norms—or to what extent the market and modernization might generate a backlash of conservative reactions affecting women's participation in it.[8]

7. There is an extensive literature on the subject; for a nonexhaustive list, see Anker and Hein 1986; Joekes 1987; Ong 1987; Standing 1999; Çağatay and Berik 1990; Elson 1991; Çağatay and Özler 1995; Blumberg et al. 1995; Anker 1998; Seguino 2000; Fussell 2000; Kabeer 2000.

8. Charusheela and Zein-Elabdin (chap. 8 in this volume) further discuss issues of women and modernization.

In sum, the market can have positive and liberating effects, such as breaking down patriarchal traditions like arranged marriages that limit individual autonomy, but can also encourage sexist practices and have negative consequences for those who suffer from discrimination and market exploitation. The literature on female labor in export industries provides a variety of examples of discriminatory practices against women, even when there has been an increase in women's autonomy and bargaining power as well (Hein 1986; Ong 1987; Pyle 1990; Cravey 1998; Fussell 2000; Seguino 2000; Salazar Parreñas 2001).

Beyond Self-Interest?

I don't need money, I want the river's color back.

The above quote, attributed to Silas Natkime, son of the Waa Valley Chief in Irian Jaya, Indonesia,[9] highlights the value placed on a clean river over that of money and symbolizes one of the dilemmas of development—the choice of whether to give priority to ecological or economic outcomes. It also reflects a reaction against the pollution caused by an uncontrolled market. Thus, we can add environmental degradation to Polanyi's list of criticisms of market society pointing to the need for some forms of planning or market interventions that would counteract not only disruptive strains but also the domination of economic self-interest over all aspects of political and social life. This is not just history. As we observe the unfolding of global markets in the late twentieth and early twenty-first centuries, these strains and criticisms of market society— à la Polanyi and also Marx—have reappeared. To be sure, the global market has displayed a dynamism that resulted in the ability to supply unprecedented amounts of goods and services and to generate new forms of wealth. It has, however, also generated new imbalances leading to economic and social crises, such as those in Africa and Latin America during the 1980s and 1990s and in Eastern Europe and Asia in the 1990s, with continuing serious strains during the 2000s in countries such as Argentina.

Evidence linking globalized markets with increasing inequality and poverty has been growing (ECLAC 1995; Freeman 1996; UNDP 1996, 1998, 1999; World Bank 2000). Similarly, high unemployment and underemployment in many areas, including both high- and low-income countries, disrupt the social fabric of communities. Rodrik (1997) has argued that globalization undermines social cohesiveness, and calls for compensatory policies and social insurance

---

9. "Goldrush in New Guinea" 1995.

systems. Some Latin American authors have referred to "socially unsustainable development" as a result of the tensions generated by neoliberal policies. Fast-track trade liberalization is undermining the capacity of some countries to survive in a global economy, and the tendency for the financial sector to dominate in setting policies has created strains in other sectors. Moreover, the recent economic and financial crises have raised new questions about the instability of financial markets and have intensified the debate about the need for global reforms and national controls over capital flows. Fifty years after Polanyi wrote *The Great Transformation*, his call for subordinating the market to the priorities set by democratic societies resonates as an urgent need, even though reforms would have to accommodate the new realities of the early twenty-first century.

All this poses challenges for feminism. Can feminism contribute to the quest for new directions toward human development? Can the alternative models discussed by feminists be used as guidelines for constructing alternative societies?

Researchers have shown on different occasions that voting patterns of most women—and those of some men—are based on modes of evaluating society's needs, human welfare, and the function of politics that include a sense of solidarity with the weakest members of society.[10] Far from seeing these modes as "backward" or "irrational," they can be perceived as a source of inspiration leading to alternative ways of organizing society, based on nonhegemonic conceptual and theoretical tools and models. Although this means not accepting economic man's objectives as the desired norm, it does not imply rejecting markets. It does, however, call for subordinating markets to the objectives of truly democratic communities. The goal is to place economic activity at the service of people-centered development and not the other way around; or to strive for productivity and efficiency not for their own sake but as a way to increase collective well-being. Hence, just as it is possible to think of Christianity without hell, it is possible to reduce the social costs of bankruptcy.

All of this implies placing issues of distribution, equality, ethics, the environment, the nature of individual happiness, collective well-being, and progressive social change at the center of our agenda. The urgent task for economists and social scientists is to translate these broad objectives into theoretical models and specific policies and actions. In her critique of the World Bank and the IMF, Diane Elson (1994) pointed out that, despite their initial laudable focus on human-friendly goals, they have tended to promote policies "more like business-centered development than people-centered development." The

---

10. See Benería 1999 for an elaboration of gender-related voting patterns.

outcomes of the neoliberal policies that have been predominant during the past two decades have displayed similar characteristics.

People-centered development also calls for transforming knowledge by re-thinking conventional approaches to theory and decision making. As Elizabeth Minnich put it: "Behind any particular body of accepted knowledge are the def-initions, the boundaries, established by those who have held power. To disagree with those boundaries and definitions, it has been necessary to recognize them; to refuse them is to be shut out even from debate; to transgress them is to mark oneself as mad, heretical, dangerous" (1990, 151). Definitions, boundaries, and power all have a historic specificity. For example, in societies of the former So-viet Union, the transition created a fluid situation in which the old "accepted knowledge" has been replaced by the new hegemonic thinking linked to the market. The negative effects of the transition on women raise many questions regarding the market's inability to generate gender equality. Will this lead to a new search for alternatives? Will women play an important role in this pro-cess? Would women's agency prevail within truly democratic processes? These questions are, to a greater or lesser extent, relevant for all market economies.

The current crises in global capitalism appear to have brought a turning point in the triumphant progress of Davos Man during the past two decades, and an increasing number of people are decrying his excesses. Economic in-security and labor market "informalization" are on the increase across many countries (Standing 1999; Benería 2001). The Asian crisis generated a break in the Washington Consensus and the notion that "there is no alternative" to the neoliberal model seems increasingly less acceptable. The post-Seattle and post-Genoa mood and the growing uneasiness regarding the uneven results of globalization are indications that, as Polanyi pointed out for the 1920s, unreg-ulated markets are likely to lead to continuing economic crises and perhaps to more "great transformations" on the left. The present danger is that new pro-posals for global governance might be introduced in a top-down fashion and without a real worldwide democratic debate. Feminism has been important in the struggle for solutions at the decentralized, local, and institutional levels, always fighting discrimination and inequalities. It has changed institutions and decision-making processes, incorporated new agendas in the politics of daily life, affected national policies, made an impact on international agendas, and been influential in bringing "human welfare first" to the center of debates on economic and social policy. While continuing these efforts, feminism now also has to meet the challenges posed by globalization and its impact at different levels.

Almost fifty years ago, Polanyi wrote that thinking of people first cannot be successful unless it is disciplined by a total view of man and society very different from that which we inherited from market economy. The main message of this chapter is that this effort must be transformative and based on a "total view of wo/man and society." Rather than dismissing this view as "soft," "idealistic," and "female," we must continue to take up the challenge, linking this effort with the many manifestations of uneasiness about the results of uncontrolled global markets.

References

Afshar, Haleh, and C. Dennis, eds. 1992. *Woman and adjustment policies in the Third World*. London: Macmillan.

Anker, Richard. 1998. *Gender and jobs: Sex segregation of occupations in the world*. Geneva: International Labor Office.

Anker, Richard, and Catherine Hein, eds. 1986. *Sex inequalities in urban employment in the Third World*. New York: St. Martin's Press.

Arrighi, Giovanni. 1994. *The long twentieth century*. London: Verso.

Aslanbeigui, Nahid, Steve Pressman, and Gale Summerfield, eds. 1994. *Women in the age of economic transformation*. London: Routledge.

Azis, Iwan. 2001. Contrasting perspectives of the IMF and alternative views on the Asian crisis: Analytic hierarchy process and game theoretic approach. Paper presented at the Global Tensions conference, Cornell University, March 9–10.

Barrig, Maruja. 1996. Women: Collective kitchens and the crisis of the state in Peru. In *Emergences: Women's struggles for livelihood in Latin America*, edited by John Friedmann, Rebecca Abers, and Lilian Autler, 59–78. Los Angeles: UCLA Latin American Center.

Bello, Walden, Nicola Bullard, and Kamal Malhotra, eds. 2001. *Global finance: New thinking on regulating speculative capital markets*. Bangkok: Focus on the Global South.

Bem, Sandra Lipsitz. 1993. *The lenses of gender: Transforming the debate on sexual inequality*. New Haven, Conn.: Yale University Press.

Benería, Lourdes. 1999. The enduring debate over unpaid labor. *International Labor Review* 138 (3): 287–310.

———. 2001. Shifting the risk: New employment patterns, informalization, and women's work. *International Journal of Politics, Culture, and Society* 15 (1): 27–51.

Benería, Lourdes, and Martha Roldán. 1987. *The crossroads of class and gender: Industrial homework, subcontracting, and household dynamics in Mexico City*. Chicago: University of Chicago Press.

Bergmann, Barbara. 1995. Becker's theory of the family: Preposterous conclusions. *Feminist Economics* 1 (1): 141–50.

Blumberg, Rae Lesser, Cathy Rakowski, Irene Tinker, and Michael Monteón, eds. 1995. *EnGendering wealth and well-being: Empowerment for global change*. Boulder, Colo.: Westview Press.

Bridger, Sue, Rebecca Kay, and Kathryn Pinnick. 1996. *No more heroines? Russia, women, and the market*. New York: Routledge.

Butler, Judith. 1993. *Bodies that matter: On the discursive limits of "sex."* New York: Routledge.

Çağatay, Nilüfer, and Gunseli Berik. 1990. Transition to export-led growth in Turkey: Is there a feminization of employment? *Review of Radical Political Economics* 22 (1): 115–34.

Çağatay, Nilüfer, Diane Elson, and Caren Grown. 1996. Introduction to *Gender, adjustment, and macroeconomics*, special issue of *World Development* 23 (11): 1827–36.

Çağatay, Nilüfer, and Şule Özler. 1995. Feminization of the labor force: The effects of long-term development and structural adjustment. *World Development* 23 (11): 1883–94.

Cornia, Giovanni, Ricard Jolly, and Frances Stewart, eds. 1987. *Adjustment with a human face*. Vol. 1. Oxford: Clarendon Press.

Cornwall, Richard. 1997. Deconstructing silence: The queer political economy of the social articulation of desire. *Review of Radical Political Economics* 29 (1): 1–130.

Cravey, Altha J. 1998. *Women and work in Mexico's maquiladoras*. Lanham, Md.: Rowman & Littlefield.

Croson, Susan. 1999. Using experiments in the classroom. *CSWEP Newsletter,* winter.

Daly, Mary, ed. 2001. *Care work: The quest for security*. Geneva: International Labor Office.

ECLAC (Economic Commission for Latin America and the Caribbean). 1995. *Social panorama of Latin America*. Santiago de Chile: ECLAC.

Elson, Diane, ed. 1991. *Male bias in the development process*. Manchester: Manchester University Press.

————. 1992. From survival strategies to transformation strategies: Women's needs and structural adjustment. In *Unequal burden: Economic crises, persistent poverty, and women's work*, edited by L. Benería and S. Feldman, 26–48. Boulder, Colo.: Westview Press.

————. 1994. People, development, and international financial institutions: An interpretation of the Bretton Woods system. *Review of African Political Economy,* no. 62: 511–24.

England, Paula. 1993. The separative self: Androcentric bias in neoclassical assumptions. In *Beyond economic man,* edited by Marianne Ferber and Julie Nelson, 37–53. Chicago: University of Chicago Press.

Epstein, Gerald, Julie Graham, and Jessica Nembhard, eds. 1990. *Creating a new world economy*. Philadelphia: Temple University Press.

Feldman, Shelley. 1992. Crisis, Islam, and gender in Bangladesh: The social construction of a female labor force. In *Unequal burden: Economic crises, persistent poverty, and women's work*, edited by L. Benería and S. Feldman, 105–30. Boulder, Colo.: Westview Press.

Ferber, Marianne A., and Julie A. Nelson, eds. 1993. *Beyond economic man: Feminist theory and economics*. Chicago: University of Chicago Press.

Floro, Maria, and Kendall Schaefer. 1998. Restructuring of labor markets in the Philippines and Zambia: The gender dimension. *Journal of Developing Areas* 33 (1): 73–98.

Folbre, Nancy. 1982. Exploitation comes home: A critique of the Marxian theory of family labor. *Cambridge Journal of Economics* 6 (4): 317–29.

————. 1994. *Who pays for the kids? Gender and the structures of constraint*. New York: Routledge.

————. 2001. *The invisible heart: Economics and family values*. New York: New Press.

Frank, Robert, Thomas Golovich, and Dennis Regan. 1993. Does studying economics inhibit cooperation? *Journal of Economic Perspectives* 7 (2): 159–71.

Freeman, Richard. 1996. The new inequality. *Boston Review*. December-January.

Frieden, Jeffry. 1991. *Debt, development, and democracy*. Princeton, N.J.: Princeton University Press.

Friedmann, John, Rebecca Abers, and Lilian Autler, eds. 1996. *Emergences: Women's struggles for livelihood in Latin America*. Los Angeles: UCLA Latin American Center.

Fussell, Elizabeth. 2000. Making labor flexible: The recomposition of Tijuana's maquiladora female labor force. *Feminist Economics* 6 (3): 59–80.

The future of the state: A survey of the world economy. 1997. *Economist*, September 20.

Gagnier, Regenia. 2000. *The insatiability of human wants*. Chicago: University of Chicago Press.

Gilligan, Carol. 1982. *In a different voice*. Cambridge, Mass.: Harvard University Press.

Goldrush in New Guinea. 1995. *Business Week*, November 20.

Guyer, Jane. 1980. Households, budgets, and women's incomes. Boston University, Africana Studies Center Working Paper no. 28.

Hacker, Andrew. 1997. Good or bad, greed is often beside the point. *New York Times*, June 8.

Haney, Lynne. 2000. Global discourse of need: Mythologizing and pathologizing welfare in Hungary. In *Global ethnography: Forces, connections, and imaginations in a post-modern world,* edited by M. Burawoy et al. Berkeley: University of California Press.

Harris, Rachel. 1997. Where have all the majors gone? *Athena* (spring): 18–19.

Hein, Catherine. 1986. The feminization of industrial employment in Mauritius: A case of sex segregation. In *Sex inequalities in urban employment in the Third World,* edited by Richard Anker and Catherine Hein, 277–312. New York: St. Martin's Press.

ILO (International Labor Office). 1998. Women in the world of work. Paper prepared for *1999 world survey on the role of women and development,* Geneva, Switzerland, June 1–3.

In praise of the Davos Man. 1997. *Economist,* February 1.

Joekes, Susan. 1987. *Women in the world economy.* New York: Oxford University Press.

Kabeer, Naila. 2000. *The power to choose: Bangladesh women and labour market decisions in London and Dhaka.* London: Verso.

Kotz, David. 1995. Lessons for a future socialism from the Soviet collapse. *Review of Radical Political Economics* 27 (3): 1–11.

Lawler, Edward, and Shane Thye. 1999. Bringing emotions into social exchange theory. *Annual Review of Sociology* 25:217–44.

Marwell, Gerald, and Ruth Ames. 1981. Economists free ride; does anyone else? (Experiments in the provision of public goods). *Journal of Public Economics* 15 (3): 295–310.

McCloskey, D. 1993. Some consequences of conjective economics. In *Beyond economic man,* edited by M. Ferber and J. Nelson, 69–93. Chicago: University of Chicago Press.

Minnich, Elizabeth Kamarck. 1990. *Transforming knowledge.* Philadelphia: Temple University Press.

Moghadam, Valentine. 1999. Gender and democratic reforms: A framework for analysis and evidence for Central Asia, the Caucasus, and Turkey. In *Gender and identity construction: Women of Central Asia, the Caucasus, and Turkey,* edited by Feride Acar and Ayse Giimes Agata, 23–42. Boston: Brill.

Nelson, Julie. 1993. The study of choice or the study of provisioning? Gender and the definition of economics. In *Beyond economic man,* edited by M. Ferber and J. Nelson, 23–36. Chicago: University of Chicago Press.

O'Grady, Mary Anastasia. 1997. Don't blame the market for Argentina's woes. *Wall Street Journal,* May 30.

Ong, Aiwa. 1987. *Spirits of resistance and capitalist discipline: Women factory workers in Malaysia.* Albany: SUNY Press.

Polanyi, Karl. 1957. *The great transformation.* Boston: Beacon Press.

Pyle, Jean. 1990. Export-led development and the underemployment of women: The impact of discriminatory employment policy in the Republic of Ireland. In *Women workers and global restructuring,* edited by Kathryn Ward, 85–112. Ithaca, N.Y.: Cornell University Press.

Rodrik, Dani. 1997. *Has globalization gone too far?* Washington, D.C.: Institute for International Economics.

Sachs, Jeffrey. 1991. *The economic transformation of Eastern Europe: The case of Poland.* Memphis, Tenn.: P. K. Seidman Foundation.

————. 1997. *Economies in transition: Comparing Asia and Eastern Europe.* Cambridge, Mass.: MIT Press.

Sahn, David, Paul Dorosh, and Stephen Younger. 1994. Economic reform in Africa: A foundation for poverty alleviation. Cornell University, Cornell Food and Nutrition Policy Program, Working Paper 72, September.

Salazar Parreñas, Rhacel. 2001. Transgressing the nation-state: The partial citizenship and "imagined global community" of migrant Filipina workers. *Signs* 26 (4): 1129–53.

Seguino, Stephanie. 2000. Accounting for gender and Asian economic growth. *Feminist Economics* 6 (3): 27–58.

Seguino, Stephanie, Thomas Stevens, and Mark Lutz. 1996. Gender and cooperative behavior: Economic man rides alone. *Feminist Economics* 2 (1): 195–223.

Soros, George. 1998. *The crisis of global capitalism*. New York: Public Affairs Press.

Sparr, Pamela, ed. 1994. *Mortgaging women's lives: Feminist critiques of structural adjustment*. London: Zed Press.

Standing, Guy. 1999. Globalization through flexible labor: A theme revisited. *World Development* 27 (3): 583–602.

Strassmann, Diana. 1993. Not a free market: The rhetoric of disciplinary authority in economics. In *Beyond economic man*, edited by M. Ferber and J. Nelson, 54–68. Chicago: University of Chicago Press.

Strober, Myra. 1994. Rethinking economics through a feminist lens. *American Economic Review* 84 (2): 143–47.

Tohidi, Nayereh. 1999. Guardians of the nation: Women, Islam, and Soviet modernization in Azerbaijan. In *Gender and identity construction: Women of Central Asia, the Caucasus, and Turkey*, edited by Feride Acar and Ayse Giimes Agata, 249–92. Boston: Brill.

UNDP (United Nations Development Program). 1995, 1996, 1998, and 1999. *Human development report*. New York: Oxford University Press.

Vernon, Raymond, ed. 1988. *The promise of privatization*. New York: Council on Foreign Relations.

World Bank. 1996. *From plan to market*. World Development Report. New York: Oxford University Press.

————. 2000. *Attacking poverty*. World Development Report. New York: Oxford University Press.

WuDunn, Sheryl. 1998. Bankruptcy the Asian way. *New York Times*, September 8.

6

The Application of Mainstream Economics Constructs to Education: A Feminist Analysis

. . . Myra H. Strober

In recent years, neoclassical economics has been highly imperialistic, extending its philosophy and methodology into matters as diverse as law, politics, marriage, and fertility (Lazear 2000). Education has not escaped its colonizing influence. This has been a mixed blessing. While neoclassical economic analysis at times provides useful insights for educators, it is often incomplete. Sometimes it is simply wrong (Winston 1997). This is not surprising, for the neoclassical economic model's narrow framing of human character, human purpose, and means to achieve well-being are ill-suited to convey the complex and transformational goals of the education sector.

In several fundamental respects, education and mainstream economic models are at odds. The key neoclassical economic constructs—scarcity, self-interest, competition, value, efficiency, and choice—originally developed to understand market transactions, are often inappropriate when applied in an educational context. And while mainstream economics equates well-being with the accumulation of goods and services, educators actively

For helpful conversations and e-mail discussions, I thank Cecile Andrews, Eamonn Callan, Jay Jackman, Biddy Martin, Julie Nelson, Elizabeth Strober, David Tyack, and Rick Wilk. For comments on an earlier version, I thank Judith Brandenburg, Elizabeth Cohen, Anne Colby, Larry Cuban, Deb Figart, Edie Gelles, Cassie Guarino, John Krumboltz, Lisa Petrides, Marilyn Power, and members of the Feminist Studies Seminar at Stanford (particularly, Carol Delaney, Estelle Freedman, Barbara Gelpi, Patricia Karlin-Newman, Paula Lee, Joanne Martin, and Cecilia Ridgeway). For a more complete discussion, see Strober (forthcoming).

disagree with the view that the person who dies with the most toys "wins" (Noddings 1984).

Leaders in the field of education who have thought seriously about educational goals are concerned not only with teaching students skills that will aid them in the workplace, but also, more broadly, skills that will help them to achieve their human potential, initiate an examination of the meaning of their lives, and fulfill their sense of duty and responsibility. These educators want to initiate students into a lifelong quest for knowledge and appreciation of the life of the mind and see educational institutions as places to seek wisdom and self-understanding as well as knowledge. Further, they wish to develop students' emotional intelligence, helping them to understand that a rich life includes experiencing not only the "good" emotions of happiness and love, but also learning to deal with the more difficult feelings of anger, sadness, fear, envy, and apathy (Goleman 1995). They wish to teach students to develop deep relationships that include mutual caring and becoming integral members of their community and polity (Bellah 2000).

These ideas are reflected in the preamble to the National Education Association (NEA) Code of Ethics of the Education Profession: "The educator strives to help each student realize his or her potential as a worthy and effective member of society. The educator therefore works to stimulate the spirit of inquiry, the acquisition of knowledge and understanding, and the thoughtful formulation of worthy goals" (NEA 2002). In several of its resolutions, the NEA indicates its interest in and support of education to achieve aesthetic and emotional intelligence, particularly "learning and practicing positive interpersonal communication skills and conflict resolution" (NEA 2001–2, 18).

Although both economics and education seek to increase well-being, in practice, neoclassical economics defines well-being much more narrowly than does education, and the neoclassical economic definition often crowds out the more expansive and more difficult to measure definitions of educators. Similarly, while economic theory treats altruism as anomalous (except insofar as the altruist egotistically benefits from the altruistic act), educators find that some individuals, including young children, behave altruistically because they have a genuine concern for other people's welfare (Sobel and Wilson 1998; Colby and Damon 1992).[1] In higher education, in particular, numerous institutions are

---

1. For an interesting selection of economists' (and others') writing on altruism, see Zamagni 1995, and particularly the introduction, by Zamagni, which discusses the extent to which economists' conceptions of *Homo economicus* will need to be changed in order to accommodate the existence of altruism. For a discussion of the role of normative and social motivations in economic actors' decisions, see Winter and May 2001.

seeking to educate students for civic responsibility and help them to develop strong ethical values (Colby 2000). These educators wish to enhance altruism in their students, not treat it as anomalous.

Thus, when applied to education, mainstream economics needs considerable leavening. This chapter argues that feminist economics, which has emerged over the last fifteen years, provides a useful tempering of the neoclassical model. Taking issue with some of neoclassical economics' basic constructs and developing a feminist pedagogy for the teaching of economics, feminist economists provide a worldview, theoretical constructs, and teaching practices that are more consonant with the goals of educators.

The Feminist Critique

Feminist economics' critique of neoclassical economics began for the purpose of improving women's economic condition (Strober 1994), but the rethinking that has resulted has led to a questioning of many of the discipline's core concepts, central assumptions, methods of analysis, policy recommendations (Ferber and Nelson 1993), and pedagogy (Aerni and McGoldrick 1999). The feminist reconceptualization is meant to benefit not only women, but also men, children, and indeed our society as a whole.

This critique of mainstream economics is extremely varied and wide-ranging and its practitioners come from multiple countries and numerous "schools" within economics: mainstream, institutional, and Marxist, to name a few. They also come from various "schools" of feminism: liberal, radical, Marxist, and separatist. Moreover, many feminist economists are as interested in the relationships among race, gender, and class as they are in gender alone, and there are multiple cultural and ethnic visions of what feminist economics means (see Saunders and Darity, chap. 4 in this volume; Charusheela and Zein-Elabdin, chap. 8 in this volume). The feminist analyses brought to bear in this chapter should not, therefore, be taken to represent all of feminist economists' thinking about these matters.

To avoid misunderstanding, it is important to know what feminist economics is not. It is *not* essentialist; it does not hold that there are fundamental (essential) differences between women and men and does not therefore suggest that women need a different economics than men. Feminist economics is also *not* about fundamental differences between female and male economists and therefore does not hold the view that female economists do economics in a way that is different from what male economists do, or even that female economists have a special pipeline to understanding women's economic oppression. Some of the insights that female economists have, however, may come from experiences that most male economists do not have.

Feminist Economics and Pedagogy

Feminist economists' pedagogical concerns have been about both the content of economics courses and about classroom practices (Aerni and McGoldrick 1999). With respect to content, the emphasis has been on including material on race and gender (Bartlett 1997; Feiner 1993; Feiner and Morgan 1987; Feiner and Roberts 1990; Ferber 1984, 1989, 1997) and on teaching beyond the neoclassical perspective (Aerni et al. 1999; Ferber 1999; Schneider and Shackelford 2001; Strober 1987).

With respect to both content and classroom practices, feminist economists have been interested especially in inclusiveness, calling for increased attention on the part of faculty to student diversity, particularly regarding learning styles, backgrounds, and interests (Aerni et al. 1999; Ferber 1999; Schneider and Shackelford 2001); and for a more interdisciplinary approach to economic analysis (Strober 1987; Aerni et al. 1999; Schneider and Shackelford 2001). They have also urged faculty to make explicit the value system underlying economic analysis (Schneider and Shackelford 2001).

Feminist pedagogy in economics has stressed the importance of cooperation in learning (Aerni et al. 1999). It has also noted the value of allowing emotion back into the classroom and the impossibility of separating affective and cognitive learning (Strober 1987). Finally, it has demonstrated how to incorporate service learning into economics classes (McGoldrick 1998, 1999) and has emphasized that, in promoting learning, the *process* of education is as important as its content (Aerni et al. 1999).

Mainstream Constructs and the Feminist Critique
Applied to Education

The next several sections summarize a feminist critique of four constructs of the mainstream economic model, the application of this critique to the field of education, and a brief review of the major ways in which feminist pedagogy illustrates the points being made. Understanding the ways in which the underpinnings of the neoclassical economic model clash with the underlying purposes of educational leaders should lead to a reassessment of the wisdom of uncritically importing economic thinking into education. Understanding feminist economic analysis and its applications to feminist pedagogy should lead to recognition of the ways in which feminist economics can be useful in education.

Scarcity, Self-Interest, and Competition

At the heart of the neoclassical economic model is economic man, *Homo economicus*. Portrayed as a wholly self-interested person with unlimited wants, living in a world where resources and therefore the goods and services these resources produce are limited, *Homo economicus* faces ever-present scarcity and must compete with others to fulfill his wants. Feminist economics questions the centrality of scarcity and self-interest in mainstream theory and the assumption that only through competition do people achieve well-being (England 1993, chap. 1 in this volume; Strober 1994).

Scarcity results from an imbalance between what one has and what one wants. Since neoclassical economic theory postulates that all human beings have unlimited material wants but finite resources, each must, by definition, face scarcity. In the mainstream view, affluence cannot end scarcity, for even affluent people want ever more material goods and services. In the more imperialistic versions of neoclassical economic theory, which deal not only with the material realm, but with all human wants, the assumption is that even if material needs were met, human beings would have other unlimited wants, for example, for more time. No matter whether scarcity is applied only to the material world or to all of life, in neoclassical economic analysis, it can never be eliminated.

In fact, however, a feminist analysis suggests that when we look at the nonmaterial world, we find many aspects of life that are not subject to the "laws" of scarcity. Love may be a scarce resource in the sense that some people may always crave more of it, but it is not scarce in the sense that once you give it to others you have less of it for yourself. Indeed, as the song goes, "Love is something, if you give it away, you end up having more." Empathy is another example of a resource that multiplies itself as it is practiced.[2]

Mainstream economics has little to say about empathy. Indeed, it portrays a far more self-interested *Homo economicus* than did Adam Smith, who wrote: "However selfish soever man may be supposed, there are evidently some principles in his nature, which interest him in the fortune of others, and render

---

2. For a discussion of the extent to which love and empathy are renewable, see Hirschmann 1992.

their happiness necessary to him, though he derives nothing from it, except the pleasure of seeing it" (Smith 1969, 47).

Interest in the fortunes of others is absent from mainstream analyses, which instead emphasize envy, the so-called Jones effect, where the increased well-being of others results in people seeking additional goods and services for themselves in order to keep up with "the Joneses." Mainstream analyses do not consider the possibility that if my neighbor buys a new car, I might simply take pleasure in her pleasure, without necessarily wishing I could have a new car too.

The failure of textbooks and faculty to consider possible empathic responses to economic situations and the exposure of economics students to repeated emphasis on self-interested behaviors appear to have powerful negative effects. In experimental research using games, economists have shown that the more neoclassical economics courses students take, the less likely they are to be public-spirited, as measured by the proportion of the tokens they contribute to support a particular public good (e.g., Frank, Gilovich, and Regan 1993). Analysis suggests that this relationship is not simply correlative, but rather causal. Interestingly, among both economics majors and noneconomics majors, women are more likely to be public-spirited than men (Seguino, Stevens, and Lutz 1996).

If resources are scarce, and each person looks out only for him or herself, then, the neoclassical story goes, to achieve well-being one must compete to get one's due. Mainstream economics rarely considers cooperation as a mode of motivating and organizing economic activity, in part because of a fear that cooperation can so easily become collusion, to the detriment of the consumer. Yet, as experiments using games have shown, there is a great deal of cooperative behavior in economic situations. Moreover, markets cannot flourish without some degree of trust and cooperation among buyers and sellers (see Fisher and Brown 1988).

By creating a scarcity of good grades and other rewards, educators have grafted the notions of scarcity and competition onto the educational system. There is no inherent scarcity of good grades or other rewards, such as prizes. The norm that not everyone can have an A, that some students must get lower grades, has been socially constructed. By creating a scarcity of good grades and therefore competition for those grades, consciously or unconsciously educators emulated the reward system of the competitive model. Thus, school teaches students to march to the beat of extrinsic motivation, where the reward is not simply learning the material, but rather competing with others to get a good grade.

Does all of this competition promote excellence? Would students work less hard if they were not competing with one another? Does competition promote better learning? An extensive review of the literature leads Alfie Kohn to the following clear conclusion: "Superior performance not only does not *require* competition; it usually seems to require its absence" (1986, 46–47).

Educational psychologists John Krumboltz and Christine Yeh (1996) argue that the competitive grading system has ill effects for teachers as well as for students. Instead of permitting a learning process where students and teachers form a partnership, which the authors contend would enhance teachers' job satisfaction, the competitive grading system forces teachers into the far less satisfying role of critics, who must seek and find fault with students' work. Moreover, Krumboltz and Yeh think the current system places too little onus on teachers when students do not learn. As they put it: "If every student achieved all the objectives of a given course, every student would earn an A—an unacceptable state of affairs in the current view. Thus teachers are reinforced for using methods that ensure that some students will not succeed" (325).

An alternative to classroom competition is cooperative learning. Instead of pitting students against one another to provide the correct answer for the class, the instructor puts students into teams that work cooperatively. In that setting, students succeed when both they and their teammates can demonstrate that they understand the material. Sometimes, in the so-called jigsaw exercise, the instructor shapes the learning by providing each student with a crucial piece required to solve a group puzzle, so that only those groups that cooperate can complete the task.

Research on the effects of cooperative learning finds that it has positive results. Robert Slavin (1990, 32) reports that as long as cooperative learning incorporates individual accountability as well as group goals, most studies find "moderate, but important" positive effects of cooperative learning methods on student achievement as compared to the achievement for students in control groups. He also finds that there are "impressive" positive effects on noncognitive outcomes such as self-esteem, pro-academic peer norms, cooperation, altruism, the ability to take another's perspective, and race relations (53).

Feminist economists consider cooperative learning to be an important component of feminist pedagogy. They advocate moving from "the sage on the stage" model where the classroom is organized hierarchically and power resides exclusively with the instructor to an environment where there is a learning community, where students learn from one another as well as from the instructor and where "students are actively engaged in the production of knowledge as opposed to being the passive recipients of teacher-imparted 'truth'" (Shackelford 1992, 571). When classrooms are organized to create learning communities through cooperative learning, the structure of the class itself challenges the notions that good grades are scarce, that people care only about their own well-being, and that only competition can promote well-being.

Well-Being and Value

Adam Smith recognized two types of value, use value and exchange value. Exchange value is the price that a good or service commands in the marketplace. Use value, on the other hand, is the value of a good or service to an individual, regardless of its exchange value. For example, a particular photo may have high use value to an individual even though its price in the market might be zero.

Mainstream economists today justify ignoring use value and concentrating solely on exchange value on the grounds that economics is interested only in *economic* value and *economic* well-being and that exchange value comes closest to measuring these economic concepts. They then go on to use an individual's (or family's) income as a measure of individual (or family) well-being. In the aggregate, well-being, the so-called standard of living, is measured by per capita income, which is gross domestic product (GDP) or national income (NI) divided by population. Of course, even mainstream economists recognize that there is economic value in nonmarket goods and services, household production and volunteer work being the most obvious examples. Still, despite this recognition, they equate value with exchange value.

Over time, by repeatedly equating value with exchange value, mainstream economists have given markets the power to become the arbiters of economic value. If one item commands a price in the market that is twice as high as another, the first item is said to have an economic value that is two times greater than the second. Eventually, the qualifier "economic" is omitted when speaking of value, and if a price of one item is twice the price of a second, the first is simply said to have twice the value of the second.

Feminist economists have challenged this concept of value and the notion that only exchange value promotes well-being. In particular, feminist economists have argued that nonmarket work and caring labor outside of the market are essential to well-being (Folbre 1995; Himmelweit 1999).

This challenge by feminist economists to the notion that only market transactions produce value is critical for the education sector, because increasingly the idea has gained currency that only those benefits of education that increase a student's contribution in the market have value and that the primary purpose of education is to produce more productive workers with higher earnings. Of course, the rationale for public primary and secondary schooling in the United States has always included a vocational mission, and it was always assumed that education would promote individual success. But these were never viewed as the sole purpose of education, or even its primary purpose. Building a better society and furthering democracy were always the major arguments for public education (Reese 2000). The missions of higher educational institutions in the United States are more difficult to summarize since they vary so widely. Still, it would be close to the mark to say that preservation, dissemination, and furtherance of knowledge have been their collective aim. In addition, there has been wide agreement that not only students themselves but also society as a whole would benefit from fuller utilization of knowledge and more educated leaders (Hofstadter and Smith 1961).

Mainstream economists divide the value derived from education into three categories: investment benefits to the individual, consumption benefits to the individual, and benefits to society above and beyond those to the individual. These last are the so-called external benefits, such as having an educated public that is able to evaluate candidates' positions, render competent verdicts on juries, and in general appreciate democracy. Investment benefits have exchange value; consumption benefits have only use value. Only investment benefits and, to an extent, external benefits are of interest to human capital theorists, the neoclassical economists who study education as an economic investment. They ignore consumption benefits—such as the pleasures of education at the time it is undertaken and future pleasures that result from being well educated. As neoclassical analysis permeates the public's thinking, the benefits of education are increasingly viewed as merely preparation for work.

The hegemony of human capital theory may be seen in the budget allocations of the education sector. The subject areas that receive the greatest resources are those associated with earning a living. Conversely, those subjects that are not associated with vocational development are often starved for resources, particularly when it is necessary for educational institutions to tighten their belts. For example, since few people earn an income by pursuing music and art, these subjects are thought to yield merely consumption benefits and are far more likely to be targeted for budget cuts in K–12 education than math or science, which are viewed as central to preparation for work. In higher education, the humanities suffer at the expense of the sciences and the professions. In the same vein, human capital theory helps shape such decisions as who is admitted to graduate programs; people who are "too old" to get a substantial return on their investment are not admitted.

There is little in the curriculum that teaches students the skills they need to be good friends, mates, or parents. Young children may get report cards that grade their ability to "work and play well with others," but for older children, adolescents, and young adults, the development of such abilities is viewed as outside the central mission of the education system. Few and far between are courses that help students draw lessons from great literature about unraveling moral dilemmas or finding meaning in life (Simon 1997). Art and music are marginalized and seen as quite expendable. Programs that teach emotional intelligence are truly rare (Goleman 1995).

Once again, we find that feminist pedagogy is at variance with the neoclassical view and more consonant with the goals of educational leaders. Feminist pedagogy sees the *process* of education as vital to what students learn. Economics itself may help students to earn higher salaries in the labor market, but the lessons they learn in a feminist economics classroom about the importance of inclusiveness and cooperation are, arguably, equally important to the education process. Similarly, the lessons service learning teaches students about the emotional and cognitive rewards of community service and the understanding students develop about the noneconomic assets of members of the community who are not financially well off are viewed by feminist economics as critical benefits of feminist pedagogy, despite the fact that they may never be used to create exchange value in the labor market.

Efficiency

According to neoclassical economic theory, the more efficient are production and distribution, the greater the output of goods and services, and since producing more goods and services is equated with greater welfare, efficiency is seen as leading to an increase in people's well-being. However, this may not be the case.

When surveyed, people in industrial societies often say that they believe that an increase of 10 to 20 percent in their income would make them happier. But when social scientists look at the relationship between income and happiness, they find little evidence to support such a belief. In economically advanced societies, those in poverty are less happy than are others; but for those in the top four quintiles of the income distribution, there is little correlation between income and happiness. For them, happiness is more strongly related to such factors as good health, self-esteem, a loving relationship, friendships, and challenging work with adequate leisure than it is to level of income (Myers 1992).

Although neoclassical economists see efficiency as simply a means to increase output, in fact efficiency represents a particular style of operation and way of being. In order to decide whether it is worth being maximally efficient, so that maximum output (or income) can be attained, it is necessary to look at the trade-off between the benefits and costs of efficiency.

What are some of the costs of efficiency? One of them is enjoyment. It is ironic that neoclassical economics, which is so strongly rooted in utilitarianism, has moved so far from a concern with matters of pleasure and fun. Rather, the emphasis is merely on obtaining well-being from goods and services. The fact that producing in the most efficient way may lead to a boring and alienating production process is disregarded, as is the possibility that many people might be quite willing to sacrifice some "product" (goods and services) in order to be able to enjoy their work more.

Because school is seen mainly as preparation for the workplace, notions of efficiency that dominate in work organizations have come to dominate in schools as well. Education is viewed in terms of a production function where the "output" is produced by a series of "inputs"—teachers, educational materials, buildings, administrators, and students themselves. Emphasis is placed on efficiently using inputs to maximize output. Few seem to pay attention to whether school is enjoyable, or whether students are learning to love learning.

Another problem is that "output" is such a fuzzy concept in education. Presumably, the output of the education system is knowledge (just as, presumably, the output of the medical system is good health). However, it is exceedingly difficult to measure "knowledge." For what we really want to measure is not just cognitive knowledge that is learned and retained for a test, but the extent to which cognitive and affective knowledge are retained over a period of time and the ways they are put to use.

Focusing on efficiency causes us to lose sight of these complexities. Ensuring efficiency requires that we measure output. But since that is too difficult, we settle all too quickly for those proxies for knowledge attainment that are relatively easy to measure. Thus, the output of the education system we focus on comes to be short-term cognitive recall that can be measured by performance on standardized multiple-choice tests.

In recent years, in both K–12 and higher education, the "accountability" movement's interest in efficiency has taken the form of pushing for more and more standardized testing. Affective knowledge (including self-esteem and caring about others), emotional intelligence (including anger management), love of learning, ability to express oneself in front of a group, and ability to work cooperatively have all been sacrificed as outcome variables because they are too difficult to measure. Similarly, there is little or no evidence of concern regarding the negative effects of frequent testing on curriculum when teachers teach "to the test," putting nothing into lesson plans except what will later require recall for standardized tests. There is even less concern about discouragement for those children who experience repeated failure when, for one reason or another, they are not ready or able to learn the material on the test.

In the 2000 presidential candidate debates, Gore and Bush sought to outdo each other in calling for more testing as the way to improve the efficiency of the K–12 education system. The focus was not on improving the system, for example by putting more resources into education, but on more testing. The assumption seemed to be that if students had more tests to take, and teachers as well as administrators were rewarded if their students did well on the tests, they would have the right incentives to improve the efficiency of the system. The No Child Left Behind Act proposed by President Bush in 2001 and enacted into law in 2002, which mandates annual testing for all students in grades 3–8, is based on this assumption.

As a result of this emphasis on efficiency and learning what can be easily measured, there is, for example, very little in the secondary school curriculum that is geared toward simply having fun with learning or toward appreciating learning for its own sake. It is not surprising then, that, except for the hidden curriculum (playground activities, the formation of friendships, etc.), many young people find school a boring and dour place.

In a world where output is measured by performance on standardized tests, learning is seen as most efficient when teachers concentrate on cognitive learning and disregard other learning outcomes. The message of standardized testing is that it doesn't matter how students *feel* about what they learn, or indeed how they feel about learning in general. What is important is that they be able to answer cognitive questions correctly on tests. But the separation of cognition and emotion in the quest for efficiency in learning contributes to diminished excitement in the classroom and to students' alienation from learning. Hence one of the major purposes of education, the creation of a lifelong love of learning, is defeated.

A great deal is lost when efficiency of knowledge production becomes the watchword in higher education. Creativity does not march to the drum of efficiency. Neither does the attainment of wisdom. On the contrary, wisdom requires extended contemplation. Moreover, faculty whose pay increases are tied to research output that is measured annually will be much less likely to undertake complex, risky, or long-term projects, in many cases to our collective detriment. We should be careful what we wish for.

Feminist pedagogy is sensitive both to the important role that emotion plays in education (Strober 1987) and to the importance of creating other evaluation procedures in addition to exams. In classrooms that are truly communities of learners, students have ample opportunities to display their knowledge. Class participation, discussions in groups, and portfolios that include journals and essays all help faculty to evaluate students above and beyond their performance on tests (Shackelford 1992). In the context of service learning, there are even more opportunities for evaluation (McGoldrick 1998, 1999).

Choice and Markets

Choice is central to neoclassical economic theory, for faced with perpetual scarcity and unlimited wants, it is through the making of choices that *Homo economicus* maximizes well-being. Being quintessentially rational, he spends life evaluating options, weighing costs against benefits, and making choices that maximize utility.

Markets are also a paramount mainstream construct, since maximization of economic well-being requires that *Homo economicus* and the businesses he creates specialize in production and then go to market to exchange goods and services with others. Markets, taking account of both supply and demand, ensure prices and quantities that create "equilibrium" conditions (at least until some factor that affects supply or demand changes). Moreover, if they are properly competitive, markets not only yield the lowest possible price for consumers, but also ensure that successful producers earn just enough to stay in business. Those who are unsuccessful must exit that market and try their hand at something else.

According to neoclassical theory, in determining prices of all goods and services and also all factors of production, including labor, markets determine the distribution of income and wealth. Therefore, it is argued, unless the sellers have monopoly power or collude, markets must be allowed to operate without interference.

This story of how choice and markets operate is appealing on several dimensions. It has elements of both the supernatural and "hard" science and may even tap into the unconscious. It also salves the conscience of those who might be concerned about receiving more than their share by varnishing the status quo with a veneer of justice.

The supernatural quality of markets is best seen in Adam Smith's concept of "the invisible hand." A kind of secular deity magically transforming individuals' inherent self-interest into societal beneficence, markets determine not only the value of goods and services and the value of everyone's labor and capital, but also everyone's fair share of those goods and services. In addition, the neoclassical economic model, which intentionally imitates physics, with its "laws" of behavior and its emphasis on the concept of equilibrium, appeals to the modern desire for scientific specificity. There is something reassuring about human behavior that obeys well-understood laws and is so orderly that it can be conceptualized as coming to "rest" when various forces have all been accounted for.

Although mainstream economists argue that first and foremost economics is the study of people's choices, this was not always so. Adam Smith saw economics not only as a problem of exchange but also a problem of provisioning, "the creation and distribution of the 'necessaries and conveniences of life.'" One of the fundamental insights of feminist economics is that economics should be first and foremost the study of provisioning (Nelson 1993).

What does it mean to concern oneself with "provisioning"? It means being concerned with everyone having the basic goods and services consistent with a society's social norms. It means being concerned not only with goods and services for oneself, but also for others. It means speaking out when some people go hungry or malnourished even though there is enough food produced to ensure all the world's population an adequate diet. It means being willing to regulate and monitor production and trade, so that consumers are provided with adequate information and so that the basic quality of goods and services is ensured. It means opening educational and economic opportunities to all. It would be a giant step for mainstream economics to consciously change its focus from analyzing choices to concern with studying the provision of material well-being.

The shift to concern with provisioning would also be important for education. It would mean that education would provision every student, regardless of race, gender, or socioeconomic status, with knowledge for living life. It would give students information and understanding to make better-informed decisions about such diverse matters as love, friendship, family relationships, parenting, community involvement, jobs and careers, leisure, political involvement, health, and financial planning. It would help them to develop a moral compass and a basis for discovering life's meanings.

Feminist pedagogy takes provisioning seriously. It is centrally concerned with providing education for all students by seeking out teaching styles that are appropriate for various kinds of learners, by assuring that the content of economics courses is also relevant for women and minorities, and by seeking to engage all students in their courses.

The notion that learning could be improved by introducing choice and markets into K–12 public education was first put forward by conservative economist Milton Friedman (1955, 1962). Public education, he argued, was a monopoly that provided too little choice for parents. If public schools had to compete with one another, and particularly if they had to compete with private schools for public dollars, they would produce "output" that was more to parents' liking.

Of course, parents with high incomes have always had choices with respect to their children's education. They can choose to send their children to an excellent (and expensive) private school, or they can choose to move to a school district with high-priced homes that provides sufficient property tax revenues to support high-quality public schools. The current "choice" movement in education argues that parents with low incomes should also have choices about where their children go to school and that having choices will improve their children's educational outcomes. The No Child Left Behind Act of 2002 requires that local education authorities using Title I funds must spend up to 20 percent of these allocations to provide school choice to students.

The schools available for inclusion in a choice system could, of course, all be public, but most frequently proponents argue strenuously for private schools to be included. One vehicle that permits low-income parents to choose private schools, which they otherwise couldn't afford, is a voucher, a document from the state or locality that parents present to the private school, which in turn redeems it for some dollar amount. A second vehicle is a charter school, a nonpublic school (either nonprofit or for-profit) funded by the state.

The argument for including private schools in parents' choice sets is often that private schools have better average test scores than public schools. This claim, however, needs careful evaluation. Because of the positive correlation between student test scores and family socioeconomic level, it is necessary to account for differences in family socioeconomic level when looking at differences in test scores between public and private schools. Also, families who send their children to private school may, all else being equal, be more interested in education than other parents, so that their children's higher test scores may reflect parental interest and assistance in addition to any value added from the private school itself. Finally, since private schools are selective, children with learning or behavior problems are often excluded. Thus, the average test scores for private and public schools are not based on the same kind of population (see Goldhaber 1999; Carnoy 2000).

In extending the market metaphor to education, those advocating school choice argue that if parents have a choice, they will take their children out of poor schools (where average test scores are low) and enroll them in better schools (where average test scores are high). As a result, better schools will expand, poor schools will contract or go out of "business" altogether, and everyone will be better off.

However, if we abandon abstract theory and look at the real people behind the supply and demand curves and the particular service that is being provided, it is unclear how either increasing the size of "good" schools or decreasing the size of "bad" schools (or closing them altogether) would improve student test scores. What we know about so-called effective schools, those that have fewer behavior problems, higher test scores, and lower drop-out rates, particularly in low-income neighborhoods, is that they have excellent principals who are able to motivate teachers, parents, and students with a personal, hands-on management style. If such schools were to admit more pupils, either by running double sessions, adding portable classrooms, or taking over an additional school, it is likely that the very resource that is so fundamental to their success would be changed. The effective principal would be unable to have an equally personal hands-on style in a large school. Indeed, research indicates that large schools are not effective, in part because they are too difficult to manage well and in part because students feel lost and "unmonitored" in them. Parents might well apply to have their children admitted to a successful school, but if the school admitted all who applied, new students would be disappointed and old students would find that their situation had worsened.

If improving schools overall by making successful ones larger is not a sensible strategy, neither is improving schools by reducing the size of, or closing, unsuccessful ones. If a school is reduced in size because some parents choose to withdraw their children, it might well decline in quality. It is likely that the children with the highest test scores, whose parents might be more knowledgeable about and interested in their children's education, would be the most likely to leave. If these children leave, and if peer learning is important, those children who remain in the poor school will have even fewer resources than before. Similarly, as morale declines, the best teachers in such a school might well leave, since they are likely to have job opportunities elsewhere that the poorer teachers don't have. Perhaps, ultimately, the school would be so "bad" that it would be closed. Then what?

If we closed a school, we would have to immediately reopen it, presumably with better management and better teachers. But the problem is that we don't have better principals and better teachers. If we did, they would already have been at the school. The problem is not that parents and children don't have choice, but that they don't have good schools. Proponents of choice believe that there are good managers and good teachers out there, but that they don't want to (or can't) work effectively in a system that is bureaucratized and heavily unionized. They want education to be improved by reopening schools that have been closed and running them as new entities.

Given that existing good schools, both public and private, are unlikely to expand to accommodate all the children whose parents want them to attend good schools, many parents who wished to move their children would have to find new schools with an unproven track record. In addition, these schools might not be in their neighborhood. Their children might have long commutes to get there. They might not be able to get there unless their parents had a car. They might have to be separated from old friends and be fearful of making new ones. With all these negatives and an unknown outcome from a new school, how many parents would choose to move their children? Making such a decision is not exactly akin to changing one's dry cleaner when the old one goes out of business. Further, why should parents have to move their children? Why shouldn't school districts provide children with good education?

Advocates of a market model that requires individual parents to take action to improve their children's schooling make no mention of providing good schools either to help the most needy or to further the common good. Who would take care in such a system of the needs of the most disadvantaged children, those whose parents are unable for one reason or another to help them attend a better school? What institutions would serve to socialize all children to be citizens of a single national entity?

There are serious problems in education. Some of them have to do with the fact that many children are not learning the cognitive material they need to succeed in the labor market. Others have to do with the fact that children are not learning what they need to succeed in life. To solve these problems we need provisioning, not choice. We need more resources, not a market model.

Public schools in the United States are starved for resources, especially as compared to other advanced countries. For example, a recent study of thirty member countries by the Organization for Economic Cooperation and Development (OECD) found that total government spending on educational institutions in the United States was 4.8 percent of gross domestic product in 1998 as compared to the international average of 5 percent (Wilgoren 2001). In other words, the United States would have had to spend another $20 billion on education in 1998 for its expenditures to have reached the average percentage of GDP spent on education by OECD member countries. The same study reported that the average salary of a U.S. teacher with fifteen years of experience was only 99 percent of the average U.S. per capita income. Among member countries as a whole, teachers earned 136 percent of their country's average per capita income.

In part because of relatively low teacher pay, one of the major problems that U.S. schools face today is an inability to attract and retain excellent teachers. Eighty percent of K–12 teachers and half of high school teachers are women. Before the 1970s, when medicine, law, academia, and business were effectively closed to women, teaching was the most attractive occupation for bright women. For decades, schools had a bargain; they could employ women at low wages and be assured that they would not be bid away by more lucrative possibilities. Those days are over. While increasing salaries would not solve all of the problems of attracting and retaining teachers (working conditions, including quality of management, opportunity to grow as a teacher, and student behavior, including violence, would still be important), it would certainly help. Also, flexibility on the part of the educational establishment in recruiting and employing teachers (including making it possible to teach part-time and providing on-the-job training in pedagogy) would help ensure a sufficient supply of teachers who have competence in their subject matter and are also able to teach.

Additional resources are also needed to permit the renovation of buildings. But providing more resources to the education sector won't be enough. The resources need to be well managed, not only at the school level, but also at the district and state levels. Figuring out how to manage school systems in large cities is one of the most daunting challenges the United States faces. It is time to lay the mainstream economic model aside and focus on the real challenges in education, the need to provide adequate resources for schools and to develop effective systems of educational management.

Conclusion

Neoclassical economics panders to the most basic, least lofty, goals of humanity. Indeed, for most of Western history, greed was seen as a vice—not as a characteristic to be indulged, but as one that required self-control and sublimation. Making the fulfillment of unlimited individual wants the centerpiece of theory is not only quintessentially narcissistic, as Feiner (1995) has suggested, it is also potentially dangerous, as when failure to curb insatiable wants leads nations to war and to destruction of the environment. Moreover, it impedes human development. Instead of aspiring to self-actualization, as Abraham Maslow's theory suggests people will do once their more basic human needs have been met, people get "stuck" with an ever-present sense of scarcity of material goods and services and never get beyond it to seek fulfillment of their human potential.

Of course, some of the lessons that economics teaches are surely worth remembering: opportunity costs (and hence trade-offs) always exist; money should be spent where it is most beneficial; people respond to incentives; second- or third-round unintended effects need to be anticipated; market mechanisms are a means of holding people accountable. However, just as economics teaches that individual and business decision making involves weighing costs against benefits, extending the economic model and particular economic constructs to nonmarket behavior also involves costs and benefits. It is curious that a discipline so imbued in benefit/cost analysis sees the extension of neoclassical economic analysis to education as an unmitigated plus.

Feminist economics has had a difficult time gaining acceptance within economics. It is still marginalized. Perhaps the education sector will see more quickly than the economics profession that feminist economic analysis and feminist pedagogy can be extremely useful.

References

Aerni, April Laskey, Robin L. Bartlett, Margaret Lewis, KimMarie McGoldrick, and Jean Shackelford. 1999. Toward a feminist pedagogy in economics. *Feminist Economics* 5 (1): 29–44.

Aerni, April Laskey, and KimMarie McGoldrick, eds. 1999. *Valuing us all: Feminist pedagogy and economics.* Ann Arbor: University of Michigan Press.

Bartlett, Robin L. 1997. *Introducing race and gender into economics.* London: Routledge.

Bellah, Robert N. 2000. The true scholar. *Academe* 86:18–23.

Carnoy, Martin. 2000. School choice? Or is it privatization? *Educational Researcher* 29 (7): 15–20.

Colby, Anne. 2000. Moral and civic education for college students. Unpublished manuscript, Carnegie Foundation for the Advancement of Teaching, Menlo Park, California.

Colby, Anne, and William Damon. 1992. *Some do care: Contemporary lives of moral commitment.* New York: Free Press.

England, Paula. 1993. The separative self: Andocentric bias in neoclassical assumptions. In *Beyond economic man,* edited by Marianne A. Ferber and Julie A. Nelson, 37–53. Chicago: University of Chicago Press.

Feiner, Susan F. 1993. Introductory economics textbooks and the treatment of issues related to women and minorities, 1984 and 1991. *Journal of Economic Education* 24 (2): 145–62.

———. 1995. Reading neoclassical economics: Toward an erotic economy of sharing. In *Out of the margin: Feminist perspectives on economics,* edited by Edith Kuiper and Jolande Sap, 151–56. London: Routledge.

Feiner, Susan F., and Barbara A. Morgan. 1987. Women and minorities in introductory economics textbooks: 1974–1984. *Journal of Economic Education* 19 (4): 376–92.

Feiner, Susan F., and Bruce B. Roberts. 1990. Hidden by the invisible hand: Neoclassical economic theory and the textbook treatment of race and gender. *Gender and Society* 4 (2): 159–81.

Ferber, Marianne A. 1984. Suggestions for improving the classroom climate for women in the introductory economics course. *Journal of Economic Education* 15 (2): 160–68.

———. 1989. Gender and the study of economics. In *The principles of economics course: A handbook for instructors,* edited by Philip Saunders and William Walsted, 44–60. New York: McGraw Hill.

———. 1997. Gender and the study of economics: A feminist critique. In *Introducing race and gender into economics,* edited by Robin L. Bartlett, 147–55. London: Routledge.

———. 1999. Guidelines for pre-college economics education: A critique. *Feminist Economics* 5:135–42.

Ferber, Marianne A., and Julie A. Nelson, eds. 1993. *Beyond economic man: Feminist theory and economics.* Chicago: University of Chicago Press.

Fisher, Roger, and Scott Brown. 1988. *Building relationships as we negotiate.* London: Penguin.

Folbre, Nancy. 1995. Holding hands at midnight: The paradox of caring labor. *Feminist Economics* 1:73–92.

Frank, Robert H., Thomas Gilovich, and Dennis T. Regan. 1993. Does studying economics inhibit cooperation? *Journal of Economic Perspectives* 7 (2): 159–71.

Friedman, Milton. 1955. The role of government in education. In *Economics and the public interest*, edited by Robert A. Solo. New Brunswick, N.J.: Rutgers University Press.

———. 1962. *Capitalism and freedom*. Chicago: University of Chicago Press.

Goldhaber, Dan. 1999. School choice: An examination of the empirical evidence on achievement, parental decision making, and equity. *Educational Researcher* 29 (8): 16–25

Goleman, Daniel. 1995. *Emotional intelligence*. New York: Bantam.

Himmelweit, Susan. 1999. Caring labor. In *Emotional labor in the service economy,* edited by Ronnie J. Steinberg and Deborah M. Figart, 27–38. Annals of the American Academy of Political and Social Science 561. Thousand Oaks, Calif.: Sage.

Hirschman, Albert O. 1992. Against parsimony: Three easy ways of complicating some categories of economic discourse. *Rival views of market society and other recent essays,* 142–60. Cambridge, Mass.: Harvard University Press.

Hofstadter, Richard, and Wilson Smith. 1961. *American higher education: A documentary history*, vol. 1. Chicago: University of Chicago Press.

Kohn, Alfie. 1986. *No contest*. Boston: Houghton Mifflin.

Krumboltz, John D., and Christine J. Yeh. 1996. Competitive grading sabotages good teaching. *Phi Delta Kappan,* December.

Lazear, Edward P. 2000. Economic imperialism. *Quarterly Journal of Economics* 115:96–146.

McGoldrick, KimMarie. 1998. Service learning in economics: A detailed application. *Journal of Economic Education* 29 (fall): 365–76.

———. 1999. The road not taken: Service learning as an example of feminist pedagogy in economics. In *Valuing us all: Feminist pedagogy and economics*, edited by April Laskey Aerni and KimMarie McGoldrick, 168–83. Ann Arbor: University of Michigan Press.

Myers, David G. 1992. *The pursuit of happiness*. New York: William Morrow.

National Education Association. 2001–2002. Resolutions B-37 and B-39, pp. 17–18. Available at www.nea.org/resolutions.

———. 2002. Code of ethics of the education profession. Available at www.nea.org/aboutnea/code.html.

Nelson, Julie A. 1993. The study of choice or the study of provisioning? Gender and the definition of economics. In *Beyond economic man*, edited by Marianne A. Ferber and Julie A. Nelson, 23–36. Chicago: University of Chicago Press.

Noddings, Nel. 1984. *Caring: A feminine approach to ethics and moral education*. Berkeley: University of California Press.

Reese, William J. 2000. Public schools and the elusive search for the common good. In *Reconstructing the common good in education: Coping with intractable American dilemmas*, edited by Larry Cuban and Dorothy Shipps, 13–31. Stanford, Calif.: Stanford University Press.

Schneider, Geoff, and Jean Shackelford. 2001. Economics standards and lists: Proposed antidotes for feminist economists. *Feminist Economics* 7 (2): 77–89.

Seguino, Stephanie, Thomas Stevens, and Mark A. Lutz. 1996. Gender and cooperative behavior: Economic man rides alone. *Feminist Economics* 2:1–21.

Shackelford, Jean. 1992. Feminist pedagogy: A means for bringing critical thinking and creativity to the economics classroom. *American Economic Review* 82 (2): 570–76.

Simon, Kathy G. 1997. The place of meaning: A study of the moral, existential, and intellectual in American high schools. Ph.D. dissertation, Stanford University.

Slavin, Robert E. 1990. *Cooperative learning: Theory, research, and practice*. Englewood Cliffs, N.J.: Prentice-Hall.

Smith, Adam. [1759] 1969. *The theory of moral sentiments*. Indianapolis: Liberty Classics.

Sobel, Elliott, and David Sloan Wilson. 1998. *Unto others: The evolution and psychology of unselfish behavior*. Cambridge, Mass.: Harvard University Press.

Strober, Myra H. 1987. The scope of microeconomics: Implications for economic education. *Journal of Economic Education* 18 (spring): 135–49

———. 1994. Rethinking economics through a feminist lens. *American Economic Review* 84 (2): 143–47.

———. Forthcoming. Feminist economics: Implications for education. In *Feminism confronts Homo economicus*, edited by Terence Dougherty and Martha Fineman.

Wilgoren, Jodi. 2001. Education study finds U.S. falling short. *New York Times*, June 13: A28.

Winston, Gordon C. 1997. Why can't a college be more like a firm? *Change* 29 (5): 33–37.

Winter, Soren C., and Peter J. May. 2001. Motivation for compliance with environmental regulations. *Journal of Policy Analysis and Management* 20 (4): 675–98.

Zamagni, Stefano. 1995. *The economics of altruism.* The International Library of Critical Writings in Economics 48. Aldershot, U.K.: Edward Elgar.

7

Economics, Policy Analysis, and Feminism

. . . Rebecca M. Blank and Cordelia W. Reimers

Perhaps any woman who chooses to pursue a full-time career in a nontraditional profession such as economics should be considered to be a feminist, whether she identifies herself as one or not. In fact, at least three types of economists might identify themselves as "feminist economists." The first are theorists who challenge and critique standard economic theories and models, identify the gender biases in what appear to be gender-neutral theories, and try to build alternative theories; the second are empirical economists and policy analysts whose concern about the inequities that face women leads them to focus at least part of their research on gender issues; and the third are economists, either theoretical or empirical, who in their other professional roles, as teachers, administrators, and participants in professional organizations, try to break down barriers facing women. The same individual may, of course, embody two or even all three of these types.

We see ourselves as meeting the second and third definitions. We are empirical economists and policy analysts, with all of the requisite credentials by which economists define themselves. We have worked for many years as academic researchers and teachers, written a great deal about "women's issues," and served in short-term full-time government positions, as well as a variety of policy advisory boards. In short, we are both highly involved in policy questions and part of the "mainstream" economics community.

We also consider ourselves feminists. We support women's involvement in nontraditional roles and positions in society; we support equal recognition, equal opportunities, and equal pay for women's efforts; we believe men should be more deeply involved in household work and caregiving within families; and we believe that as a broader range of opportunities are available to women and more and more women take advantage of these opportunities, this will open up new options for men as well.

This chapter is more autobiographical than most papers we write, but perhaps that is appropriate for this volume, since one of the primary claims in the feminist literature is that women's lived experiences are integral to their feminist perspectives. It is perhaps even necessary to be somewhat autobiographical, since we explore the question of whether our feminist commitments make any difference to how we fulfill our professional roles as economists and policy analysts. Our feminism affects our choice of models, our choice of topics, how we present our work, and our behavior in our other professional roles.[1]

Choosing Models by Which to Represent Reality

The Usefulness of the Standard Economic Model . . . with Constraints

Our work has consistently used as a starting point the mainstream economic model of optimizing behavior by individuals and firms, subject to constraints. Some feminists reject this model because of the conclusions some economists have drawn from it, but the model can also be used to draw quite different conclusions. We find it to be a powerful analytic tool, more useful than any other available for understanding differences in outcomes in a market society and for exploring the probable consequences of alternative policy options. At the same time, our feminist concerns lead us to be skeptical of the "purer" forms of this model, in which markets are frictionless and everything works for the best. We are more open than many economists to going beyond the perfectly competitive model to take account of frictions and market imperfections.

In the standard microeconomic model, individuals bring certain preferences (goals, desires) to a situation and attempt to maximize their satisfaction given those preferences, subject to the institutional and personal constraints they face. Thus, a woman is viewed as entering the labor market with a "taste" for certain types of work or for a certain combination of market work and home-based work. She also brings given levels of education and experience, which open up a given set of opportunities to her. The wage that she receives

---

1. For a short discussion of a similar set of issues, see Blau 1981.

is partially determined by these opportunities and constraints and is assumed to be a fixed constraint—she is offered a job at a given wage that she cannot change through negotiation. But her preferences might lead her to trade off wages for more flexible hours or to accept a job in retail trade with very different characteristics than a job in finance.

The fundamental properties of this model are that it is *choice-based*, it recognizes that *individual tastes* might vary, and it recognizes the presence of *unchangeable constraints* (at least in the short term). The interesting part (in our opinion) comes when one begins to consider what the constraints are and how to model their interaction with preferences and tastes. Our feminist perspective leads us to be skeptical of the simpler forms of this model, in which everyone has full information, constraints are easily characterized by one or two variables (such as a single market wage rate), and everything is considered a viable choice (hence, if it was not chosen, it must not be preferred). These stripped-down versions of the economic model often define away many of the interesting issues that confront women as they make work and family decisions.

For instance, the model predicts that "compensating" wage differences will arise in the labor market in response to workers' preferences among various job characteristics, so that, all else equal, undesirable jobs will command higher wages than desirable jobs. It is sometimes claimed that this can explain the gender gap in wages. But it does not explain why the wage differentials almost always seem to favor men's jobs, when many predominantly female jobs are also arduous and unpleasant. For instance, Altonji and Blank (1999) review the literature on labor-market discrimination against women and conclude that there is clear evidence that women's wages are affected by considerations beyond their productive characteristics and the nature of their jobs.

Similarly, models of household decision making often assume complete agreement on the part of the husband and wife. A household typically is modeled as having one coherent set of preferences and making a single choice. This ignores situations in which husbands and wives might have different preferences and ignores all issues of conflict or bargaining. In contrast, Lundberg and Pollak (1994) provide an alternative model of household decision making as a bargaining situation. Phipps and Burton (1998) show that women's expenditure choices differ from men's, so that increases in wives' incomes result in different spending patterns than do increases in husbands' incomes.

Despite its limitations, we believe the economic model, even in a relatively simple version, can serve a useful purpose if it is used to provide a null hypothesis against which more complicated possibilities can be compared. As already suggested, the choice-based economic model provides a framework within which to examine the effects of frictions and market imperfections. The model provides a way to think about the impact on outcomes of limited information, of transaction costs, of discrimination in wages, or of other constraints. What difference does it make if employers discriminate, compared to a world in which they do not? What difference does it make if women's labor-market choices are constrained by firms that offer health benefits only to those who work more than thirty-five hours each week? What difference does it make if child care costs $10 per hour versus $5 per hour? The economic model allows one to think rigorously about such questions in a way that we find highly useful.

Suitably extended, the standard economic model can help us understand the problems that women face, by highlighting the ways in which optimizing behavior on the part of firms as well as male (and even female) workers can produce gender and other inequities. It powerfully illuminates the economic "trap" women are in, because their greater child-rearing and household responsibilities produce differentials in the labor market, and those differentials in turn reinforce the unequal division of responsibilities in the home. This vicious cycle is difficult to break, which helps explain why women's progress has been so slow.

The standard model also focuses attention on the power of market forces to undo the best-intentioned policies unless they are carefully designed. It shows how some policies may lead to very different outcomes than initially intended, because of incentive effects on behavior. For example, President Clinton proposed making paid family leave mandatory and financing it by an insurance system akin to Unemployment Insurance (UI), with experience-rated employer premiums as in UI. This means that firms employing women of child-bearing age would bear higher costs, through these taxes. This might well improve the well-being of women who retain their jobs, but make employers less willing to hire women in this age group. Or it could lead employers to try to pass the cost of the tax along to workers (economists call this "shifting the incidence" of the tax) and pay lower wages in jobs that are disproportionately filled by women. For instance, Gruber (1994) shows that employers shift the incidence of mandated maternity benefits, so that workers receive lower wages. Ruhm (1998) also finds some evidence that women pay for entitlements to extended parental leave by receiving lower relative wages. These possibilities should affect how paid family leave policies are designed. For example, financing such leaves with a premium set as a flat percentage of the wage of all workers would be more neutral with respect to the age and gender of employees. This would spread the cost of family leave among the entire workforce, so that the larger society shared some of the costs of child rearing.

Another example of the power of the economic model is its usefulness for the analysis of child-care issues. Is child care a "lumpy good," that is, a good that can be purchased only in certain set quantities? How will differences in child-care prices affect female labor supply? What if child care adds to the cost of transportation and commuting? The economic model provides an explicit way to model these different aspects of the child-care market and to explore the effects of child-care prices on women's behavior, as Kimmel (1995, 1998) has done. Similarly, one can consider how child-care subsidies would affect behavior, how the effects of subsidies to parents might differ from those of subsidies to child-care centers, and how a tax credit might have a different impact than a child-care voucher program. The economic model provides a systematic framework for exploring all these questions, as Blau (2003) discusses.

In short, the search for explanations for the observed inequalities in outcomes between men and women can make us aware of the real-world violations of the pure competitive-market version of an economic behavioral model and lead us to model more realistically constrained situations. We believe such an effort can produce valuable insights. Thus, properly handled, the mainstream economic model can be a powerful tool for designing and analyzing policies to help women and for alerting us to possible unintended policy consequences. But we also recognize that the standard economic model has its limitations, which leads us occasionally to seek alternatives.

Going Beyond the Standard Economic Model

Our interest in understanding the realities of women's lives makes us open to models and perspectives from other disciplines. In part because of our feminist interests, our own reading and thinking draws more on research from outside the traditional bounds of economics than that of many economists. (Just saying that one reads social science research outside economics may be taken as a radical statement in some economics circles!) This means both keeping somewhat abreast of feminist writings and also being familiar with a variety of sociological and psychological models that incorporate key ideas that economic models often discount or ignore. We give four examples here.

Sociological models often place the concept of "community" at the center. In many sociological writings, the whole is much more than the sum of the parts. In fact, the community and its social norms may provide shape and definition to individual lives; that is, individuals are defined by the community as much as the community is defined by individuals' actions. For instance Wilson's (1987) classic study of changes in ghetto communities talks about the interaction of larger economic forces with behavioral changes. There are substantial sociological literatures on the role of social networks, on peer effects, and on the role of social capital.

This is quite different from standard microeconomic models, in which there is often no concept of the aggregate except as the summing up of individuals' behaviors. To the extent that larger social constraints are recognized at all, they are usually in the background of economic models, whereas sociological models place the understanding of these social and cultural factors at the center of concern.

In trying to understand the impact of policies upon women's families and on their economic behavior, it is often useful to supplement the standard economic model with some of these more sociological concepts. For instance, specific social norms may be highly important influences on the labor market choices of immigrant women (Reimers 1985a). The lack of employed friends in a welfare recipient's social network may limit the effectiveness of welfare-to-work programs designed to assist women who have been out of the labor force. The role of peer effects and social pressure to conform may be important in understanding teenage sexual behavior and fertility outcomes. While the economic model can be used to address these issues, the addition of sociological perspectives may enhance one's understanding of them.

Economists have not been entirely blind to these issues. Case and Katz (1991) look at the effects of peer networks on teenage behavior. Borjas (1995) studies the role of social networks in economic outcomes among immigrant groups. Glaeser, Laibson, and Sacerdote (2002) discuss the role of social capital in economic models.

A second approach we find useful is found in the organizational behavior literature that focuses on how institutional structure can influence action. While the economic model allows one to study the impact of institutional constraints, these constraints are typically taken as given. Those interested in organizations, however, provide more detailed descriptions of institutional structure and how it interacts with individual behavior (Baron and Bielby 1985). Institutionalists are concerned not just with the presence of organizational constraints, but with how such constraints arise, how they are maintained, and how they might be changed.

Our understanding of how women's labor market opportunities have changed over time may be improved by case studies of specific business institutions, showing how their structure has responded to internal and external pressures to hire and promote women. For instance, Wallace (1976) provides case studies of how the institutional structure of AT&T was set up (prior to changes mandated by gender and race discrimination suits) to provide very different job opportunities to men and to women. Alternatively, to understand the ways in which welfare caseworkers respond to clients, it may be highly useful to consider the structure of the public assistance bureaucracies in which caseworkers operate, the pressures these organizations place on employees, and the incentives they offer. A unique study by Bloom, Hill, and Riccio (2001) shows that the effectiveness of welfare-to-work programs is at least partially determined by the management attributes and administrative structure of the welfare office.

A third set of theoretical approaches from outside economics is useful because it helps us understand preference formation. While the standard economic model takes individual preferences as given (and often as fixed over time), other disciplines can provide insights into where individual preferences are likely to come from and how and why they may change. Psychology, anthropology, and sociology all provide models of preference formation (although they typically don't use that term) that explain how individuals' beliefs, desires, and sense of need might be formed. These models can help us understand the socialization and acculturation of children as they grow to adulthood. They can help us understand why women may develop systematically different preferences than men (leading to consistently different occupational or job choices). For instance, Laws (1976) shows how the work environment acts to modify women's work motivation. Models of preference formation can also indicate why policy changes may result in adaptive changes in expectations and behavior over time. For instance, so-called hysteresis hypotheses about high and sustained European unemployment rates suggest that negative macroeconomic shocks raised unemployment in the short run, while high unemployment led to a depreciation of skills or a loss of job contacts that led to higher unemployment in the long run (Lindbeck and Snower 1990).

Finally, we are perhaps more interested in history than most economists (other than economic historians). We are not economic historians ourselves, but we use historical works to learn how institutions and social norms have evolved over time. The discipline of history does not provide alternative theoretical insights or models so much as it provides evidence about the impermanence of current constraints. The explosion of scholarship in social history and women's history in the last twenty-five years has been a particularly rich source of new ideas and information about the issues we are particularly concerned with—the history of the family, child-rearing practices, women's roles in society, and social policies to support and help care for children, the elderly, and other dependent members of society (Kessler-Harris 1982; Gordon 1994; Gabaccia 1994; Jones 1995).

For the topics we study, the biggest inadequacies of the economic model lie in exactly the areas outlined above. Economic models often ignore the concept of social norms and the behavioral effects that emerge from membership in distinct communities and often take little notice of institutions. Thus, they fail to consider the nuances of institutional behavior and how these can interact with individual behavior. Instead, they treat preferences and tastes—key elements in choice-based behavior—as firmly established without accounting for where they come from, and take current institutional arrangements and social customs as given and unchanging. Theories not based on economics and evidence from other disciplines can help us understand these issues better and can, in turn, make us more effective analysts of policies and their impacts on outcomes.[2]

Choosing Topics on Which to Work

Probably the main way in which our feminist interests influence our actions as economists is through the topics we choose to research and the questions we think are important. The same concerns that make us feminists also lead us to ask certain questions and to focus on certain issues.

A Concern with Equity and Distributional Issues as Well as Efficiency Issues

The marked inequities that women have historically faced in the labor market and the high rates of poverty among some groups of women make distributional issues quite important to anyone interested in understanding women's lives. Because modern economics has focused much more on efficiency than on equity, issues of distribution have received less research attention. The rise in earnings inequality during the 1980s changed this situation somewhat, as large numbers of researchers investigated this change. This literature has, however, been focused on wages and has not stimulated much new research on income inequality or on other economic inequalities.

The inequalities faced by women include the differentials in male and female employment opportunities, which continue to persist even after controlling for a rich set of background variables. For instance, Blank (1989) shows that the cyclical response of single women's employment and earnings

---

2. We note that some of these views are shared by other authors in this volume. For example, see Nelson, chap. 3, for more about organizational behavior; England and Folbre, chap. 2, about specific business institutions; Saunders and Darity, chap. 4, about institutions and history; and England, chap. 1, about preference formation.

is different from that of married couples. The disproportionate representation of women (especially single mothers) among the poor raises questions about earnings opportunities, as well as about policies to provide assistance to this group (Blank and Schmidt 2001). The fact that tax code changes and proposed Social Security reforms differentially affect men and women also suggests interesting questions about how policy changes interact with differences between men's and women's choices and outcomes (Reimers and Honig 1996).

We do not believe that policy should be determined by efficiency considerations alone or that every efficiency-enhancing policy is necessarily a desirable one. Rather, we believe that in some cases one must first seek policies that address equity issues, and then choose the more efficient among these. In short, in cases where there might be an equity-efficiency trade-off, we put more weight on equity than many economists do.

In other situations, there may also be goals other than equity that need to be weighed against efficiency. For instance, efficiency and quality might sometimes be in conflict, particularly in the provision of services. One might be willing to accept a less efficient bureaucracy overseeing social services for the elderly or for children, for the sake of closer monitoring of outcomes and higher quality, as suggested by Blank (2000). Here again, we do not want to assume (as many economists do) that efficiency is the primary concern.

An Interest in Specific Topics That Relate to Women's Concerns

Our general concern with women's issues has led us to focus much of our research on topics that are usually assumed to be of particular interest to women. This general interest has certainly been reinforced over time by our own life experiences. (One of us married and had children early, and spent several years raising children full time before studying economics in graduate school; while the other married and had children late, after establishing an academic career.) For instance, it is well-nigh impossible for an economist to participate in the often-chaotic market for child care or elder care without wondering why these markets are so poorly organized. Among the topics that our experiences have led us to explore are married women's allocation of time between labor market and home-based activities (Reimers 1985a); the role that part-time work plays in women's labor market opportunities (Blank 1990, 1998); and the impact of public assistance policies on the behavior and well-being of less-skilled women (Blank 1997).

With these choices of research topics, we realize that we run the risk of being labeled within the profession as economists who work on "women's issues." (One of us was explicitly advised as a graduate student not to work on "women's issues" before completing a body of work that would establish her as a "real" economist.) Our response to this is a mix of amusement that our colleagues still use such categorizations and frustrated recognition that younger female economists may be less able to shrug off these labels.

Particularly as we have gained more seniority, we are happy to accept this characterization and do not find it as critical a comment as those who make it typically intend it to be. One of us studied at Columbia when the "new home economics" was being developed and used by both male and female economists to analyze married women's labor force participation, fertility, household production, and welfare participation. Far from being marginalized, those who worked on these "women's topics" were in on the most exciting intellectual game around at the time. We have, however, also chosen to work on other topics as well as "women's issues," and that has helped to broaden our professional reputations. One of us deliberately chose a dissertation topic that dealt with male behavior, partly because of data availability, but also partly to avoid being stereotyped.

Today, we feel somewhat vindicated by the growing public interest in issues of family and work, in policies relating to less-skilled women, and in women's labor market roles. We believe that our work on topics of particular concern to women has placed us at the center of a key set of policy debates and has opened opportunities for public policy involvement that would not have existed if we had not pursued these interests.

In looking at the growing body of first-rate research on topics relating to women's lives and behavior, it is clear that female researchers are highly important to this literature. While male scholars have made significant contributions, more women find these research questions compelling. One of the strongest arguments for the greater inclusion of women in the economics profession is that they frequently bring different questions to the table and generate research that would not otherwise be done.

An Interest in Specific Policies That Disproportionately Affect Women

Much of our policy work is not specifically focused on women. Even so, a good deal of this work deals with areas where the policies have a different or a disproportionate effect on women. This includes research on the consequences of Social Security reform for lower-income groups (Reimers forthcoming), of health insurance benefits on low-wage and part-time workers (Blank 1990), and of changes in the structure of pension plans (Council of Economic Advisers 1999). It also includes the responsiveness of poverty to the macroeconomy

(Blank and Card 1993) and changes in participation in the Unemployment Insurance or public assistance programs (Blank and Card 1991; Blank and Ruggles 1996).

Our feminist interests are clearly visible to anyone looking at our curriculum vitae, even if they focus only on those articles that do not include the word *women* in the title. Just as our policy interests strongly direct us toward policy-relevant research topics, our feminist interests lead us to select policy questions that particularly impact women's lives.

Presentational Issues

Being feminists affects not only *what* we study, but also influences *how* we study it and how we present our results and conclusions. We deeply believe that these "presentational issues" are as important as the topics chosen, in part because they help to establish social norms and role models within the profession and to transmit signals to younger economists about "how to do research." We would note at least three ways in which our presentation is affected by our feminist concerns.

First, we make an effort to analyze the experiences of women as well as men in our studies and to investigate gender differences in outcomes. The vast majority of the empirical literature in labor economics still uses data for men alone. Worse yet, this is not always made clear in a paper's title and discussion, which often give the impression that the results apply to all individuals, when in fact they are based on all-male samples. This is typically done with a comment such as "We want to focus on a group of attached workers" or "We want to abstract from questions about family and child-care choices." We frequently find these excuses invalid (and speak up in seminars, asking the question, "Why didn't you include women in your sample?"). A growing number of women in the United States and many other countries are long-term workers who are very attached to the labor market, and their experiences should be included in the analysis. At the very least, when an all-male sample is used, that should be made clear throughout the paper. We make a practice of doing this in our own writing.

Moreover, the presumption that men are not affected by family and child-care choices is being increasingly thrown into question, both by the evidence that more men are engaging in a greater amount of child-care activities and by the evidence that men's work choices and wages are affected by marriage and children (Korenman and Neumark 1991). Therefore, it should not be assumed that policies such as the Family and Medical Leave Act or regulation of the child-care industry are just "women's issues" that affect women but not men.

At the same time, it should be recognized that programs such as Social Security, SSI, Medicare, and Medicaid disproportionately affect women, so that policies affecting these programs *are* women's issues. Much of the research on Social Security reform, for instance, has focused on the "macro" effects on the federal budget and the rate of return on payroll taxes among lifelong full-time workers, who are mostly male. The distributional effects on women have received much less attention, despite the fact that most Social Security beneficiaries are women.

Another recent example of the continuing inattention to women's lives in economic research can be seen in the recent explosion of work on the increase in wage inequality within the U.S. economy. A large number of studies have focused solely on wage inequality among men, mentioning women only in passing or not at all. Yet many of the reasons presented for this increasing inequality (changing technologies, expanding international trade, etc.) should be affecting women as well as men. The fact that women's wage inequality has not grown as rapidly as men's is not an argument for ignoring women in this research, but should instead interest researchers in investigating these gender differences. Blau and Kahn (1997) have done so, in one of the few papers that focus on changes in women's wage inequality. Because they live and work in the same economy, women's different experiences might provide real insight into what is and what is not driving the increase in wage inequality among males. The overall wage structure includes both men and women, and more and more jobs are open to both sexes. It therefore makes no sense to analyze changes in the wage structure as if men and women were in two separate, sealed compartments.

Another frustration is that the Census and Current Population Survey data, the only datasets with samples large enough to analyze small population groups and frequent enough to track changes in the wage distribution, lack a measure of actual lifetime work experience. This makes it difficult to analyze women's wages. Garvey and Reimers (1980), Hill and O'Neill (1992), and Gladden and Taber (2000) indicate that properly accounting for gaps in labor market experience among women is important for understanding the labor market returns faced by women. Confronted with the lack of appropriate data, many researchers have simply excluded women's wages from the analysis. We, however, have typically chosen to analyze women's wages—often with very imperfect measures of experience—rather than treat males as representative of everyone (Reimers 1985b; Reimers 1997).

A second presentational issue involves our writing and verbal presentations. We try very hard not to treat the words *male* and *person* as synonymous, but to specify carefully which sex is meant. Again, this is in contrast to much work in economics, where "economic man" is the traditional terminology. Similarly, we try not to say "work" when we mean "paid work," and not to say "leisure" when we mean "unpaid activities," including household work and child care. It is common for economists to say that a woman who is not employed is not working, no matter how much unpaid work she does, and to equate not working for pay with leisure. Our emphasis on precise and inclusive language may be dismissed as trivial by some, but language matters, as many feminist scholars have noted. We think role models who regularly and publicly use female-oriented as well as male-oriented references can over time change the accepted norms within the profession.

Other Professional Roles

A very important part of our role in the economics profession has involved our commitment to mentoring other female economists, especially younger ones, and to creating community among female economists. We make an effort to become acquainted with other women in the profession and try to recommend them as referees and conference participants. We are frequently called by departments or organizations who are hiring and asked, "Do you know anyone good for our position, and in particular do you know any good female candidates?" One of us keeps a file at her desk, which includes the résumés of women who she knows are on the market or thinking about changing jobs, that she can pull out when she gets such a phone call. One of us founded a local group of female economists, New York Women Economists, which has been meeting since 1985. Both of us have been active in the Committee on the Status of Women in the Economics Profession (an official subcommittee of the American Economic Association). Both of us organize conferences and sessions at professional meetings to make sure women's issues, such as the effects of proposed Social Security reforms on older women, get attention and women's voices are heard.

Because the economics profession remains remarkably male, we are still in a situation where creating community among female economists is a highly important activity. In the United States, women are only 6 percent of the tenured full professors in economics at Ph.D.-granting institutions. Even among untenured assistant professors of economics at these schools, only 22 percent are female (Haworth 2002). Many schools still have only one or maybe two women in the economics department, if any. This often creates a sense of isolation and marginalization. There is a good deal of evidence that the situation is no better, or even worse, in other countries, as seen in the recent discussion of gender differences in economics in Great Britain (Booth and Burton 2000).

Why would a woman who works, say, on international trade feel isolated, if she has active male colleagues in her specialty? There are many reasons. Male colleagues may not provide the same mentoring or attention to female junior colleagues as a female colleague would be likely to do. Also, male colleagues may not provide a satisfactory network of friends, because of the occasional delicacy of male-female relationships and because of different interests in how to spend free time. In addition, male colleagues may not understand some of the concerns that women have about the rules and organization of the department or university.

The most talked-about male-female career difference is that men typically do not face the same time pressures as women concerning family and children. This can be highly important—too many women in economics have felt that expressing a desire for children would be interpreted as saying, "I'm not serious about my career." One of us, when she was the only woman in her department, went to great lengths to attend meetings at inconvenient times rather than reveal conflicts between work and family, for fear such revelations would be used as arguments against hiring more women. Now, a good many male as well as female colleagues routinely put family first, so there has been some progress! The one of us who had a child quite recently has twice been told by younger men in her work environment that they appreciate the fact that she occasionally has her child at work or is open about leaving work early to deal with child-care conflicts, because it makes them feel more able to do such things as well.

But subtler issues—such as differences in how women and men perceive and talk about a potential problem within the department—can also be important. One of us, while a junior faculty member (and the only woman) recalls sitting at a faculty meeting and simply wishing someone were across the room who she felt would understand her reaction when she rolled her eyes at a particularly bombastic argument. There was a strong sense that "nobody in this room will understand why I think this guy's making a fool of himself. In fact, most of my colleagues almost surely believe he's behaving in a completely acceptable manner." Over time, this type of isolation can affect not only one's job satisfaction, but also one's job performance. One of us has experienced first-hand both the discomfort of being the only woman in her department and the comfort of being in a department with several other women and a female chair, in a college with many female administrators. Creating networks of women within economics remains an important issue, and those of us who are senior women in the field are most responsible for making sure that this happens.

Conclusions

Unlike those who describe themselves as "feminist economists," we would describe ourselves as economists who also happen to be feminists. We do not define our work primarily as feminist policy analysis. But our feminist commitments and our concerns about the well-being of women clearly influence our work and our careers.

We participate fully, and for the most part comfortably, in the mainstream of the economics profession. While working on policy issues that relate to the distribution of well-being, that relate to equity in the labor market and in society, or that disproportionately affect women, we have demonstrated our abilities as economists while acting upon our interest in women's lives. There were times at younger ages when it was not clear that we could succeed in establishing ourselves in the discipline, and there are still occasions when a colleague dismisses our work a bit quickly and it hurts. But we do not feel that we have had to choose between our interest in women's issues and our long-term investment in the profession of economics.

In part, this is because we continue to base our work on mainstream economic models. We think like most economists—at least when we first approach an issue—and this gives us credibility within the discipline. It also helps that we are both primarily empirical economists who use standard econometric methods. Our interest is in using data to explore the way the world works. This makes us markedly different from our friends who are primarily interested in feminist theory, who find the confines of the discipline much more limiting, and who engage in more direct theoretical challenges to mainstream economics.

These more fundamental challenges are deeply important for the profession, and we support our colleagues who do this sort of work, even when we ourselves disagree with their particular arguments. We believe that forums (such as this volume) that raise feminist concerns within the economics profession are very useful. A discipline can never be weakened by such challenges. It can only be enriched and invigorated.

References

Altonji, Joseph, and Rebecca M. Blank. 1999. Gender and race in the labor market. In *Handbook of labor economics*, vol. 3c, edited by Orley C. Ashenfelter and David Card, 3143–259. New York: Elsevier Science Press.

Baron, James N., and William T. Bielby. 1985. Organizational barriers to gender equality: Sex segregation of jobs and opportunities. In *Gender and the life course*, edited by Alice S. Rossi, 233–51. New York: Aldine.

Blank, Rebecca M. 1989. Disaggregating the effect of the business cycle on the distribution of income. *Economica* 56 (2): 141–63.

———. 1990. Are part-time jobs bad jobs? In *A future of lousy jobs: The changing structure of U.S. wages*, edited by Gary Burtless, 123–64. Washington, D.C.: Brookings Institution Press.

———. 1997. *It takes a nation: A new agenda for fighting poverty*. Princeton, N.J.: Princeton University Press.

———. 1998. Labor market dynamics and part-time work. In *Research in labor economics,* vol. 17, edited by Solomon W. Polachek, 57–93. Greenwich, Conn.: JAI Press.

———. 2000. When can public policy makers rely on private markets? The effective provision of social services. *Economic Journal* 110 (462): C34—C49.

Blank, Rebecca M., and David Card. 1991. Recent trends in insured and uninsured unemployment: Is there an explanation? *Quarterly Journal of Economics* 106 (4): 1157–89.

———. 1993. Poverty, income distribution, and growth: Are they still connected? *Brookings Papers on Economic Activity* 1993 (2): 285–325.

Blank, Rebecca M., and Patricia Ruggles. 1996. When do women use AFDC and food stamps? The dynamics of eligibility versus participation. *Journal of Human Resources* 31 (1): 57–89.

Blank, Rebecca M., and Lucie Schmidt. 2001. Work, wages, and welfare. In *The new world of welfare*, edited by Rebecca M. Blank and Ron Haskins, 70–102. Washington, D.C.: Brookings Institution Press.

Blau, David. 2003. Child care subsidy programs. In *Means-tested transfer programs in the United States,* edited by Robert Moffitt. Chicago: University of Chicago Press.

Blau, Francine D. 1981. On the role of values in feminist scholarship. *Signs* 6 (3): 538–40.

Blau, Francine D., and Lawrence M. Kahn. 1997. Swimming upstream: Trends in the gender wage differential in the 1980s. *Journal of Labor Economics* 15 (1, part 1): 1–42.

Bloom, Howard A., Carolyn J. Hill, and James Riccio. 2001. Modelling the performance of welfare-to-work programs: The effects of program management and services, economic environment, and client characteristics. MDRC Working Papers on Research Methodology. New York: Manpower Demonstration Research Corporation, June.

Booth, A. L., and J. Burton. 2000. The position of women in U.K. academic economics. *Economic Journal* 110 (474): 312–33.

Borjas, George J. 1995. Ethnicity, neighborhoods, and human-capital externalities. *American Economic Review* 85 (3): 365–90.

Case, Anne C., and Lawrence F. Katz. 1991. The company you keep: The effects of family and neighborhood on disadvantaged youths. National Bureau of Economic Research Working Paper no. 3705. Cambridge, Mass.: National Bureau of Economic Research.

Council of Economic Advisers. 1999. Work, retirement, and the economic well-being of the elderly. In *Economic report of the President and annual report of the Council of Economic Advisers,* 131–69. Washington, D.C.: U.S. Government Printing Office, February.

Gabaccia, Donna R. 1994. *From the other side: Women, gender, and immigrant life in the U.S., 1820–1990*. Bloomington: Indiana University Press.

Garvey, Nancy, and Cordelia Reimers. 1980. Predicted versus potential work experience in an earnings function for young women. In *Research in labor economics*, vol. 3, edited by Ronald Ehrenberg, 99–127. Greenwich, Conn.: JAI Press.

Gladden, Tricia, and Christopher Taber. 2000. Wage progression among less skilled workers. In *Finding jobs: Work and welfare reform*, edited by David Card and Rebecca M. Blank, 160–92. New York: Russell Sage Foundation.

Glaeser, Edward L., David Laibson, and Bruce Sacerdote. 2002. The economic approach to social capital. *Economic Journal* 112 (483): 437–58.

Gordon, Linda. 1994. *Pitied but not entitled: Single mothers and the history of welfare, 1890–1935.* New York: Free Press.

Gruber, Jonathan. 1994. The incidence of mandated maternity benefits. *American Economic Review* 84 (3): 622–41.

Haworth, Joan G. 2002. Report of the Committee on the Status of Women in the Economics Profession. *American Economic Review* 92 (2): 516–20.

Hill, M. Anne, and June O'Neill. 1992. An intercohort analysis of women's work patterns and earnings. In *Research in labor economics,* vol. 13, edited by Ronald Ehrenberg, 215–86. Greenwich, Conn.: JAI Press.

Jones, Jacqueline. 1995. *Labor of love, labor of sorrow: Black women, work, and the family from slavery to the present.* New York: Vintage Books.

Kessler-Harris, Alice. 1982. *Out to work: A history of America's wage-earning women.* New York: Oxford University Press.

Kimmel, Jean. 1995. The effectiveness of child care subsidies in encouraging the welfare-to-work transition of low-income single mothers. *American Economic Review: Papers and Proceedings* 85 (2): 271–75.

———. 1998. Child care costs as a barrier to employment for single and married mothers. *Review of Economics and Statistics* 80 (2): 287–99.

Korenman, Sanders, and David Neumark. 1991. Does marriage really make men more productive? *Journal of Human Resources* 26 (2): 282–307.

Laws, Judith Long. 1976. Psychological dimensions of labor force participation of women. In *Equal employment opportunity and the AT&T case*, edited by Phyllis Wallace, 125–56. Cambridge, Mass.: MIT Press.

Lindbeck, Assar, and Dennis Snower. 1990. Demand- and support-side policies and unemployment: Policy implications of the insider-outsider approach. In *Unemployment and wage determination in Europe: Labour market policies for the 1990s*, edited by Bertil Holmlund and Karl-Gustaf Loftgren, 149–75. Oxford: Basil Blackwell.

Lundberg, Shelly, and Robert A. Pollak. 1994. Noncooperative bargaining models of marriage. *American Economic Review: Papers and Proceedings* 84 (2): 132–37.

Phipps, Shelley A., and Peter S. Burton. 1998. What's mine is yours? The influence of male and female incomes on patterns of household expenditure. *Economica* 65 (260): 599–613.

Reimers, Cordelia W. 1985a. Cultural differences in labor force participation among married women. *American Economic Review: Papers and Proceedings* 75 (2): 251–55.

———. 1985b. A comparative analysis of the wages of Hispanics, blacks, and non-Hispanic whites. In *Hispanics in the U.S. economy*, edited by George Borjas and Marta Tienda, 27–75. New York: Academic Press.

———. 1997. The progress of Mexican and white non-Hispanic immigrants in California and Texas, 1980 to 1990. *Quarterly Journal of Economics and Finance* 37 (special issue): 315–43.

———. Forthcoming. Issue brief: Hispanics and Social Security. Washington, D.C.: National Council of La Raza.

Reimers, Cordelia W., and Marjorie H. Honig. 1996. Responses to Social Security by men and women: Myopic and farsighted behavior. *Journal of Human Resources* 31 (2): 359–82.

Ruhm, Christopher J. 1998. The economic consequences of parental leave policies: Lessons from Europe. *Quarterly Journal of Economics* 113 (1): 285–317.

Wallace, Phyllis, ed. 1976. *Equal employment opportunity and the AT&T case.* Cambridge, Mass.: MIT Press.

Wilson, William J. 1987. *The truly disadvantaged.* Chicago: University of Chicago Press.

8

Feminism, Postcolonial Thought, and Economics

. . . S. Charusheela and Eiman Zein-Elabdin

> Simply put, culture is alive and always on the run, always
> changeful. Our task is to look at the two strategies: culture as
> a battle cry against one culture's claim to Reason as such, by
> insider as well as outsider; and culture as a nice name for the
> exoticism of the outsiders.
>
> Gayatri Spivak, *A Critique of Postcolonial Reason*

Western women and people in the postcolonial world are both
marginalized within economic discourse.[1] Their marginalization
has been historically sanctioned by particular apprehensions of
rationality and humanity that form a hallmark of the European
modernist worldview. Modernism is based on a social vision that
includes a liberal-democratic nation-state, an industrial capitalist economy, and a series of other specific institutions of public
life and "civil society," requiring a particular mode of interaction
between individuals, between individual and state, and between
individual and society. This conception is generally offered as

---

1. *Postcolonial* has a twofold meaning. First, it stands for the postwar experience of societies colonized by Europeans in the past few centuries—currently,
Third World, "less developed," or South. In this usage *postcolonial* mainly marks
a historical period. Second, the term *postcolonial* refers to a body of thought that
analyzes Euro-American or Western cultural hegemony that began with colonialism
and continues in the current economic and political ascendancy of industrialized
countries. In this latter sense, *postcolonial* refers to a certain critical approach. We
use the term *postcolonialism* to refer to discourse and ideas, and *postcoloniality* to
emphasize the social condition of being postcolonial.

a normative ideal, with societies ranked on the basis of their closeness to or distance from it.[2]

In economics, such modernism has been most intensely expressed in the notion of "development," whether in neoclassical, Marxian, or other heterodox approaches, including feminist scholarship. As Drucilla Barker (2000) notes, despite the strides made in the field of Gender-and-Development since the publication of Esther Boserup's *Woman's Role in Economic Development* in 1970 and despite feminist critiques of modernism in economics, much development feminism remains intransigently modernist. Postcolonial thought scrutinizes the way in which the modernist worldview is applied to non-Western, or "less developed," social forms and subjectivity(s).[3] The purpose of this chapter is to provide an introductory overview of postcolonial critique, highlight its relevance for economics, and lay the groundwork for a postcolonial approach to feminist economics. While feminist critiques of the masculinized Cartesian self in *Beyond Economic Man* (Nelson 1993; Strassmann 1993) and this volume (especially England, chap. 1; Benería, chap. 5) have addressed modernism in mainstream economics, postcolonial critique goes further, uncovering modernist limits in both heterodox and mainstream analyses.

The next section surveys the concerns and contributions of postcolonialism. We then examine the relationship between postcolonial and Western feminisms, identifying both common projects and departures. After that, we discuss the major themes of the emerging area of postcolonial feminist economics and end with a short conclusion.

---

2. As applied to non-Western societies, modernism includes a host of assumptions about: (1) the nature of history, progress, culture, and cognition, with the West upholding the "modern" end and the non-West the "nonmodern" end of this spectrum; (2) what happens when members of one society are forced to reorganize the institutions of economy, polity, and culture to conform to the modernist imagination; and (3) the reasons for persistent failure to attain the hoped-for results despite ongoing efforts to put modernist social institutions and norms in place.

3. The terms *Western/non-Western, European/non-European,* and *First World/Third World* are problematic and suffer from multiple inaccuracies. We use them as conventionally adopted categories in analysis and policy formulation, bearing in mind the complex ways in which these categories shape analyses and policies and organize international relations. *Western* and *European* interchangeably refer to industrialized societies in Western Europe and those settled by Europeans in North America and the Pacific. Our discussion does not include Eastern Europe, because it does not share this history of colonialism with the postcolonial world.

The term *subjectivity* in social science derives from the root *subject* in the sense of "being subjected to." It refers to a human being as historically and culturally constituted. Here, the human is interpreted as an incomplete (not fully coherent) site of cultural and historical processes, rather than a "rational," fully meaning source of knowledge, as in the Cartesian/Kantian tradition. For a brief discussion of subjectivity, see Taylor and Winquist 2001.

Postcolonial Thought and the Critique of Modernism

Postcolonial critique is a broad field that takes up a variety of themes—the philosophy of history, culture and identity-formation, and the social and economic reorganization of non-Western life during and after colonialism. However, in general, postcolonial scholarship is marked by concern with

1. Cross-cultural *hegemony* and *domination* in all its forms (cultural, economic or political), and the consequent phenomenon of *subalternity*;
2. European *historicism* as it is applied to "other" cultures.

In the discussion below, we outline these themes and provide an introduction to key scholarship in which they have been developed.

Postcolonial writers borrow the terms *hegemony* and *subalternity* from Antonio Gramsci (1975). *Hegemony* refers to the ability of a particular social class (e.g., capitalists, men) to make everyone consider this group's interests the universal concern and thus create acceptance of a particular way of organizing society. *Subaltern*, on the other hand, refers to a subordinate person—Gramsci used the term *subaltern classes* to refer to those of lower rank (primarily peasants) dominated by the political and intellectual authority of the state in Fascist Italy. In Western thought, analyses of how cultural hegemony works to produce subjects and explorations of how to undo hegemony when one is a product of a hegemonic order have been most strongly developed in the work of poststructuralists such as Michel Foucault, Jacques Lacan, Louis Althusser, and Jacques Derrida.[4] Postcolonial critics examine how Western hegemony and non-Western subalternity has been created in and through knowledge construction since the colonial encounter. Like their Western poststructuralist counterparts, they examine how subjects and identities are formed, negotiated, and reshaped and seek strategies to undo hegemony. These issues have been most importantly articulated through the pioneering work of the literary critics Edward Said, Gayatri Spivak, and Homi Bhabha.[5]

---

4. Postcolonialism shares several analytical projects with postmodernism. However, postcolonial critique engages with European modernity through its subaltern history. For discussions of the convergences and departures between postcolonial and postmodernist visions, see Appiah 1992; Bhabha 1994; Zein-Elabdin 2001; and the mini-symposium on postmodernism and postcolonialism between McCloskey (2000); Spivak (2000); and Charusheela (2000a).

5. Primarily, Said's *Orientalism* (1978), Spivak's "Can the Subaltern Speak?" (1988), and Bhabha's "The Other Question" (1983) and "Signs Taken for Wonders" (1985). Their work has come to be known as postcolonial *theory*, a narrower field than postcolonial *thought*, and has defined the central

The appearance of postcolonial thought in the Western academy is commonly associated with Said's *Orientalism* (1978).[6] Said argued that cultural hegemony was a central element of colonial relations and a continuing aspect of how the West maintains its hegemonic power vis-à-vis the non-West. While critiques of European ethnocentrism predate Said, his book inaugurated the analysis of how European thought constructed an imagined non-Western (Oriental) Other, who was central to the creation of Europe's own modernist self-imagination. He identified orientalism in three related ways: an academic field with its own protocols; a style of thought that sets up a dualism between East and West based on perceived ontological and epistemological differences between the two; and an institution of domination that authorizes a certain treatment of the Orient based on its representation as inferior and backward. Accordingly, orientalism is not about the Orient per se. Rather, it is about a relationship of power maintained and upheld by a *discourse* of what is wrong with others (and consequently, what is right with oneself).[7]

Following Said, postcolonial critique grew with the work of Spivak and Bhabha. All three authors critique *essentialist* conceptions of "human nature" and push for alternate, *nonessentialist* approaches to cultural identity(s). *Essentialism*—a defining aspect of modernism—refers to the belief in pregiven, underlying attributes that define what it means to be a member of a particular group (e.g., male or female, Western or non-Western). Postcolonial critics do not deny the social existence of such categories, but they see no innate aspect that defines any group's experience. Rather, the categories are relational—the nature and meaning of each is socially fabricated, and known and experienced mainly through social relationships of power that define them. In developing the analytical implications of Said's insights, Spivak and Bhabha paid special attention to subaltern identity-formation, with Spivak highlighting the role of implicit meanings in the structure of language and Bhabha examining the simultaneous displacement and reconstitution of cultural meanings. In effect, the

---

problematic and approach of postcolonial critique. Postcolonial thought has since branched into a number of other disciplines, including history, philosophy, and anthropology. For reviews and critical analyses, see Williams and Chrisman 1993; Ashcroft, Griffiths, and Tiflin 1995; McClintock, Mufti, and Shohat 1997; Moore-Gilbert 1997; and Gandhi 1998.

6. As with any field, locating a point of origin is somewhat arbitrary. Several authors (e.g., Gandhi 1998) trace arguments of a postcolonial nature back to Frantz Fanon 1967a. Moore-Gilbert 1997 argues that elements of postcolonial critique can be found in earlier African-American influences such as the Harlem Renaissance.

7. A *discourse* is an overall language—not merely the stated words, but the implicit meanings, the shared, taken-for-granted, and unstated assumptions that we use when we deploy a language. It is thus a cultural product, and we become part of a culture by learning the discourse and engaging in its various discursive practices.

two have produced an outline of the *postcolonial condition*, namely, the problem of seeking alternatives to a discourse of which one is a tangible product. They have also proposed strategies for formulating alternatives.

Spivak (1988) used the term *subalternity* to refer to subordinate, oppressed groups that include not only peasants, but also tribals and poor "informal sector" workers in South Asia, who, she argued have been silenced by the epistemic violence of colonialism.[8] To describe the consequences of such violence, she used the case of the British abolition of *sati* (widow burning) to show how the sexed (female) subject is constructed under colonial rule, making the Third World woman yet another subaltern. With the debate about *sati* taking the form of a contest between a British story of "white men saving brown women from brown men" and an Indian nativist argument that "the women wanted to die," there remained no discursive space from which the sexed subaltern subject could speak (1988, 297). Spivak's solution is to resituate the debate about *sati* in its historical context to figure out how and why it unfolded as it did—a deconstructive strategy that seeks to undo the discourse around *sati*. But Spivak also knew that her solution is not available to the Other or subaltern women, who lack the position of authority possessed by the postcolonial intellectual woman schooled in the ways of the hegemonic order.

Realizing that getting heard requires authority, Spivak articulates postcoloniality around the role of the cultural critic. The postcolonial critic must (re)claim cultural authority by "reversing, displacing, and seizing the apparatus of value coding," that is, the hegemony that assigns certain value to different positions (1990, 228). This can be accomplished through the catachrestic use of historically European concepts such as democracy and citizenship. In literary criticism, *catachresis* refers to the "misuse" of terms, either occurring mistakenly or performed deliberately for rhetorical effect. In Spivak's work, catachrestic "misuse" indicates the intentional reappropriation of conventionally Western concepts into non-Western meanings and contexts. She suggests catachresis as a vehicle for postcolonial cultural struggle since one cannot simply escape or reject modernism—not only has one been marked and shaped by its structure through the colonial encounter, but one cannot not want its promises of liberation, nor should one seek to disavow them. At the same time, the

---

8. This means that violence (in a social, moral sense) operates at the level of how we organize knowledge, how we force a reorganization of institutions as a result of this knowledge, and how we fail to comprehend the protests of those having to undergo this reorganization. Spivak (1988, 281) draws this term from Foucault, who used it to describe the overhaul of the episteme (structure of comprehending self and society) in redefinitions of sanity at the end of the eighteenth century in Europe (Foucault 1973, 1980).

terms of modernist emancipation have too many hegemonic connotations—thus one needs to force new meanings onto them. Within feminist economics, attaching new meanings to the concepts of labor and work or thinking about endowments in new ways form part of a similar effort. A postcolonial approach would similarly push feminist economists to look anew at the meanings of development, progress, empowerment, and so on.

The complexity of postcoloniality as a contemporary condition emerges powerfully in the work of Homi Bhabha, who draws on psychoanalysis (e.g., Fanon 1967a) to generate a complex, ambivalent image of colonial domination. In "The Other Question" (1983), he argues that the colonial attitude toward the "native" reflected both a longing for *her* exoticism and a disavowal of *his* primitive/savage qualities, rendering the stereotypical native a site of both desire and derision. This also reveals that colonial attitudes—expressed by such diverse individuals as the colonial administrator, missionary, or wife—were themselves gendered; the derided savage is masculine, the desired exoticism is feminine. At the same time, in "Signs Taken for Wonders" (1985), Bhabha shows that colonial authority was never complete; it was constantly challenged and undermined by local interpretations and questions. Thus, he reads colonialism not as a singular tale of Western triumph but as a process of mutual transformation for both colonizer and colonized in the constant struggle over constituting and reconstituting hegemony.

Bhabha (1994) describes postcoloniality as a constant movement, inbetweenness, and ambivalence between here and there; a condition of migration, diaspora, displacement of tribal and aboriginal communities, exile, and refugee liminality.[9] It is a state of cultural *hybridity*, namely, the advanced mixing and remaking of European and other cultures that has resulted from colonialism. Hybridity undermines any appeal to notions of "authentic" identity; it also suggests that cultural relativism and multiculturalism are inadequate frameworks for capturing postcoloniality, because they both conceive of self-contained, "homogeneous national, or ethnic, cultures" (5).[10] Similarly, postcolonial thinkers reject interpretations of the binary constructs First World/

9. *Diaspora* and *exile* hold different cultural and psychological connotations. The first refers to longer-term group experiences and identity formulations, while the second denotes a more immediate, individual subjectivity. Postcolonials may experience one or both. *Liminality,* a term derived from being at the limen, i.e., a (typically psychological) threshold, is used frequently in contemporary anthropology to describe the state of people living in-between situations, cultures, and societies.

10. By *cultural relativism* we mean the anthropological tradition in which a culture's practices cannot be judged from the "outside," because outsiders have no access to its meanings and logics. Multiculturalism is an adaptation of the idea of pregiven cultural identities in order to promote "tolerance" of different ethnic groups (black, Latino, etc.). See Charusheela 2001b for a critical discussion of the ethnocentrism-relativism dilemma in economics.

Third World and North/South as pregiven, independent, or fixed identities and boundaries (also see Hall 1990: Chakrabarty 1992).[11]

The work of these pioneering authors cannot be adequately understood apart from the problem of *historicism*, which is a predominant current in European modernism. Historicism is the interpretation of history as a process that unfolds according to certain immutable laws. This notion—which typically presents a set of historical rules all leading to the universal replication of the European experience—constitutes a hegemonic discourse within which the non-West is produced as subaltern; forever immature, nonmodern, and less developed. The Subaltern Studies Collective writers (see Guha et al. 1982–1997) have been most critical of historicism. Chakrabarty (1992) criticizes the Enlightenment narrative of history as a set of stages culminating in modern (European) development, showing how it conflates capitalism with historical progress and development with the re-creation of European institutions. His critical examination of the Marxist tradition is especially relevant for the fields of economic history and development because it shows how Marx's notion of historical materialism made capitalist modernity both the definer of progress and a necessary preconditional phase for further progress under socialism. This conviction underlay Marx's tolerance of British colonialism in India as a necessary evil for modernizing precapitalist structures (Zein-Elabdin 2001).

In the postwar era, historicism surfaced through the many stages-of-growth accounts that provided the anchor for development economics. The Colombian anthropologist Arturo Escobar (1995) renders the most comprehensive analysis of modernism in this field. He ethnographically traces the emergence and expansion of the postwar project of international development from the first World Bank mission to his own country in 1949 to the subsequent mushrooming of its literature. He adapts Said's notion of orientalism to describe the parallel contemporary phenomenon of *developmentalism* as a discursive field, a framework of knowledge with a set of certain dynamics and conventions that "results in concrete practices of thinking and acting through which the Third World is produced" (11) as the less developed Other. The result is the collective subjectivity of underdevelopment or backwardness that authorizes Western development policy prescriptions.

---

11. Of course, all cultures are hybrid to varying degrees. The deployment of hybridity in postcolonial analysis undoes the modernist imagination about "other cultures." The rejection of essentialist approaches to the categories North/South or First/Third does not indicate that there is no problem of First World–Third World relations to be examined. Rather, postcolonial scholars examine the relationship between each pair of terms that creates these categories, and expose how treating them as essentialist identities upholds and re-creates that relationship.

By linking the continued operation of modernism's hegemony over the non-West directly to the discourses of historicism and developmentalism within economics, postcolonial thought challenges us to rethink our approaches to the non-West. Its critiques push us to look for theories that undo the modernist imagination of not only the individualist subject of neoclassical economics (as many feminist scholars have undertaken to undo), but also our imagination of the history and future of economic and social change.[12]

Postcolonialism and Feminism

Before we review postcolonial contributions to feminist economics, some discussion of the relationship between postcolonial thought and feminism is in order. The two share many concerns: many postcolonial scholars emphasize the role of gender in shaping subalternity, and many feminists engage questions of race and culture in their own analysis (see Saunders and Darity, chap. 4 in this volume; Benería, chap. 5 in this volume). Beyond that, postcolonial thought shares methodological concerns with postmodernist and poststructuralist strands of feminist thought. Both pay attention to how cultural hegemony is generated and maintained, and both seek to challenge the construction of center-margin relations within modernist thought. Feminism's effort to undo androcentrism parallels postcolonialism's effort to undo orientalism and developmentalism. Nonetheless, certain issues require a distinctly postcolonial feminist intervention.

There are some inherited tensions between the feminist and the postcolonial projects. Leela Gandhi (1998) points out two sources of tension.[13] The first is the historical complicity of many Western women in the project of imperial domination. Many served in the colonies in different capacities, and feminist and postcolonial efforts to resurrect elided historical figures approach this role very differently. Gandhi (1998) examines two pieces of feminist literature that illustrate this problem. The first is Jenny Sharpe's book *Allegories of Empire* (1993), which critically brings to life the problematic figure of the female imperialist. This figure is far more revealed in Pat Barr's *The Memsahibs* (1976), which

12. In addition to its disciplinary expansion, postcolonial thought has followed a distinctly regional pattern in its historical evolution—from historiography in South Asia (e.g., Guha et al. 1982–1997) to philosophy in Africa (Mudimbe 1988; Appiah 1992), cultural studies in the Caribbean/black diaspora (Hall 1990; Gilroy 1993), and postdevelopment in Latin America (Esteva 1991; Escobar 1995). The different foci of these strands of postcolonial thought reflect specific disciplinary projects for historical and epistemological reasons and are, therefore, complementary in nature.

13. For other discussions of feminism and postcolonialism, see Trinh 1989; Hutcheon 1989; Suleri 1992; and McClintock, Mufti, and Shohat 1997.

seeks to find validation for the lives of European wives, mothers, and daughters in the colonies. Barr's defensive remembrance of this colonial constituency is summarized in her statement: "For the most part, the women loyally and stoically accepted their share of *the white people's burden* and lightened the weight of it with their quiet humor, their grace and often their youth" (Barr 1976, 1; emphasis added).[14] Indeed, as Spivak (1985) demonstrates, Western feminist activism itself rose at the age of formal empire, and therefore the feminist imagination of what it means to be a liberated woman was generated partly in contrast to orientalized representations of Other women. The rights and desires of one group of women, while wrested in the name of women in general, rested on the back of subalternity for other women.

The second source of tension between feminist and postcolonial concerns is an extension of the first: contemporary feminism has exhibited much of the cultural bias of colonial Europe. This is perhaps most clear in the use of the category Third World woman, a "singular, monolithic subject," with an essential identity (Gandhi 1998, 85). As Gandhi states, "the representation of the average third world woman as 'ignorant, poor, uneducated, tradition-bound, domesticated, family-oriented, victimized,' facilitates and privileges the self-representation of Western women 'as educated, modern, as having control over their own bodies and sexualities, and the freedom to make their own decisions'" (86). The composite Third World presumes notions of both a definitive non-Western experience and of Western feminism.

The issue of development is central in the relationship between Western and postcolonial feminisms. In deconstructing the category Third World woman, Chandra Mohanty (1984) highlighted the problem of representation of the Other in Western feminism. Feminist scholarship has usually taken the notion of development for Third World women for granted, as evidenced by the massive industry of women-and-development, now reformulated as gender-and-development (GAD)—with its extensive projects, literature, experts, and training programs. Spivak (1999) discusses the limits of modernism in the reformulated discourses of GAD and demonstrates that, in practice, the GAD agenda presents incorporation into capitalist markets, the safety nets of the welfare state, literacy, and skill-based empowerment as the key solution for women's oppression in the non-West. The institutional frameworks of market

14. One example of Western feminist complicity is reflected in the difficulty Huda Sha'arawi, the Egyptian feminist (1879–1924), had in getting Western feminist allies in the International Woman Suffrage Alliance to address the role of imperialism in shaping women's lack of rights within their discussions of rights for women (Badran 1995). American-born Lady Brunyate refused to respond to Sha'arawi's letter critiquing British policy in Egypt despite having played the role of long-time friend and supporter to the Egyptian feminist (Sha'arawi 1986).

and state on which GAD projects rest their hope for non-Western women's emancipation are the same institutions identified with Western women's own emergence from subordination. However well-meaning the project, it lacks serious consideration of the transnational and local institutional contexts that shape state formation, market operation, and cultural transformation in the non-West (also see Ong 1988).

Despite these differences, common ground can be found in feminist and postcolonial struggles against domination and hegemony. Gandhi offers a clue to this potential when she suggests that the colonial encounter may be read as a "struggle between competing masculinities" (1998, 98). She argues that the nation, on either side of empire, often authenticated itself through its women—for instance, Mother India serving as a nationalist trope. Another example is the use of the veil as part of the Algerian anticolonial strategy (Fanon 1967b). Indeed, Said (1978) had pointed out that orientalism was a male-dominated practice, with orientals ranked on a parallel threshold with European women, delinquents, the poor, and the insane. These affinities suggest that the political projects of Western and postcolonial feminisms share interests in rejecting masculinized, nationalist structures.

Thus, although the relationship between postcolonialism and feminism faces some difficulties, there are also historical and theoretical grounds for solidarity. Western women and formerly colonized people are both marginalized Others of European modernity and share contemporary marginalization within economics. Both share an interest in undoing the hegemonic discourses of mainstream economics even as they approach key aspects of these discourses from different angles.

Postcolonial Feminist Economics

From our standpoint, the most significant contribution of feminist economics over the past decade has been the interrogation of economics as a hegemonic discourse (Nelson 1992, 1993; Strassmann 1993; Williams 1993; Grapard 1995; Seiz 1995; Barker 2000). However, the continuing modernism in Western approaches to non-Western women—highlighted in postcolonial feminists' critical discussions—indicates the need for a specifically postcolonial approach in feminist economics. In this section, we review the small but growing body of postcolonial scholarship in this area.

Feminist postcolonial scholarship in economics takes two forms: first, it interrogates the orientalism and developmentalism of economic discourse, and second, it contributes to the creation of alternate frameworks. In both forms, the nature of postcoloniality does not permit an easy, clean break with past discourses. Nor, given hybridity, can we fall back on multiculturalist politics or simple relativism. Instead, postcolonial insights operate critically to generate renegotiated standards for assessing approaches to analyses of and for non-Western women. Additionally, postcolonial scholarship follows a *transdisciplinary* method. Instead of drawing on material from different disciplines that maintain their philosophical core and methodological tools (the current interdisciplinary approach), a transdisciplinary method reveals the common preanalytical premises of different disciplines, for example, economics and philosophy; and forces them to lose their perceived autonomy (Zein-Elabdin forthcoming).[15] The following literatures focus partly on critique and partly on alternatives.

A number of scholars have examined the role of colonialist mindsets in classical political economy. The easy transposition of Malthusian orthodoxies of the classical period into the postwar development project of population control provides one obvious indication of the continuities between colonial cultural frameworks and the "new" frameworks of modernist economics. Dimand (forthcoming) excavates the treatment of slaves, women, and colonized Others in early political economy. His work parallels critical feminist discussions of androcentrism in early economic thought. Grapard (forthcoming) shows how one can uncover unstated assumptions in classical thought and link them to the broader cultural discourses of orientalism. She locates approaches to trade in classical political economy within the broader context of hierarchical discourses about world regions, as displayed via the use of six allegorical statues in female form representing the six regions of the globe at the 1878 Paris Exhibition.

Others have deconstructed the contemporary development paradigm to reveal the continuity between orientalist discourses in the colonial period and development discourses of the postwar era. Charusheela (1997) provides a detailed discussion of the role of orientalism and Cartesianism in defining development economics from its inception through the 1990s. Zein-Elabdin (1998) traces the notion of development through its grounding in Western Enlightenment philosophy and ideas of universal history that underlie both mainstream and Marxian visions of progress, thereby revealing their convergence in representations of non-Western societies. Both visions fail to recognize that for

---

15. Transdisciplinarity is mandated by the need for catachresis since the reappropriation of many concepts requires an inquiry into the philosophy of knowledge and being. For example, the term *development* can be reappropriated only after an inquiry into the philosophy of history and ethics, *rationality* requires an examination of the philosophy of humanist ontology, *democracy* calls for a serious interrogation of its relationship to the nation-state in political philosophy.

nonindustrial cultures, development is not merely a matter of limited macro-economic policy but a much larger, ontological question.

Suzanne Bergeron (1998) draws on postdevelopment literature (e.g., Escobar 1995) to examine the production of the development discourse, especially the subjectivities produced by the rhetoric of backwardness and primitivism. She argues that "economic development theory is an important aspect of a broader development problematic that authorizes particular visions and practices and forecloses others, participates in the establishment of expertise and silences alternative perspectives" (2). She focuses particularly on the idea of the nation, pointing out the extent to which the nation-state "has framed our concepts of the economy" (4) and showing that the idea of a national economy and how it operates implicitly assumes other modern European notions, such as citizenship and sovereignty. Bergeron (2001) develops this critique further, examining debates over financial stabilization and structural adjustment. She reveals the extent to which nonindustrialized "nations" are framed in gendered, racialized, and colonialized terms.

Postcolonial perspectives have also highlighted the limitations of developmentalism beyond the mainstream. Charusheela (2000b) shows that modernism is embedded in the otherwise critical and insightful capabilities approach. Drawing on the philosophical underpinnings of the approach as laid out by the philosopher Martha Nussbaum (e.g., Nussbaum and Glover 1995), Charusheela examines the role envisaged for literacy within this framework, showing that it depends on taking a modernist institutional organization of society as the norm for development. As a result, the framework ends up promoting approaches that worsen hegemony and fail to provide appropriate solutions to the problem of gender subordination in the non-West.

This critique can be further developed to examine the limits of the usual GAD agenda (Charusheela 2001a). GAD policies are based on microlevel, bargaining models that depend on certain assumptions about the role of the market and the state in empowering women, even as both market and state are being transformed in ways that prevent them from fulfilling this role at the macrolevel under globalization processes. In contrast, discussions of poverty, race, class, and burdens of work found within the feminization-of-poverty literatures in the West provide better structural solutions because they use Marxist-institutionalist approaches. Nonetheless, modernism also besets much Marxist feminist thought (Charusheela 2000b). Although feminists have challenged Marxism's androcentrism, many continue to hold on to its modernism by implicitly drawing on Classical assumptions about the nature of the transition to capitalism, the logic of capital accumulation, and the relationship between capitalist development and women's emancipation, which limits their analyses of non-Western contexts.

Some postcolonial literature has identified the presence of overt orientalism in contemporary economic scholarship. Jennifer Olmsted (forthcoming-b) highlights this tendency in the treatment of Islam and Muslim societies through an analysis of feminist economic texts. Olmsted discusses Grossbard-Shechtman and Neuman's (1998) use of econometric tests to examine the impact of marriage-related practices within Christianity, Islam, and Judaism on women's labor supply in Israel. Grossbard-Shechtman and Neuman list a variety of marriage-related practices, including divorce, fertility, and domestic violence, that could affect women's labor market entry. However, Olmsted notes that they do not follow with a careful examination of these practices in the three communities. Instead, their model partitions the data into religious categories, notes the presence of differences in labor market outcomes for Muslim women, and concludes that since the differences are statistically significant, they have shown how differences in marriage-related religious practices affect women's labor supply outcomes. They conclude that two models of marriage operate in Israel—one reflecting a "Christian West" culture and the other reflecting a "Moslem [sic] East" culture.[16]

As Olmsted notes, this is a methodological problem that demonstrates how orientalist assumptions can influence data organization and testing. In deciding that all differences are attributable to inherent religious beliefs, Grossbard-Shechtman and Neuman have, in effect, preanalyzed culture and have made no effort to work out the differential role of religious vis-à-vis other factors in shaping practices. Their analysis rests on assuming a stark dualism between Judeo-Christianity/West culture, on the one hand, and Islam/East, on the other, which overlooks the ways in which the three religions are closely tied historically. Moreover, by assuming that the categories Muslim, Christian, and Jewish capture primarily religious-attitudinal differences, they do not consider other specific elements, such as how levels of secularization link to socioeconomic conditions and the extent to which the three religions themselves have been

---

16. Olmsted (forthcoming-b) discusses another example of orientalism that surfaces in Bergmann's (1995) critique of Becker's theory of the family (in which he concludes that polygamy is more beneficial to women than monogamy). Olmsted shows how Bergmann makes a number of sweeping, largely unsubstantiated generalizations about the status of women in Muslim societies, including claims that "in societies that allow polygamy" (more precisely, polygyny), "women tend to have abysmal status," in summary, "they are virtual prisoners; men totally monopolize all the power, freedom, fun and games" (Bergmann 1995, 145). It is worth noting that *Feminist Economics* has published a contrasting perspective to Bergmann's view (Hale 1995). An article critically discussing Grossbard-Shechtman and Neuman's article is to follow (Olmsted forthcoming-a).

hybridized by successive historical processes and power relations, including Ottoman and British colonial rule and Israeli occupation. Olmsted's work exposes the tendency to slip into pregiven, essential categories in comparative economic analysis of cultures.

We end with three examples of scholarship that use postcolonial strategies to offer alternatives to conventional economic approaches. The first shows the usefulness of the concept of hybridity for considering conceptions of identity, the second provides an example of catachrestic strategies for redoing economic analysis, and the third shows how a culturally situated, nonessentialist interpretation of gender breaks the binarism of the development discourse.

Karen Graubart (2000) has challenged received economic histories of the gender division of labor in Latin America. She suggests that "the colonial economy of Peru was constructed in contestation: the relations of production and consumption that developed were the result of innumerable conflicts between and among indigenous and European actors, and not the simple triumph of one system over another" (537). Her analysis links the construction of gender roles in the formation of a gender division of labor to the emerging political economy of the period. Graubart (forthcoming) builds on this insight, using the concept of hybridity (*mestizaje*) to show how the now-naturalized conceptualizations of pre-Hispanic Incan culture and of the racial and cultural identity-categories Spaniard and Indian were the product of social negotiation to reconstitute and consolidate the emerging social and economic structure of early colonial Peru.

Colin Danby offers an example of catachrestic strategies, where he critically reappropriates Post Keynesian economic theory into new contexts. Danby (2002a) utilizes Post Keynesian theory to show that the gift-exchange dichotomy, often used to explain differences between nonmodern/nonmarket and modern/market production, is flawed since the concepts of both exchange and gift rest on the same underlying Walrasian vision of market exchange. He notes that many feminists have also relied on this dichotomy when distinguishing between household and market spheres. But he also argues (Danby 2000) that although the Post Keynesian notions of time and uncertainty should in principle be as applicable to alternate institutional arrangements as they are to bank-firm relations in advanced industrial states, the modernist commitments of contemporary Post Keynesian theorists have prevented them from making this move. This argument provides the basis for a reappropriation of Post Keynesian theory in which its insights about uncertainty and financial fragility can also be applied to households. By adapting the Post Keynesian cash-flow approach to firms to cultural contexts in which "nonmodern" institutions such as kinship and familial relations play a large role in structuring material life, Danby (2002b) illuminates the intersecting roles of kinship and credit/money management in household interactions, offering another dimension to our approach to households (also see Charusheela and Danby 2001).

Finally, Zein-Elabdin (1996) has addressed the nature of gender in the context of the environment-development discourse. She critiques the essentialist construction of women in the two competing positions in this debate, neoclassical economics and cultural ecofeminism. From this critique, building on the institutionalist tradition of Thorstein Veblen and Karl Polanyi, she provides an interpretation of gender as an institution that sets the parameters of women's and men's operation within the (culturally embedded) economy. She rejects the notion of a theoretical articulation of a relationship between gender, development, and the environment and instead sees a multiplicity of contextual points of interaction where women and gender relations can be examined and understood only within historically and culturally specific contexts. In this conception, there is no presumption that development is the underlying logic of all economic processes, in other words, that all institutions and processes in the "less developed" economy must result in the orientalist vision of development. She further suggests (2000) an economic approach that theorizes postcolonial economies as contemporary cultural productions and not a mere prelude to "modernity."[17]

Conclusion

Postcolonial thought explores the ways in which orientalism, historicism, and developmentalism draw on and maintain Western hegemony over former European colonies. Beyond critique, postcolonial scholars have confronted the difficulty of challenging this hegemonic discourse. Their approaches provide us with concepts and strategies for the task of creating alternatives: the strategies of catachresis and transdisciplinarity and the concepts of hybridity and nonessentialist identity. The above discussion has provided examples of the usefulness of these concepts and strategies in creating a postcolonial approach in feminist economics.

17. For a similar articulation, see the "situated subjects" approach in Charusheela 2001b.

References

Appiah, Anthony. 1992. *In my father's house: Africa in the philosophy of culture.* New York: Oxford University Press.

Ashcroft, Bill, Gareth Griffiths, and Helen Tiflin, eds. 1995. *The post-colonial studies reader.* London: Routledge.

Badran, Margot. 1995. *Feminists, Islam, and nation: Gender and the making of modern Egypt.* Princeton, N.J.: Princeton University Press.

Barker, Drucilla. 2000. Dualisms, discourse, and development. In *Decentering the center: Philosophy for a multicultural, postcolonial, and feminist world,* edited by Uma Narayan and Sandra Harding, 177–88. Bloomington: Indiana University Press.

Barr, Pat. 1976. *The memsahibs: The women of Victorian India.* London: Secker & Warburg.

Bergeron, Suzanne. 1998. *Fragments of development: Three essays on development, structural adjustment, and economic knowledge.* Ph.D. dissertation, University of Notre Dame.

———. 2001. Challenging the World Bank's narrative of inclusion. Paper presented at the Allied Social Science Associations meetings, New Orleans.

Bergmann, Barbara R. 1995. Becker's theory of the family: Preposterous conclusions. *Feminist Economics* 1 (1): 141–50.

Bhabha, Homi K. 1983. The other question: Stereotype, discrimination, and the discourse of colonialism. *Screen* 24 (6): 18–36.

———. 1985. Signs taken for wonders: Questions of ambivalence and authority under a tree outside Delhi, May 1817. *Critical Inquiry* 12 (1): 144–65.

———. 1994. *The location of culture.* London: Routledge.

Chakrabarty, Dipesh. 1992. Postcoloniality and the artifice of history: Who speaks for "Indian" pasts? *Representations* 37:1–26.

Charusheela, S. 1997. *Structuralism and individualism in economic analysis: The "contractionary devaluation debate" in development economics.* Ph.D. dissertation, University of Massachusetts, Amherst.

———. 2000a. On history, love, and politics. Mini-symposium on postmodernism and postcolonialism between McCloskey, Spivak, and Charusheela. *Rethinking Marxism* 12 (4): 45–62.

———. 2000b. Marxism, liberalism, and modernity in development analysis. Paper presented at Marxism 2000: Fourth international conference sponsored by *Rethinking Marxism.* University of Massachusetts, Amherst, September 21–24.

———. 2001a. Modernization, globalization, and women's empowerment. Paper presented at the Allied Social Science Associations meetings, New Orleans.

———. 2001b. Women's choices and the ethnocentrism/relativism dilemma. In *Postmodernism, economics, and knowledge,* edited by Stephen Cullenberg, Jack Amariglio, and David Ruccio, 197–220. London: Routledge.

Charusheela, S., and Colin Danby. 2001. A through-time framework for producer households. Available at www.bothell.washington.edu/faculty/danby/papers/prodhhweb2.htm.

Danby, Colin. 2000. LDCs, institutions, and money. *Journal of Post Keynesian Economics* 22 (3): 407–21.

———. 2002a. The curse of the modern: A Post Keynesian critique of the gift/exchange dichotomy. *Research in Economic Anthropology* 21:13–42. Special issue: *Social dimensions in the economic process,* edited by Norbert Dannhaeuser and Cynthia Werner.

———. 2002b. Lupita's dress: Care in time. Paper presented at the International Association for Feminist Economics (IAFFE) Summer Conference, Los Angeles, July.

Dimand, Robert W. Forthcoming. Classical political economy and orientalism: Nassau senior's Eastern tours. In *Postcolonialism meets economics,* edited by E. Zein-Elabdin and S. Charusheela. London: Routledge.

Escobar, Arturo. 1995. *Encountering development: The making and unmaking of the third world.* Princeton, N.J.: Princeton University Press.

Esteva, Gustavo. 1991. Preventing green redevelopment. *Development, the Journal of the Society of International Development* 1991 (2): 74–78.

Fanon, Frantz. 1967a. *Black skin, white masks*. New York: Grove Press.

————. 1967b. *A dying colonialism*. New York: Grove Press.

Foucault, Michel. 1973. *Madness and civilization: A history of insanity in the age of reason*. New York: Vintage.

————. 1980. *Power/knowledge: Selected interviews and other writings, 1972–1977*. New York: Pantheon.

Gandhi, Leela. 1998. *Postcolonial theory: A critical introduction*. New York: Columbia University Press.

Gilroy, Paul. 1993. *The black Atlantic: Modernity and double consciousness*. Cambridge, Mass.: Harvard University Press.

Gramsci, Antonio. 1975. *The prison notebooks, volumes I, II*. Translated and edited by Joseph Buttigieg. New York: Columbia University Press.

Grapard, Ulla. 1995. Robinson Crusoe: The quintessential economic man? *Feminist Economics* 1 (1): 33–52.

————. Forthcoming. Trading bodies, trade in bodies: The 1878 World Exhibition as economic discourse. In *Postcolonialism meets economics*, edited by E. Zein-Elabdin and S. Charusheela. London: Routledge.

Graubart, Karen. 2000. Weaving and the construction of a gender division of labor in early colonial Peru. *American Indian Quarterly* 24 (4): 537–61.

————. Forthcoming. Hybrid thinking: Bringing postcolonial theory to colonial Latin American history. In *Postcolonialism meets economics*, edited by E. Zein-Elabdin and S. Charusheela. London: Routledge.

Grossbard-Shechtman, Shoshana, and Shoshana Neuman. 1998. The extra burden of Moslem wives: Clues from Israeli women's labor supply. *Economic Development and Cultural Change* 46 (3): 491–517.

Guha, Ranajit, et al., eds. 1982–1997. *Subaltern studies: Writings on South Asian history and society*. Vols. 1–9. New York: Oxford University Press.

Hale, Sondra. 1995. Gender and economics: Islam and polygamy—a question of causality. *Feminist Economics* 1 (2): 67–79.

Hall, Stuart. 1990. Cultural identity and diaspora. In *Identity: Community, culture, difference*, edited by Jonathan Rutherford, 222–37. London: Lawrence & Wishart.

Hutcheon, Linda. 1989. Circling the downspout of empire: Post-colonialism and postmodernism. *Ariel* 20 (4): 149–75.

McClintock, Anne, Aamir Mufti, and Ella Shohat, eds. 1997. *Dangerous liaisons: Gender, nation, and postcolonial perspectives*. Minneapolis: University of Minnesota Press.

McCloskey, Deirdre. 2000. Postmodern market feminism: Half of a conversation with Gayatri Chakravorty Spivak. *Rethinking Marxism* 12 (4): 27–36.

Mohanty, Chandra. 1984. Under Western eyes: Feminist scholarship and colonial discourses. *Boundary 2*, 12 (3) & 13 (1): 333–58.

Moore-Gilbert, B. J. 1997. *Postcolonial theory: Contexts, practices, politics*. London: Verso.

Mudimbe, V. Y. 1988. *The invention of Africa: Gnosis, philosophy and the order of knowledge*. Bloomington: Indiana University Press.

Nelson, Julie A. 1992. Gender, metaphor, and the definition of economics. *Economics and Philosophy* 8 (1): 103–25.

————. 1993. The study of choice or the study of provisioning? Gender and the definition of economics. In *Beyond economic man: Feminist theory and economics*, edited by M. Ferber and J. Nelson, 23–36. Chicago: University of Chicago Press.

Nussbaum, Martha C., and Jonathan Glover. 1995. *Women, culture, and development: A study of human capabilities*. Oxford: Oxford University Press.

Olmsted, Jennifer. Forthcoming-a. A comment on "The extra burden of Moslem wives: Clues from Israeli women's labor supply." *Feminist Economics*.

—————. Forthcoming-b. Orientalism and economic methods: (Re)reading feminist economic discussions of Islam. In *Postcolonialism meets economics,* edited by E. Zein-Elabdin and S. Charusheela. London: Routledge.

Ong, Aihwa. 1988. Colonialism and modernity: Feminist re-presentations of women in non-Western societies. *Inscriptions* 3 (4): 79–93.

Said, Edward. 1978. *Orientalism.* New York: Pantheon Books.

Seiz, Janet. 1995. Epistemology and the tasks of feminist economics. *Feminist Economics* 1 (3): 110–18.

Sha'arawi, Huda. 1986. *Harem years: The memoirs of an Egyptian feminist (1879–1924).* Translated and edited by Margot Badran. London: Virago.

Sharpe, Jenny. 1993. *Allegories of empire: The figure of woman in the colonial text.* Minneapolis: University of Minnesota Press.

Spivak, Gayatri C. 1985. Three women's texts and a critique of imperialism. *Critical Inquiry* 12 (1): 243–61.

—————. 1988. Can the subaltern speak? In *Marxism and the interpretation of culture,* edited by Cary Nelson and Lawrence Grossberg, 271–313. Urbana: University of Illinois Press.

—————. 1990. Poststructuralism, marginality, postcoloniality, and value. In *Literary theory today,* edited by Peter Collier and Helga Geyer-Ryan, 219–44. Ithaca, N.Y.: Cornell University Press.

—————. 1999. *A critique of postcolonial reason: Toward a history of the vanishing present.* Cambridge, Mass.: Harvard University Press.

—————. 2000. Other things are never equal: A speech. *Rethinking Marxism* 12 (4): 37–44.

Strassmann, Diana. 1993. Not a free market: The rhetoric of disciplinary authority in economics. In *Beyond economic man: Feminist theory and economics,* edited by M. Ferber and J. Nelson, 54–68. Chicago: University of Chicago Press.

Suleri, Sara. 1992. Woman skin deep: Feminism and the postcolonial condition. *Critical Inquiry* 18 (4). 756–69.

Taylor, Victor E., and Charles E. Winquist. 2001. *Encyclopedia of postmodernism.* London: Routledge.

Trinh T. Minh-ha. 1989. *Woman, native, other: Writing postcoloniality and feminism.* Bloomington: Indiana University Press.

Williams, Patrick, and Laura Chrisman, eds. 1993. *Colonial discourse and post-colonial theory: A reader.* Hemel Hempstead: Harvester Wheatsheaf.

Williams, Rhonda. 1993. Race, deconstruction, and the emergent agenda of feminist economic theory. In *Beyond economic man: Feminist theory and economics,* edited by M. Ferber and J. Nelson, 144–52. Chicago: University of Chicago Press.

Zein-Elabdin, Eiman. 1996. Development, gender, and the environment: Theoretical or contextual link? Toward an institutional analysis of gender. *Journal of Economic Issues* 30 (4): 929–47.

—————. 1998. The question of development in Africa: A conversation for propitious change. *Journal of African Philosophy* 11 (2): 113–25.

—————. 2000. Economic heterodoxy and subaltern cultures. Paper presented at Marxism 2000. University of Massachusetts, Amherst, September 21–24.

—————. 2001. Contours of a non-modernist discourse: The contested space of history and development. *Review of Radical Political Economics* 33 (3): 255–63.

—————. Forthcoming. Articulating the postcolonial. In *Postcolonialism meets economics,* edited by E. Zein-Elabdin and S. Charusheela. London: Routledge.

Zein-Elabdin, Eiman, and S. Charusheela, eds. Forthcoming. *Postcolonialism meets economics.* London: Routledge.

Contributors

Lourdes Benería is professor of city and regional planning and of women's studies and director of the Gender and Global Change Program at Cornell University. She taught at Rutgers University between 1975 and 1986 and has participated in short courses and seminars at other universities in the United States and internationally. She has published several books and numerous articles on topics related to the global economy, gender and development, women's paid and unpaid work, and structural adjustment policies, particularly in Latin America.

Rebecca M. Blank is the Henry Carter Adams Collegiate Professor of Public Policy, professor of economics, and dean of the Gerald R. Ford School of Public Policy at the University of Michigan. From 1997 to 1999 she served as a member of the President's Council of Economic Advisers and before then was on the faculty at Princeton and at Northwestern University. She has published extensively and most recently is coauthor (with Ron Haskins) of *The New World of Welfare* (2001).

S. Charusheela is assistant professor of women's studies at the University of Hawai'i at Mānoa. She received her doctorate in economics from the University of Massachusetts, Amherst. Recent essays include "On History, Love, and Politics" (2000) and "Women's Choices and the Ethnocentrism/Relativism Dilemma" (2001). She has served on the editorial boards of *Rethinking Marxism* and *Feminist Economics* and is an active member of the International Association for Feminist Economics and the Association for Economic and Social Analysis.

William Darity Jr. is the Cary C. Boshamer Professor of Economics at the University of North Carolina at Chapel Hill and research professor of public policy studies at Duke University. His research interests include racial and ethnic economic inequality, North-South models of trade and growth, interpreting Mr. Keynes, the economics of the Atlantic slave trade, and the social psychological effects of exposure to unemployment. He has published over one hundred articles in professional journals and authored or edited seven books. His most recent publication (coauthored with Samuel Myers Jr.) is *Persistent Disparity: Racial Economic Inequality in the United States Since 1945* (1998).

Paula England is professor of sociology at Northwestern University, where she is also affiliated with the Institute for Policy Research. She was editor of the *American Sociological Review* from 1994 to 1996 and is the author of *Comparable Worth: Theories and Evidence* (1992). In addition, she has written numerous articles, many focused on the sex gap in pay and gender in family dynamics. She is especially interested in integrative dialogues among sociological, economic, and feminist perspectives.

Marianne A. Ferber is professor emerita of economics and women's studies at the University of Illinois, and during 1993–95 was the Matina Horner Visiting Professor at the Radcliffe Public Policy Institute. She is coauthor of *The Economics of Women, Men, and Work,* 4th ed. (2002); editor of *Women in the Labor Market* (1998); and coeditor of *Work and Family* (1991), *Academic Couples* (1997), and *Nonstandard Work* (2000); and she has published in economics, education, sociology, and women's studies journals. She continues to serve on the editorial board of several journals.

Nancy Folbre is professor of economics at the University of Massachusetts, Amherst. She is also a staff economist with the Center for Popular Economics, associate editor of the journal *Feminist Economics,* and a recent recipient of a MacArthur Foundation fellowship. Her academic research explores the interface between feminist theory and political economy. In addition to numerous articles in academic journals, she is the author of *Who Pays for the Kids? Gender and the Structures of Constraint* (1994) and *The Invisible Heart: Economics and Family Values* (2001).

Julie A. Nelson is currently with the Global Development and Environment Institute at Tufts University after having held positions including associate professor of economics at the University of California, Davis, and at Brandeis University and fellow at Harvard Divinity School. Her research areas have included the empirical study of household demand and the relation of feminist theory to economics. She is the author of *Feminism, Objectivity, and Economics* (1996) and numerous articles in leading journals in economics and women's studies. She is an associate editor of *Feminist Economics.*

Cordelia W. Reimers is professor of economics at Hunter College and the Graduate School of the City University of New York, where she has taught since 1982. In recent years she has been a visiting scholar at the Russell Sage Foundation and a senior economist at the Council of Economic Advisers. Prior to joining the faculty at CUNY, she taught at Princeton University. Her research has focused on racial and ethnic differences in labor market outcomes and on Social Security and retirement behavior.

Lisa Saunders is associate professor of economics at the University of Massachusetts, Amherst. She specializes in transportation and labor economics. She has published papers on airline and trucking deregulation, urban transportation to work, and the effect of government regulations on transportation industry output and employment. Another set of her publications has examined racial differences in earnings by region and industry, and trends in racial differences in commute time to work.

Myra H. Strober is a labor economist and professor of education and of business (courtesy) at Stanford University, where she teaches in education, business, and feminist studies. She is coauthor of *The Road Winds Uphill All the Way: Gender Work and Family in the United States and Japan* (1999) and has written numerous articles on occupational segregation and on work and families. She is the founding director of Stanford's Center for Research on Women (now the Institute for Research on Women and Gender) and past president of the International Association for Feminist Economics.

Eiman Zein-Elabdin is associate professor of economics at Franklin and Marshall College. Her interests include development, postcolonial studies, gender, and ecology. She is a former economist with the government of Sudan. She has served as a consultant to the U.N. Development Program, as editorial advisor for the *Encyclopedia of Political Economy,* and on the editorial board of the *Journal of Economic Issues.* She has published in several journals and books. She is currently editorial consultant for *Explorations in Postcolonial Studies*, published by SUNY Press.